# PRISONERS OF THE PAST

# PRISONERS OF THE PAST

South African Democracy and the Legacy of
Minority Rule

## STEVEN FRIEDMAN

WITS UNIVERSITY PRESS

Published in South Africa by:
Wits University Press
1 Jan Smuts Avenue
Johannesburg 2001

www.witspress.co.za

First published 2021

http://dx.doi.org.10.18772/12021066840

978-1-77614-684-0 (Paperback)
978-1-77614-685-7 (Hardback)
978-1-77614-686-4 (Web PDF)
978-1-77614-687-1 (EPUB)

Project manager: Lisa Compton
Copyeditor: Lisa Compton
Proofreader: Simone van der Merwe
Indexer: Margie Ramsay
Cover design: Hybrid Creative

The past is never dead. It's not even past.

— WILLIAM FAULKNER, *Requiem for a Nun*

# CONTENTS

# INTRODUCTION

In one of those polarised arguments which are typical of South African political debate, a quarter-century of democracy has either changed everything – or
nothing. Both views are right and both wrong.

This claim is made not to appear cute. It reflects an important reality which the
debate largely ignores: that a society can both change and remain the same. This
book argues that this is precisely what has happened in South Africa since formal
democracy was achieved in 1994. It aims to show that, while much has changed,
the society still operates in ways which share strong features with realities before all
adults were allowed to vote and all citizens were able to enjoy, at least in principle,
the freedoms which are central to democratic citizenship.

The view that nothing has changed might sound good in speeches but does not
bear serious scrutiny. It should be trite to point out that, under apartheid, most
South Africans could not live or move where they pleased. Or that most people
were denied, because of their race, the opportunity to study where they wished
or to occupy the jobs best suited to their talents and inclinations. Some of these
restrictions were eased as the apartheid state tried to reform in order to survive,[1]
but not all were. When formal democracy began in 1994, black South Africans still
laboured under severe restrictions. Today, none of them apply. South Africans are
far freer today than before apartheid ended.

Nor is there substance to the claim that the first 25 years of democracy have
brought no social and economic changes. This period witnessed a strong growth in
a black professional and business class which was only beginning to emerge when
democracy dawned.[2] This growth is a consequence of ending racial restrictions and
of affirmative action policies introduced since 1994. Programmes implemented
since democracy's advent have enhanced access to assets for people living in poverty. Contrary to claims that democratic government has offered nothing to most
South Africans, access to electricity, water and other public goods has grown significantly.[3] The most significant gain of all for people denied access to the middle class

has been the extension of more than 17.7 million social grants.[4] Over four million people are receiving antiretroviral treatment for HIV and AIDS[5] in response to a citizens' campaign for adequate treatment whose success would not have been possible without the rights extended by democracy and the opportunities it creates to pressure politicians to respond to public demands.

But much has remained the same. Poverty and inequality persist, a product of the continued division of the population into economic insiders who enjoy access to the benefits of the formal economy and outsiders who do not.[6] Even among the insiders, there is no equality between the pre-1994 white incumbents and the new black entrants: the black middle class, whose growth democracy has enhanced, includes many people precariously balanced just beyond economic hardship, 'one pay cheque away' from poverty.[7] The new black insiders face obstacles – and prejudices – which the older insiders do not experience. Black professionals and business people are among the angriest South Africans because they enjoy qualifications and opportunities which their parents and grandparents were denied but they experience many of the same racial attitudes as previous generations endured. The cultural preferences of the minority still dominate.[8] Black students rebel against this, demanding the decolonisation of higher learning.

How to explain this apparent contradiction between change and continuity? Perhaps the most common approach among those who agree that society has changed since 1994 is to see the transition from racial minority rule as an unfinished journey: the society has made progress but much work remains.[9] Yet the patterns of the past persist not because the current path of change is still getting around to tackling them. They survive because that path is incapable of dealing with them. The changes since 1994 may be real, but they are also all that is possible within the current development path because it does not fundamentally alter how the economy and society operate.

To put this another way: In 1994, the new democracy inherited a society of insiders and outsiders. The insiders were all white and the outsiders all black (even if some, in the former Bantustans, had a stake in the system which made them outsiders). Since 1994, a significant number of outsiders have become insiders: the black South Africans who are now able to occupy positions and play roles which apartheid reserved for whites. But the rest remain outsiders – in the economy and society, although not in the political system. So South Africans can now vote and enjoy freedoms denied to most by minority rule – anyone who thinks this is trivial has forgotten or never knew the humiliations of apartheid. Some have also been able to use these freedoms to claim a better life and more dignified treatment. But many are condemned by the current path to remain economic and social outsiders.

They will not become insiders if the elites who decide the society's fate simply try harder to do what they have been doing since 1994. The outsiders will win inclusion only if the elite and the society set out on a new path. To illustrate, think of South Africa in 1994 as a country whose economy and society were controlled by an exclusive club, composed of only white people. Since 1994, the club has taken on new, black members. But it remains an exclusive club because many cannot gain admission – and most of the new members lack the same powers and privileges enjoyed by the old ones.

This path was chosen not, as we are sometimes told, because the political leadership who negotiated the settlement which produced democracy were slaves of the white establishment. It was selected because the new political elite agreed with the old economic and social power holders on one crucial point: that the goal of the new democracy was to ensure that what whites enjoyed under apartheid would be available to all. That being so, there is no need to change the way in which things have been done for decades in the economy and social institutions; all that is needed is to ensure that everyone can do them. It is the key reason why the core pre-1994 patterns remain. Neither elite saw any need to change them.

It needs no pointing out why the old elite wanted to retain that to which it was accustomed. The old insiders have an obvious stake in protecting past patterns. The new elite saw it the same way because, in its view, to deny everyone what whites enjoyed was to expect the black majority to settle for second best. During the negotiations, an African National Congress (ANC) official who was later to become a Cabinet minister argued that sections of the white establishment were arguing for privatisation because they did not want black politicians 'to get [their] grubby paws' on the state-owned companies the old elite had used to advance its interests. Similarly, it could be argued that large corporations should not be broken up because black people would not benefit from controlling them. Or that curbing the lifestyles of the affluent would deprive black people of the way of living which only whites once enjoyed. Instead of insisting that the economic and social habits of the minority were wasteful and a bar to progress, the new governing elite insisted that the minority's lifestyle should be available to all. Since it is impossible to extend to everyone what a minority enjoyed because it used force to deny opportunities to the vast majority, this inevitably meant that some would enjoy the fruits of this choice but most would not.

This may explain why the negotiation process which ended apartheid did not tackle these issues. The compromise of 1993 settled only one question – the denial of citizenship and rights to the vast majority. This issue was crucial and no progress on any others was possible without addressing it. But it was not the only issue: the power which is wielded outside government does not disappear because everyone can vote. Although the negotiation period saw a plethora of forums which sought to negotiate change in all aspects of social and economic life,[10] their impact was limited. The bargained compromises which produced a new constitution extending equal rights to all were not accompanied by similar agreements on how the economy and social institutions (schools, colleges and universities, for example) should change to dissolve the exclusive club. And so core patterns remain unchanged. The unspoken consensus between the two elites was to leave things largely as they were, not because the new political elite feared a backlash if it sought to change them, but because it wanted to leave them intact.

While this process has peculiarly South African features, its broad patterns are not unique to this country. On the contrary, processes in which societies change but their core patterns do not have been described and analysed by the economic historian Douglass North, who, in his attempt to understand why societies could experience political change and yet remain on the same economic growth path, used the term 'path dependence'.[11] While North's perspective is open to challenge, this emphasis on structural continuity even when real change is occurring expresses the experience of South Africa's democracy. So too do the three elements which Scott Page, a scholar influenced by North, has identified as the components of path dependence: behaviour patterns, what people do and do not value, and the social relationships which people form.[12]

Understanding South Africa's development path since 1994 as a case of path dependence enables us to move away from a common but misleading view of the country's democratic journey. In this view, the negotiations of the early 1990s produced a settlement which resolved the problems of the past and laid a foundation for an inclusive democracy. But corrupt politicians abused democracy and squandered the promise of its beginnings. So, the society's health requires it to return to the period before these corrupt actors did their damage. A business leader has claimed that the unemployment rate would be little more than half its 2019 level had the administration of former president Thabo Mbeki not been replaced by that of Jacob Zuma.[13] The Zuma administration did great damage. But corruption did not disrupt an economy and society which worked for all. Rather, corruption was a symptom of the fact that they worked for far too few. To cite one example, the unemployment rate has been above 20 per cent throughout the democratic period[14] regardless of who was head of government. Corruption is a symptom of the reality that the society remains too firmly trapped in its past. The remedy lies not in returning to the past but in escaping from it. It requires not only undoing the damage caused by corruption but addressing the path dependence which created it.

This book analyses South African path dependence and suggests ways to escape it. It examines the particular features of path dependence and how a modified version of North's insight into this reality helps us to make sense of developments in South Africa. It also examines the work of two social thinkers, Mahmood Mamdani and Harold Wolpe, who in different ways enable us to enhance our understanding of path dependence. The book concludes with a discussion of ways in which the society might escape the burden of its past.

The book aims to contribute to the debate on how to understand South Africa's past, present and possible future, and to shed light on where the country is and where it could be headed. It also aims to encourage a more accurate understanding of why South Africa faces social and economic difficulties and what might be done to overcome them. As long as debate remains trapped in the oft-repeated but inaccurate claim that an essentially sound society and economy was diverted from its promising growth path by the corruption of some politicians, the country will remain trapped in an unproductive past. A scholarly study may not change how South Africans understand their present and imagine a better future. But it is not beyond the bounds of realism to hope that this book may influence the way some people see these issues and that this may, in turn, influence the political debate.

Much of this book was written before Covid-19 reached South Africa. An analysis of how the virus may change the society is beyond its scope. But because *Prisoners of the Past* proposes a way out of the realities which made Covid-19 so difficult to contain and magnified the damage it caused, the epidemic has made the argument offered here crucial to the challenges now facing South Africa.

# 1

# The Past Is Too Much With Us:
# South Africa's Path-Dependent Democracy

In early 2018, an illusion which had underpinned South Africa's mainstream debate ended. But, in the main, the debate did not notice.

For several years prior to 2018, the mainstream account – promoted by journalists, commentators, many politicians, and citizens on social media – lamented the country's fall from grace. The presidency of Jacob Zuma, who was widely associated in the public mind with corruption and patronage, was compared unfavourably to the days before 2007, when he won the ANC presidency. This comparison underpinned an account of South Africa's reality after 1994. The new democracy, this view claimed, had been the envy of the world, the product of a transition in which the political class had placed the national interest first and produced a constitution of which the country could be proud. For almost a decade and a half, the new democracy flourished. But in 2009, when Zuma became state president, it fell into the hands of the greedy who destroyed the dream and turned South Africa into a society 'in tatters'.[1] Only new leadership could restore it to its former state.

The new leadership duly arrived in the form of current president Cyril Ramaphosa. Although he had served as deputy president in Zuma's government, Ramaphosa was the unofficial head of the ANC faction which opposed Zuma and so was associated in the minds of many with opposition to corruption. Surveys[2] and the 2019 election results showed that he was popular among voters. Business people also appeared to place their trust in him: since he had spent years in business before returning to politics, they assumed that he favoured not only clean government but market-led economic growth. In almost every way, Ramaphosa seemed to be the polar opposite of Zuma. If the standard account was accurate, then, the new presidency would surely trigger growth and renewal.

But while Ramaphosa and his allies did make significant changes to the criminal justice system and state-owned enterprises, both of which had been key targets of the patronage politics of the Zuma era, the problems which were meant to begin vanishing under new leadership have remained. There was no economic revival – on the contrary, even before Covid-19 arrived, the economy faltered, falling into recession in 2018, followed by weak or negative growth in 2019.[3] Unemployment reached 29 per cent in mid-2019.[4] Despite the removal of board members and senior management at state-owned companies who were accused of corruption and their replacement by people with personal credibility, virtually all these enterprises fell into financial crisis. Some battled to pay salaries,[5] while the largest and most important, the power utility Eskom, was forced to introduce rolling power cuts and needed a large infusion of public funds to remain in operation.[6] The public debate continued to paint the government as corrupt[7] and incompetent.[8]

For those doggedly committed to the mainstream account, there was an escape hatch. Ramaphosa presided over a deeply divided ANC which seemed to have agreed, at the conference which elected him, to share leadership positions between his faction's and Zuma's – its national executive committee, which runs the ANC between conferences, was evenly divided between the two. It could be argued that the people who caused the problem still wielded power. But that argument was less credible than it seemed. The divisions had not stopped the Ramaphosa-led governing party from making changes, and the key positions in the national Cabinet were dominated by ministers loyal to his faction. It was fashionable among commentators to insist that he was in charge of government (although not the ANC)[9] – which meant, of course, that the new president's difficulties within his party did not prevent him from getting government to adopt his programme. Why, then, was there no clear movement towards a stronger economy and more effective government after Zuma's departure?

Most mainstream explanations remained firmly within the paradigm which insisted that the country's fate depended on the quality of its head of government. Ramaphosa, they suggested, was not the saviour he had appeared to be (at least to some). He was, in one view, not firm or decisive; he was regularly accused of lacking courage by failing to implement whichever measures the person levelling the accusation felt were required.[10] For others, the problem was that he was not a new broom after all: he was happy to serve as Zuma's deputy president and so was no alternative.[11] In this view, the entire governing party was corrupt and it did not matter which individual or faction presided over it. These claims missed crucial realities.

The complaints about Ramaphosa's indecisiveness ignored the fact that, in a society as divided and fractious as South Africa's, doing what some people wanted inevitably meant doing what others did not want. Often, those who did not want policy had enough power to defeat it; and so 'timidity' may be the only route to change. One example of the 'leadership' many wanted was the decision, in 2018, of the Eskom board to inform trade unions that it was not willing to grant any wage increases – precisely the aggressive cost-cutting which is popular in business and among the media. But this decision triggered industrial action which forced Eskom to impose 'load shedding', rolling blackouts[12] that caused dismay among precisely those voices which had loudly advocated 'getting tough with the unions' but seemed unwilling to pay the price. While some in business blamed the government for capitulating to the unions, they did not explain how they would have maintained power supply which, they insisted, should not be disrupted.

Nor is this the only case in which 'decisiveness' seemed likely to cost much and reap little. Ramaphosa may have chosen to conciliate his opponents rather than confront them, not because he is a brilliant strategist, but because this was where his temperament inclined him. But the concrete effect may have been to avoid courses of action which would have caused great economic damage. The view that there was no difference between the Ramaphosa group and its opponents ignores the fact, mentioned earlier, that the new ANC leadership introduced significant changes which aimed to restore the status quo before Zuma became president.[13] More importantly, as we shall see shortly, it misses the reality that the factional divide within the ANC runs deep because it reflects the contrasting interests of those whom path dependence has included in the market economy and those it has excluded, ensuring that the two groups had very different priorities.

The change in leadership in early 2018 was significant: leaders who wanted what those who shaped the mainstream debate wanted replaced those who did not. The non-appearance of the promised revival surely meant that, contrary to the mainstream account, the actions in office of Zuma and his faction were not the only reasons for the economic and social problems they were said to explain: the causes clearly ran deeper. Closer examination shows that the difficulties persisted after Zuma left office because they existed for a long time before he arrived. The constitutional settlement which ushered in democracy in 1994 was an important break with the political past, but it left much of its economic and social realities intact. These persistent realities explain why the post-Zuma reality is not nearly as different from his term in office as the mainstream accounts hoped it would be.

## A PLACE FOR SOME: ECONOMIC INCLUSION AND EXCLUSION

Apartheid was, of course, built on creating a divide between the included and the excluded.

The primary divide was that between black and white, but there were secondary exclusions too. Some black people were allowed to live in the cities permanently, but most could live in urban areas only if they were working on a contract which required them to return annually to ethnically demarcated rural areas. People classified coloured and Indian were allowed to occupy skilled jobs and belong to trade unions with official bargaining rights; black African workers were not.[14] In the Western Cape, people classified coloured were given job preference over Africans and harsher restrictions were placed on the right of Africans to live there, making the province the only area in the country where Africans were not in the majority.[15] These examples of exclusion among the excluded were symptoms of a wider reality in which political, economic and cultural institutions were designed to serve whites and to exclude the black majority. The primary form of exclusion – the fact that only whites (and latterly people classified coloured and Indian for segregated and subservient parliaments) could vote – ended with the settlement of 1993. But this does not necessarily end the other forms of exclusion. In the economy, while exclusion is no longer entirely racial, it survives and, as before 1994, its effect is to exclude millions of black citizens from the benefits of the formal economy.

That this exclusion cannot be explained by the Zuma presidency is illustrated by data at the tail end of the presidency of Thabo Mbeki – the period in which the economy was, according to the mainstream account, operating as it should. In the fourth quarter of 2008, unemployment fell to its lowest level since credible records were available. While this seems to support the view that the problem began with the Zuma presidency the following year, this 'record low' was 21.5 per cent[16] – higher than the unemployment rate in the Netherlands at the height of the Great Depression.[17] In 2006, more than half the population (51 per cent) received incomes below Statistics South Africa's lower-bound poverty line, while two-thirds were below the upper-bound line (the two differ in their calculation of what is needed to sustain a household).[18] South African poverty rates are higher than those of middle-income countries with a lower gross national income.[19] Then, as now, it was trite to point out that South Africa's level of inequality, measured by the Gini coefficient, was the highest in the world. So too is inequality of opportunity,[20] which, according to the 2010 official census, had not changed significantly since 1994.

While it was customary at the time to blame inequality on the post-1994 government's claimed inability to provide services and programmes which addressed the needs of people who had been excluded by apartheid, the census showed that the government was extending basic services to many more people. The problem was, rather, continued inequality in the formal market.[21] To reinforce the point, a study of government programmes since 1994 found that they had transferred assets to people in poverty – but without significantly altering inequality.[22] So the key problem was not government failure to provide relief (although the programmes could, it was widely agreed, be run better). It was that the formal economy still bred inequality.

A further indicator of persistent patterns of the past was the survival, in robust health, of racial inequality. In 2010, according to the Johannesburg Stock Exchange, black South African investors owned only 18 per cent of the available share capital in the top 100 listed companies.[23] By 2009, the percentage of black professionals in accounting, engineering and law remained at 12 per cent, 24 per cent and 21 per cent respectively.[24] Clearly, despite government affirmative action programmes, which were repeatedly denounced by white critics as a sign that white men were being swept aside, whites remained dominant in business and the professions. Most significant of all, research in the same year showed that white incomes had increased faster than those of other races since democracy was achieved.[25] The period since 1994 was not one in which the country made slow progress towards racial equality in the economy. It was one in which those who had gained from apartheid benefited disproportionately from democracy.

If economic growth is taken as a measure, evidence seems to support the claim that the economy was growing until Zuma took over and has been in decline since. In 2007, Mbeki's last full year in office and his last as president of the ANC, South Africa's growth rate was 5.5 per cent. This followed four consecutive years in which growth exceeded 4.5 per cent. These levels were never reached during Zuma's term and, in his last four years in office, growth did not reach 2 per cent. In the first year of his term, 2009, the economy contracted by 1.5 per cent.[26] It seems easy to conclude that Mbeki's economic management ensured a growing economy while Zuma's prompted the reverse. But 2008, during which Mbeki resigned after the ANC withdrew its support for him, was also the year of a global financial crisis. As the sharp decline in 2009 cannot be attributed to Zuma's presidency since he had not yet begun to act in ways that alienated investors, the only plausible explanation is the impact of the crisis. Similarly, poverty fell until 2011, when it began increasing.[27] It is reasonable to assume that this reflected the economy's limited ability to adjust to the 2009 crisis, not the impact of a change in government.

The economy, which had been partly closed to the world as sanctions were imposed in the last years of minority rule, opened up in the 1990s. Smaller, open economies are highly sensitive to international shocks, and the global crisis might have ended the growth spurt regardless of other constraints. But the fact that, a decade and two very different presidencies later, growth has not been restored suggests an explanation other than that offered by the mainstream. It says not that a healthy economy (measured by its capacity for growth rather than its impact on poverty) was brought to its knees by abusive governance, but that an economy still riddled with structural flaws grew in the tailwinds of a strong world economy only to lose steam when the end of the global boom exposed its weaknesses. This explanation is particularly convincing in the light of an important analysis by the economist Dani Rodrik[28] which found that external shocks turned many African economies from successes to failures because the shocks exposed the weakness of domestic institutions. Similarly, the change in South Africa's economic fortunes was a consequence of structural weaknesses which were exposed by the global crisis, not of a change in political leadership. This does not deny that the patronage politics which reigned during Zuma's tenure was severely damaging, but it does challenge the notion that the economy which he and his faction damaged was fundamentally sound.

In the decade or so since these indicators were measured, some have worsened, some have improved. As noted earlier, in 2019 unemployment stood at 29 per cent, giving apparent credence to the view that the Zuma years had taken a great toll. Black participation in the upper echelons of the economy had increased slightly and black ownership on the stock exchange was measured at 27 per cent in 2017.[29] Since Zuma and his allies sought to justify patronage politics by claiming they were engaged in 'radical economic transformation' which was challenging the power of 'white monopoly capital', these figures could be taken to show that the Zuma years harmed the formal economy as the government also set about reducing racial inequality (among the elite only). But the figures do not show clear movement in either direction. The unemployment rate was 31 per cent in 2003[30] (again during Mbeki's tenure), while the late Zuma-era figures reflected a 5.75 per cent decline in black ownership compared to the previous year.[31] These and similar figures since 1994 show that the similarities between the Mbeki and Zuma periods far outweigh the fluctuations. Unemployment has remained stubbornly high, as have inequality and poverty, while whites dominate the upper echelons of the economy. All of these realities were, of course, features of the (later) apartheid economy.

Again, it must be stressed that this does not mean nothing has changed since 1994, and still less that, as some rhetoric insists, the position of most South Africans has worsened. Black participation in business and the professions has grown since 1994. While the term 'black middle class' is hotly contested, there is a significant and growing number of black South Africans who have benefited from new opportunities and now occupy professional and managerial posts. What the figures do show is that the core features of the pre-1994 economy remain intact. It remains highly concentrated: in 2018, 80 per cent of the listed assets on the stock exchange were owned by just 20 companies.[32] It also excludes many: barriers to entry are high,[33] and the core promise of a market economy – that people who display initiative and ability will be included and rewarded – fails to describe South African realities. This economy, like apartheid's, excludes more people than it includes. According to one estimate, 20 per cent more adults are unemployed in South Africa than in peer economies.[34]

Edward Webster, the first South African scholar to use 'path dependence' to explain current realities, applied the theory to the labour market. He argued that 'the founding interlocking apartheid institutions of the Mineral Energy Complex (MEC) have ensured continuity beyond the change in political regime in 1994'.[35] Writing in 2013, he noted that violent industrial conflict had returned to the workplace after a 'surge in militancy over the past five years'. Strikers were bypassing the established institutions and employers were 'hostile to the institutions of collective bargaining'. For Webster, 'legacies of the past' which placed pressure on bargaining were the persistence of migrant labour; a 'predominantly white management and a black labour force'; high structural unemployment; and 'most importantly … a labour market deeply segmented by race, gender and ethnicity'. The labour market's core, where workers earn regular wages and enjoy union rights, was 'increasingly under threat from those workers who are either outsourced into precarious and lower-paid jobs, or who are retrenched'. Beyond this 'new working poor' lies a third zone of unemployment and 'informal subsistence activities'.[36] Bargaining between unions and employers was, he added, providing a subsistence lifeline to the unemployed – but the power of workers in the formal system was eroded by unemployment and poverty, prompting heightened conflict.

At the time Webster offered this analysis, the bargaining system seemed to be buckling under path dependence. Worker militancy appeared to be fuelled by 'unsecured lending', a euphemism for the fact that workers were borrowing more than they could afford.[37] There were two reasons, both rooted in the past. First, the society's inequalities created a culture in which conspicuous consumption is a measure of personal status. According to the census, more households owned television sets than refrigerators,[38] indicating that it is more important to impress family and friends than to store perishable food. This was rooted in pre-1994 realities. The white affluence apartheid produced was often flaunted as a sign of status and merit: the assumption that expensive consumption signalled worth became pervasive. Since many workers cannot afford the goods which confer status, they borrow more than they can repay. (This culture also helps fuel crime, which, in a society which values consumption, some choose as the route to respect and self-esteem.)[39] Second, poverty and unemployment compel workers to share their pay with those who cannot find work – it is estimated that on average each miner's wage feeds eight to ten people.[40] This is an obvious consequence of continued exclusion.

The militancy which Webster described subsided, although industrial conflict remains a reality. But the patterns of the past have not only caused conflict; they also shape attempts to manage it. One of the great advances of the post-1994 period is said to be the 1995 Labour Relations Act, often cited as evidence of the new order's commitment to change. But, while the law did enhance worker and trade union rights to a degree, the 'new labour relations system' it purported to introduce was not new at all. Its structure was much the same as that of the 1924 Industrial Conciliation Act, which aimed to defuse conflict between employers and white workers and introduced a statutory bargaining system from which black African workers were excluded. The bargaining councils introduced by the 1995 law were essentially the 1924 system extended to all workers. Its only innovation was a provision for workplace forums, which were meant to offer an opportunity for unions and employers to discuss workplace issues, but these have hardly been used. Unions were suspicious of the forums, and employers do not seem to have done much to persuade them to accept them. So the only novel feature of the system has fallen into disuse because the bargaining parties prefer the familiar to the new. This makes the claim that 'a new system' was created by the new democratic order largely an illusion.[41]

Webster's observation that the exclusion of many from the economy created obstacles to growth and stability is increasingly the subject of wide consensus. In 2016, a deputy managing director of the International Monetary Fund, David Lipton, delivered an address in Johannesburg during which he asserted that one-third of the population was excluded from the benefits of the mainstream economy.[42] Many who study the economy would see this as an underestimate. For Lipton, the cause was collusion between formal business and government, who agreed on rules which excluded millions. This broadly describes reality in the economy since at least 1910, when the unified South African state was born.[43] Support for inclusive growth has become a mainstream preoccupation and is a key stated concern of Ramaphosa's government.[44] But this does not necessarily mean a recognition that exclusion is a consequence of patterns which hardened before 1994 and survived political change.

The brunt of exclusion is borne by people in poverty. But they are not the only victims. Inevitably, an economy using the skills and abilities of a minority of its people will be stunted, not only because it deprives itself of energies and talent, but also because it limits its consumer market. It was noted earlier that some who cannot afford to buy goods and services borrow beyond their means; many others go without. Bargaining between employers and trade unions is much more difficult given that workers are demanding pay to feed not only their households but the jobless who depend on them. The continuation of past patterns obstructs the entire economy and explains why it is not growing as fast as its middle-income peer countries.[45] It also explains why the middle class also experiences stagnating living standards.[46]

The economy did not fall ill when politicians used the new democracy to damage the strong markets and industries white South Africa created before 1994. It has been ill for a long time because, as it always has done, it excludes most people from its benefits. South Africa's economic problem is not that democracy changed what needed to be preserved. It is that democracy has changed too little. The weaknesses are a product of leaving intact the essentials of an economy built for the few.

## The Dynamics of Exclusion

It needs constant emphasising that the survival of economic exclusion does not mean that the economy has not changed since 1994.

First, as mentioned earlier, the post-1994 government extended services to people deprived of them under apartheid. This has enhanced the quality of life of millions: by 2014, 83 per cent of households enjoyed access to basic sanitation, compared to 50 per cent in 1994; 95 per cent enjoyed free basic water, compared to 60 per cent; and 86 per cent of households had electricity, compared to 50 per cent.[47] This enhanced the quality of life of people who received these services and, to a degree, offset continued income poverty.[48] The extension of the social grants programme has had a marked effect on livelihoods, providing resources which beneficiaries use to bolster local economies.

Second, the fact that poverty remains high does not mean that everyone who was poor under apartheid is still poor now. On the contrary, the evidence shows widening income gaps between, for example, people residing in cities and those living in the countryside.[49] A key feature of the past two decades is that, while inequality between races remains high, 'inequalities within the African population have increased'.[50] The period since 1994 saw the expansion of a growing black middle class. So inclusion is no longer defined purely by race – a significant section of black South Africa has been incorporated into the mainstream economy.

But race has not been replaced by class as the South African fault line. As noted earlier, racial inequality is stubbornly high. Nor have new black entrants to business and the professions been absorbed seamlessly. By 2017, black Africans occupied only 14 per cent of senior management positions, and only 3 per cent of shares on the stock exchange were directly black-owned.[51] The view of many black professionals and business people mentioned earlier – that while they enjoy qualifications and opportunities denied to their parents and grandparents, they still encounter many of the same racial attitudes[52] – is supported by research.[53] The strong sense by many black professionals that they have been absorbed into the 'insider' club on terms which suggest that older (white) members enjoy status, power and opportunity that are denied them means that race remains a core source of division, just as it was under apartheid. So both racial and social inequality remain features of post-1994 reality.

## THE POLITICS OF INCLUSION AND EXCLUSION

In a variety of ways, the division between economic insiders and outsiders shapes politics as well as the economy. Most visibly, it has moulded the politics of the governing party and, through it, national politics. The divide between insiders and outsiders defines and explains the factionalism which has riven the ANC.

One consequence of economic exclusion is that politics has become for many a route to the middle and affluent classes. People who find their path into the market economy blocked see politics as a substitute, and so those who can do so attach themselves to politicians and parties in the hope of gaining the sustenance and respect offered by a middle-class income.[54] Middle- or upper-level activists also see politics as a way to gain the status and benefits which are products of (relative) affluence. They respond to the courtship of owners of private wealth in the hope of enriching themselves, perpetuating, although in a less formal manner, the close ties between government and business of the apartheid period.[55] This creates an obvious opportunity for those who want to buy influence over government. These private resources – and public money where possible – may be used to distribute money and jobs in exchange for political support. This patronage politics – labelled 'state capture' by its opponents – was, during the Zuma years, largely associated with the Gupta family, immigrant Indian businessmen who were said to have bought huge influence over the government and governing party. But evidence presented to the commission convened to investigate 'state capture' allegations confirmed that patronage was by no means restricted to them.[56] It was also the political strategy employed by the ANC faction which supported Zuma.

The faction which opposed Zuma, and which coalesced behind his successor, Cyril Ramaphosa, represented and comprised people who had been absorbed into the formal economy and had become, in varying degrees, 'insiders'. Ironically, aspects of the absorption process bore important resemblances to the strategy of the patronage faction, although it was far more subtle and did not necessarily require corrupt behaviour. The political transition created fertile ground for a marriage of convenience between the new political elite and its old economic counterpart. In the early 1990s, the political elite returned from exile or emerged from the under-ground without the necessaries of middle-class life, let alone those expected of prospective government ministers. At the same time, white business owners knew they needed to build a relationship with the likely new government and those who would serve in it. Businesses or business people helped provide the houses and flats, the cars and the places for children at suburban schools which the elite-in-waiting lacked. When white businesses began to realise that they needed black partners, the only potential candidates many knew were the political activists whom they had met across the negotiation table when the two sides began talking from the late 1980s. And so activists were offered business partnerships and seats on company boards, not because they had a record of business success, but because they were politically connected. (Chapter 3 elaborates on the relationships between the two elites.)

Ramaphosa was a beneficiary of this process. When he left politics in 1996 for business, he was a prized addition to boardrooms and his companies were sought-after partners in ventures. In 2012, these relationships were highlighted in a way which damaged his credibility and also offered important insights into the role which activists-turned-business-people were expected to play. Ramaphosa was a non-executive member of the board of the Lonmin mining company which mined platinum in the North West province. During a strike at the company, security guards were killed and the company blamed striking miners. Ramaphosa was asked to contact the minister of police to urge him to do more to curb this violence. He sent an email asking the minister to take 'concomitant action' against the 'plainly dastardly criminals' whom he blamed for the violence. The next day police opened fire on striking miners, killing 34.[57] Ramaphosa insisted he had no role in the killings and was merely asking the minister to enforce the law; the official inquiry into the Marikana killings found that he was not responsible for the shootings.[58] But this did not alter the implication of the emails: that Ramaphosa's role on the board was to act as an emissary to the government. He was 'effectively trading his access to the business stake in the mining companies for his political influence with the ANC government'.[59] This greatly strengthened claims that white-owned businesses saw their black directors and senior managers as conduits to the government, not partners in a common business endeavour – and the view that black people had joined the business 'club' as junior members only.

Nevertheless, this incorporation gave a section of the ANC leadership and support base a very obvious stake in the health of the market economy. This was not shared by the patronage faction, which relied on the state to attract the interest of would-be capturers or as a source of money. The stake in the formal market-place was shared by trade unions and their members, who might lack many of the advantages of other members of the club but did depend on the market economy for their wages or salaries. This gave them a clear interest in defending that economy when it was threatened by the patronage faction.

An incident which encapsulated the conflicting interests of the two factions was Zuma's dismissal, in December 2015, of the finance minister, Nhlanhla Nene. Nene was removed because he refused to approve large projects favoured by the patronage group[60] and was replaced by a little-known member of Parliament, Des van Rooyen, who had clearly been placed in the position because he would approve the spending. This prompted resistance from a remarkable coalition which stretched from the left of the trade union movement to executives of the major banks. Within days, Van Rooyen was replaced by Pravin Gordhan, a former finance minister who opposes the patronage faction.[61] Zuma's quick retreat was prompted largely by the fact that three of the ANC's top six leaders also opposed Nene's dismissal. The president's attempt to remove a minister who stood in the way of patronage projects was, there-fore, successfully resisted by a coalition which, divided on everything else, shared an interest in protecting the market economy from the costs imposed on it by this manoeuvre. The incident revealed the fault lines which dominated politics at least until the Covid-19 epidemic of 2020: a battle between those who saw the state as their primary economic vehicle and those who needed the market (as well as the state in varying degrees). This reflected the reality that apartheid's end incorporated only some of the excluded, preserving a divide between those who directly bene-fited from the market and those who did not.

The battle within the ANC – and in the wider political arena – was not one between insiders and outsiders. Patronage politicians were not outsiders, nor did they speak for them. They found it useful to use the language of 'radical eco-nomic transformation', but this was a tactic of expediency. Using the state to secure resources, directly or from businesses or individuals seeking to influence govern-ment decisions, does not challenge economic exclusion: it is an attempt by some insider politicians to rise up the ladder and perpetuates a pattern of relationships between some businesses and politics which solidified in the apartheid era. It seeks not to abolish the inequities inside the club but to gain a greater share of the benefits.

If the internal battle within the ANC leaves outsiders unrepresented, so too does politics more broadly. Political parties may seek votes from outsiders but they do not speak for them, even when they use rhetoric which claims that they do. The insiders' control over the national debate is so profound that it renders outsiders invisible: the contest between 'left' and 'right' is a debate between insiders in which outsiders remain mute.[62] This point is expanded on later (Chapter 5), but an anecdote conveys some of its flavour: A leader of the Economic Freedom Fighters (EFF), often assumed to be the voice of the dispossessed, was asked by a radio interviewer how he came to own two houses. He replied that, 'like every young South African', he used his first salary cheque to buy a home.[63] The remark was that of an insider entirely blind to the circumstances of outsiders. Youth unemployment ensures that most young South Africans do not receive a first salary cheque. Those lucky enough to get one do not earn enough to buy a house. That the speaker represented a party which claims to speak for the dispossessed illustrates how deeply the insiders have rendered the world of everyone else invisible. But while outsiders' role in politics is relegated to voting and, at times, demonstrating on the streets, the divide between them and the insiders shapes democratic politics.

## White Privilege for All

A need to defend the market economy is not the only commonality between the old economic elite and its new political counterpart. The divide between insiders and outsiders is a consequence of an unspoken consensus between them which also informs much politics and insider debate – that the goal of democratic South Africa should be to ensure that everyone enjoys the privileges whites were favoured with under apartheid.

After 1994, two imperatives prompted the political leadership elected by the majority to seek to inhabit, not change, the patterns established by white rule. First, apartheid was, for much of its life, an efficient racial oligarchy which ensured white wealth, comfort and security. Whites possessed political rights and a high standard of living: by the time apartheid ended, only 1 per cent of whites lived in poverty.[64] Public policy ensured that the economy, public services and city planning served the needs of the racial minority. It hardly needs explaining why the white economic elite (indeed, all whites) should want to establish what they had as the norm in which black people were to be included. For the new political elite, to end the system was to deprive blacks of the privileges that whites possessed. Racial equality meant, therefore, that black people should now have the same benefits that whites alone had once held.

But not everyone could enjoy what whites had under apartheid. Once legal discrimination ended, all citizens could not possibly have what a few had only because the law and violence were used to deny everyone else: inevitably, there would not be enough to go around for most people. The point was underscored by events in Johannesburg's Alexandra township in the last few years of apartheid. Alexandra was once one of the few urban areas in which black people possessed property rights under apartheid. The system's planners sought to destroy this and turn the area into a vast barracks for migrant workers. A residents' committee led by local notables successfully resisted these plans by securing agreement that the township should be developed, not demolished. The committee told university-based town planners whom it asked for help that it wanted Alexandra to become a 'garden city' like those whites inhabited.[65] The academics replied that there were too many people in the township and too little land: a 'garden city' was possible only if tens of thousands of residents were removed from their homes. The committee remarked, angrily, that the town planners, who were white, lived in garden suburbs but were claiming that blacks could not have the benefits of the same surroundings. It insisted that Alexandra residents enjoy what the white planners enjoyed. And so, the 'garden city' plan was implemented – and tens of thousands were displaced. The removals set off a spiral of conflict between people who considered themselves the real residents of Alexandra (those who had owned or rented land) and those they considered new arrivals. This continues into the present.[66]

The tragedy of Alexandra exemplifies the post-1994 path of South Africa's economy and society. During apartheid, Alexandra could be developed only by leaving white privileges and entitlements untouched. After 1994, trying to extend to all what the privileged few obtained by force ensures, as it did in Alexandra, that only some will benefit at the expense of many others. The exchange between the residents' committee and the planners ignored what was not possible under apartheid but could have been addressed after 1994: that the people of Alexandra could never all be accommodated unless those in the neighbouring suburbs made do with less. In this case, this meant opening land for township residents. More generally, the elites who decided the course of post-1994 South Africa did not seriously address the reality that the minority would have to give up some of what it had enjoyed if everyone was to enjoy full economic citizenship. And so, the need to negotiate new economic rules which would open opportunity was ignored.

A similar dynamic was prompted by an understandable concern of the new elite: to counter the prejudice that blacks were incapable of running a state with an industrial economy. The Mbeki administration was acutely aware of this bias and determined to refute it. Its chief concern was to convince whites at home and elsewhere that a black administration could perform the tasks whites were believed to value. But Mbeki's presidency could only show whites that a black-led government was efficient at doing what they valued by adopting what were assumed to be their (whites') standards. This ensured a focus on making existing arrangements run better.[67] One way in which this was expressed was a frequent stress on ensuring that South Africa became 'world class', which meant, in effect, meeting the norms of the global North.[68] This perpetuated attitudes which saw Europe and the US as models and ensured that their cultural influence would persist. And so, the institutions and patterns of the past are preserved by the new elite as well as the old.

One of the many consequences is a debate on jobs which is based on assumptions that defy logic. Political parties and lobby groups compete to convince voters and decision-makers that their policy will create millions of formal sector jobs[69] – despite the fact that domestic realities and global trends show that, regardless of the growth level, millions of people will not work in formal businesses. The illusion prevents a productive discussion of ways to ensure that those who cannot work in formal jobs can engage in productive activity which will offer them an adequate livelihood. 'Job creation' remains an unquestioned cornerstone of the national debate, not because evidence supports it, but because it holds open the illusion of a return to white life in the 1960s, when secure work in a formal factory, office or shop was the norm – in which the privilege which apartheid bestowed on whites can be extended to all.

## ISLANDS OF POWER: OLD PATTERNS IN A NEW POLITICAL ORDER

Another aspect of the way 'new' political realities preserve pre-1994 patterns challenges the common notion that post-1994 South Africa is a 'dominant party' system in which, although regular elections are held and citizens are endowed with democratic rights, one party dominates the political system and society.[70]

But winning elections does not necessarily mean dominating society. Despite repeated successes in national elections, the ANC dominates some areas only – in others, different parties and social interests dominate. This pattern operates in a manner which preserves realities that prevailed before 1994.

The ANC is seen in much academic literature[71] and public debate[72] as a dominant party because it has won every general election since 1994 with at least 57 per cent of the vote and controls eight of nine provinces. ANC dominance is seen as a threat to democracy because it is said to centralise power in one party, reducing minorities to political spectators.[73] But if we look beyond national voting numbers and examine power realities, we find that no party imposes its will on all of society. This is a consequence of racial and other identity divisions and of a reality often ignored by theories of 'party dominance': social power – the capacity to wield power in society through control of intellectual and material resources – can enable political minorities to set the agenda regardless of election results.

One effect of these realities is an ironic divide in the major cities between middle-class and affluent suburbs on the one hand, and (mainly) low-income townships on the other. It is ironic because opponents of the 'dominant' party enjoy political, economic and social freedoms which its supporters do not. In the suburbs, which, two decades after the end of apartheid, remain predominantly white, the official opposition, the Democratic Alliance (DA), dominates. If we see the suburbs not purely as a physical space but as a metaphor for the areas of public space and life dominated by the middle class and the wealthy, they have become almost monolithic in their opposition to the government. It is rare to see comment in the media – by readers, listeners or viewers or by journalists – sympathetic to the ANC. While this initially seemed to be a response to Zuma, it has survived his departure from the presidency. No force is used to impose uniformity – social convention and a shared world view ensure an echo chamber. This is obviously in sharp contrast to election results and it creates an anomaly. When few voices in the mainstream public debate present the perspective of a party which, despite a decline, still attracts almost 60 per cent of the vote – and, in 2019, despite its worst national result yet, was still 37 percentage points ahead of the next biggest party – democratic debate takes on an almost surreal air since it excludes more than half the electorate.

By contrast, in the townships and shack settlements where the ANC's support has been concentrated since 1994 (and still is to a significant degree, although it no longer monopolises the vote in many areas), democracy is constrained, not necessarily by the state or national leadership of the governing party, but by local political elites who are often connected to the local state, in particular the police. The elites use these connections to suppress independent and opposing views, particularly when those who hold them threaten the elites' monopoly on local power. Ironically, democracy has brought freedom to those areas where the ANC is relegated to the margins, but this is far less the case in those areas where the party carries majority support. And even in some areas where the ANC seems to dominate public life, it is debatable whether the party really is the source of local elites' power or merely the vehicle through which they exercise it.[74]

The township reality does not mean that the ANC compels voters to support it: voters in these areas can and do vote against it. In 2012, after the Marikana shootings, the ANC lost a municipal by-election in the area. In the same year, following media reports that huge amounts had been spent renovating Zuma's homestead in Nkandla, in rural KwaZulu-Natal, the ANC lost a by-election in Nkandla which handed control of the municipality to the Inkatha Freedom Party (IFP).[75] Opposition control continues despite (or because of) the fact that Zuma personally campaigned for the ANC after stepping down as state president.[76] Like the DA, the ANC relies for its support on deeply rooted sentiment among its voters. The claim by a US scholar that ANC support is 'politically engineered'[77] – which implies that it convinces voters that they share an identity and experience they do not really have – shows deep ignorance of black experience in a society in which race remains pervasive,[78] and the ANC is still seen by many grassroots voters as the party which resists racism. A research finding that urban people living in poverty believe that the ANC 'brought freedom and democracy to South Africa'[79] is not a product of party strategy. It is a reflection of the degree to which racial domination and responses to it shape political identities.

Despite changes as ANC support erodes, election results still reflect the persistence of social and economic patterns which are products of racial minority rule – in this case, residential segregation. While this has been weakened, the pace has been relatively slow. Race and political identity often coincide: racial minorities remain concentrated in suburbs; their black counterparts still live mainly in townships and shack settlements. And so voting districts are, to varying degrees, homogeneous. As a consequence, the DA is as dominant in its strongholds as the ANC is in its. Historically, the IFP dominated those areas of KwaZulu-Natal in which traditional authorities wielded power.[80] Although it lost support after the ANC persuaded some traditional leaders that it could better serve their interests, the IFP continues to dominate some hostels and parts of rural KwaZulu-Natal. The party has also experienced a modest but significant revival in its traditional strongholds.[81] Ethnic identity ensures dominance of geographic areas by a party other than the ANC.

An analysis of voting statistics in Johannesburg in the 2011 local elections[82] reveals, not surprisingly, that in township wards, which are still almost exclusively black, the ANC received 80–90 per cent of the vote; the DA was usually second but received only 4.5–8 per cent. The only exception was the one ward which houses a hostel for Zulu-speaking workers: here the IFP won. The DA's dominance of suburbs was more pronounced. In areas in which only suburban voters live, the DA's share of the vote ranged from 78 to 87 per cent. In these areas, the ANC vote varied between 11.5 and 19.5 per cent. The DA's share began dropping only in those suburban wards which incorporate township or inner-city areas and so also include concentrations of black voters. It is remarkable that the DA won roughly the same share in its strongholds as the ANC did in its, because it is common for suburban householders to employ black domestic workers who are unlikely to vote for the DA. And so among homeowners and tenants rather than domestic workers, DA dominance was so huge that the results began to look like the outcome of plebiscites in authoritarian regimes: the DA probably won 95 per cent or more of the votes cast by owners and renters of property. In the decade since then, the ANC's share of the township vote has declined. The DA's hold over the suburban vote, however, remained fairly constant until the 2019 election, when it suffered losses to the Freedom Front Plus, which appeals to Afrikaans-speaking right-wing white voters. Nonetheless, the DA remains electorally dominant in the suburbs.

These realities ensure that while elections have, since 1994, been free and fair, they have rarely been competitive. The ANC, DA and, in some cases, IFP monopolise parts of the country or cities where their rivals offer only token resistance, preferring to solidify support in their own fiefdoms than to launch a fruitless challenge in their rivals' bastions. This pattern began in 1994, when the information analysis department of the Independent Electoral Commission identified 165 'no-go areas' in which a party was able to prevent rivals from campaigning.[83] The problem was most pronounced in KwaZulu-Natal, where the ANC and IFP controlled their respective areas by force. In that election, peace was largely preserved by the fact that excluded parties kept out of their opponents' no-go areas. (An ANC canvasser was murdered in the KwaZulu area of the province[84] and other incidents of violence were reported, but they were not as severe as anticipated.) By the second election, force no longer prevented competition between parties. But, while parties no longer risked life and limb by campaigning in their opponents' strongholds, they did waste resources and energy which could be better employed getting their own supporters to the polls. The coercion of 1994 was replaced by social power. Over the past few years, the ANC's hold over its strongholds has diminished as it faced challenges from breakaway parties, the Congress of the People and the Economic Freedom Fighters. The DA has also begun campaigning in townships and shack settlements. But the ANC remains by far the largest party in townships and shack settlements; the DA largely dominates the suburbs.

The DA's dominance reflects social reality. The affluent areas, supposedly under the heel of a dominant party, are in reality sites of a power which neutralises ANC influence: residents' social and economic life is barely touched by the ANC. Suburban householders routinely complain about the quality of city governance, and are sometimes inconvenienced by power or water outages or inadequate road maintenance. But they have ample access to private companies who sell services previously provided by the state – there are more active private security guards in South Africa than police and army officers combined.[85] Schools and hospitals are usually privately owned. Boom gates which bar public access to suburban streets and 'gated communities' seek to create mini-cities entirely shielded from most citizens.[86] Influential business and professional associations, as well as residents' and ratepayers' associations in the suburbs, are out of the ANC's control. Because they are better able to organise and gain access to officials, suburban residents secure much higher levels of the public services they still use than do residents of the townships and shack settlements.[87]

## The Power of the Social

The social power of the suburbs also shapes public debate: their concerns shape the media and the academy. Aubrey Matshiqi observes: 'White people remain a cultural majority. And it is their world view that continues to dominate the shaping of social and economic relations.'[88]

Much public commentary which claims to 'speak truth to power' is an attempt to defend the hierarchy of the past. Thus a journalist, in an article comparing the moral excellence of a white Constitutional Court judge to the immorality of a black state president, declares that because the judge grew up as a white person in poverty under apartheid, he had 'endured much the same hardship and discrimination as the most unfortunate of his compatriots',[89] despite the fact that those compatriots were subject to a battery of racial laws from which even the poorest whites were exempt. Social power ensures that the standards and concerns of the minority dominate the national debate.

While it seems unlikely that a society which experienced three centuries of minority rule would be free of inherited problems after achieving democracy, the national debate blames all ills on post-1994 governance, and references to the influence of the past are dismissed as lame excuses. This implies that political change created an entirely new and workable society which is being ruined by majority rule. Some commentators have insisted that the misdeeds of the current government are more serious than those of apartheid's rulers,[90] despite the fact that democratic government has not deprived nine-tenths of the population of basic rights simply because they belong to the 'wrong' race. The debate assumes that difficulties are the consequence not of deep-rooted problems embedded in the past, but of the actions of the governing party and its leadership since 1994: 'The failures of the ANC, both real and perceived, have emboldened many among those who bene-fited from white minority rule to such an extent that it is no longer obvious that the ravages of apartheid are part of the present.'[91] Majority rule is still seen as a problem, not a solution – a view which, of course, underpinned the thinking of apartheid's architects and supporters.

The dominant culture is not exclusively white; it also has black adherents. Nor does it repeat the values of apartheid. These have been largely discredited. As Sam Nolutshungu pointed out during apartheid, it and its ideology could never absorb blacks into the power structure or convince them to endorse its values – it could only subordinate them. (In systems where all enjoy formal rights, people who are dominated may be persuaded that they are really equal. A system which denies a racial group rights denies explicitly that all are equal.)[92] But while the change of 1994 ended the apartheid framework, it did not replace it with a non-racial alternative. It prompted a change to values of older origin – those of the British colonialism which preceded the Afrikaner nationalist victory of 1948. While the dominant values in post-1994 South Africa do not explicitly support colonialism, they assume that all should aspire to 'Western' values. Over four decades ago, the philosopher Richard Turner wrote of South African white liberals that they 'believe that "western civilisation" is … superior to other forms, but also that blacks can, through education, attain the level of western civilisation.'[93] Since 1994, this view has become dominant in much of cultural and intellectual life. It even dominates, at times, those who claim to be rebelling against it, just as the Mbeki administration could attempt to refute claims of black incompetence only by embracing the values of those who harbour this prejudice.

It is extremely rare in academic or policy debates or public conversation to see other African countries as useful models for policies and practices. It is far more common to look to Europe, North America or Australia. This is generally so whatever the race or political allegiance of the participants. During constitutional negotiations, all the parties showed intense interest in German and Canadian fed-eralism, none at all in that of Nigeria or India.[94] Discussions of negotiated economic compromises focus on Sweden, Germany or Ireland – never Mauritius, whose eco-nomic development depended heavily on economic bargaining.[95] These biases are pervasive in the media and the academy, where they have prompted protests from students demanding the 'decolonisation' of the university.[96] They also shape the world view of the suburbs. The past's influence is particularly pronounced since the assumptions which now hold sway are not those which dominated between 1948 and 1994 but are those of an earlier era.

In the townships and shack settlements, power can appear in a far more obvious – and at times violent – guise. Developments in these areas must be placed in social and economic context. The townships were systematically underdeveloped by apartheid; economic opportunities were deliberately limited. Research finds that, since democracy was established, these areas have seen the emergence of both a new elite and a new underclass: the most significant form of enrichment and power for the new elite is local government.[97] The ANC is a conduit for the elite but has also been the vehicle for protest by the underclass.

These areas are sites of sustained protest. While much reportage and commentary assumes that protest is new – a product of disenchantment with the ANC after Zuma took office – it has been an almost constant reality since 1976, when the Soweto uprising began. Only in the mid-1990s, in the first flush of democratic enthusiasm, did protest briefly subside.[98] But while it is usually directed at ANC-run local authorities, the protest is often led by local ANC activists and branches – either because they are articulating local grievances[99] or because individuals hope that, by mobilising protest, they will enhance their leverage and gain places on election lists.[100] An ANC activist summed up the reality: 'The greatest enemy of the ANC here is the ANC itself.'[101] Even where protesters are ANC members, police action is often harsh, and police appear to act in concert with ANC branches or community policing forums on which local politicians serve.[102] Where protest is led by independent organisations, the use of violence to retain the dominance of local elites becomes more severe.

By the early 2000s, evidence began to surface of the use of force against local protesters.[103] The shooting of activist Andries Tatane, in the Free State town of Ficksburg,[104] and repeated violence directed at leaders of the shack-dweller organisation Abahlali baseMjondolo[105] are merely the most publicised of the uses of violence by local elites: 'A thuggish local elite is able to arise through a combination of criminal, extralegal and quasi-state activities; while elements of this elite may enter into partnership with ANC representatives and officials in local government, they are also independent, since their economic base is independent and, in fact, depends on the inability of state officials to enforce the law in their territory.'[106] The ANC's local dominance ensures that the new elites, who seek the resources of the state, must engage with it – but it is they who are using, rather than being used by, the ANC. While relationships with local ANC politicians and officials play a role in enabling the elites to continue to impose themselves, they may operate in precisely the same way if another party were in power.

Attempts to turn townships and shack settlements into the unchallenged fiefdoms of local bosses are not entirely successful. Residents have used democratic rights to organise: citizens' organisations are active in many townships. The environment in which they operate is constrained, but options for collective action are never entirely closed. We have seen that the ANC is not insulated from local electoral defeats. But the rights which democracy has bestowed are curtailed by dynamics that constrain free political expression. While closeness to the state helps to bolster that power, local elites are independent enough from the ANC and the state to make them another form of social power which preserves pre-1994 patterns.

## YESTERDAY AND TODAY

The contrasts between suburbs and townships neatly mirror past realities even if they take on a different form.

Before 1994, the suburbs enjoyed superior services, provided by a government concerned to attend to their needs. Owners and tenants could vote and, provided they did not identify with black people, speak their minds. They were sites of economic, political and social inclusion. The townships were places of exclusion. People had no vote, services were poor if they were available at all, and the government was interested in the excluded only as sources of labour or threats to order. Speaking their minds, as people in the suburbs did, invited repression. Today, township residents and people in shack settlements have the right to vote and are, in theory at least, represented by a government concerned to serve them. But the areas in which they live repeat the patterns of the past.

Townships and their residents have benefited from development they were denied by apartheid. They have also paid a price for change, as upwardly mobile former residents have moved to the suburbs. But the core reality, that some enjoy a much fuller citizenship than others, remains. So too does the fact that the excluded are black, even if the included are not all white. This exemplifies the wider South African reality. A quarter-century of democracy gave black South Africans opportunities and access to resources which were not available when only whites could vote. Political rights enabled people to send messages to politicians and, at times, to campaign effectively for government which better serves their needs. But the patterns of inclusion and exclusion remain. Within the insider group, subtle racial barriers anger black professionals and business people. Outside it, people remain excluded from wages, salaries, and the political leverage and voice which access to them brings.

This reality contradicts the claim that the successful transition to democracy was damaged by patronage politicians. The transition was always partial because while the structure of the political system changed, that of the economy and the society's institutions did not. Democracy did open opportunities for all. But continued economic exclusion and the dominance of assumptions which underpinned minority rule, albeit in the pre-1948 period rather than during apartheid, ensured that core features of the old order were also key elements of the new.

# 2

# Path Dependence: What It Means and How It Explains South Africa

The analysis thus far has used the term 'path dependence' without detailing what it means and how it offers a lens through which to view post-1994 realities. This chapter discusses the theory of path dependence and its usefulness in making sense of contemporary South Africa.

## NORTH AND PATH DEPENDENCE: UNDERSTANDING INSTITUTIONS

Douglass North, an American economic historian whose work on institutions won him the Nobel Prize in 1993, was not a student of economic exclusion. His academic concern was chiefly to understand why some economies seemed unable to grow over extended periods: 'What accounts for the survival of societies and economies which are characterized by persistent poor performance?'[1] His interest in path dependence, which he defined as 'a term used to describe the powerful influence of the past on the present and future',[2] was a product of his attempt to answer these questions.

Unlike many mainstream economists, North was not wedded to models which claim that humans act rationally only when they behave as computers, weighing the economic costs and benefits of each action and choosing the option which brings them most benefit or least cost. These models, he believed, only work in an abstract world in which there are no rules governing trade and so people can transact with each other without any cost. But in the real world, people are forced to pay a price to trade because every society needs rules to ensure that people transact only in ways consistent with its values. These rules are the institutions which govern economic life: 'When it is costly to transact, then institutions matter. And it is costly to transact'.[3] Institutions, according to North, are 'the humanly devised constraints that structure political, economic and social interaction'. They consist of 'both informal constraints (sanctions, taboos, customs, traditions, and codes of conduct) and formal constraints (constitutions, laws, property rights)'.[4] Throughout history, humans have devised institutions to 'create order and reduce uncertainty in exchange'.[5] These institutions and the degree to which they are enforced determine the cost of transacting. They also impose constraints which can aid or obstruct economic growth. Institutions are effective (economically) if they make it more possible for people to reap the benefits of trading.[6] If they do, they stimulate growth.

For North, economic activity is always pursued within rules, whether these are expressed in formal laws or in informal beliefs and habits. Because formal and informal rules are important, in societies in which the formal laws change, the transaction costs – and thus the ability of economies to grow – may not alter if the informal institutions which influence behaviour remain unchanged. A change of political system, and the adoption of new laws and policies, alter the formal rules but not necessarily the informal institutions. If North is right, economies perform well not because their citizens are better at doing what makes economies grow, but because their institutions – informal as well as formal – make it easier for them to grow.

Unlike conservatives, who view traditional belief systems and the institutions they produce as precious resources to everyone in the society where they hold sway, North notes that institutions are 'not necessarily or even usually created to be socially efficient'. Rather, they 'are created to serve the interests of those with the bargaining power to create new rules'.[7] Institutions are therefore a product of who holds power; they may survive even if they are inefficient, as long as they serve the interests of power holders. They are likely to change only when the power holders are replaced by others with an interest in different institutions. But if power changes hands and institutions remain the same, the economy's patterns will not change. This is crucial to our understanding of South African realities.

## 'Locked In' or Moving On

The key role North gives institutions in shaping economic performance is crucial to his interest in path dependence.

He is quick to acknowledge that he did not invent the term 'path dependence' or the idea that change does not always happen when it seems logical to expect it. He cites two authors who analyse the way in which particular technologies become dominant even though they may not be the most economically efficient. The first is Brian Arthur, who examined how 'chance' elements or 'historical events', not economic efficiency, dictate the choice of one technology over another. Arthur argues that random events could trigger a process in which 'a technology that by chance gains an early lead in adoption may eventually "corner the market" of potential adopters with the other technologies being "locked out".'[8] What presumably attracted North's attention is that Arthur examines a process of 'lock-in', in which a technology is established as the only way of performing a function even though it can be shown that another technology, available at the time, would have done the job better and at less cost.

While Arthur's discussion of the topic consists mainly of abstract modelling, the other author North cites, Paul David, makes the same point by way of a familiar and easily understood example: the 'QWERTY' typewriter or computer keyboard, so called because the top row of letters begins with this sequence. David outlines an understanding of path dependence which helps clarify the concept and its relevance for North. He notes that 'it is sometimes not possible to uncover the logic (or illogic) of the world around us except by understanding how it got that way'. More specifically, 'a *path-dependent* sequence of economic changes is one in which important influences upon the eventual outcome can be exerted by temporally remote events'.[9] The QWERTY keyboard is an example.

Computer users are so used to seeing QWERTY as natural and normal, David explains, that attempts in the 1970s to persuade manufacturers to change to the DSK (or Dvorak Simplified Keyboard) persuaded no one. But DSK, patented in 1932, is more efficient than QWERTY. Typists who use it (presumably because they have access to the few machines which employ this keyboard layout) have 'long held most of the world's records for speed typing': a 1940s study showed that if typists were retrained to use DSK, the cost of their training would be recovered in ten working days. One computer company installed a switch on its machines allowing the user to shift to DSK, which, its advertising material proclaimed, would allow people to type 20–40 per cent faster. But few users flicked the switch and QWERTY continues to dominate. Before DSK, seven other improvements on QWERTY were patented in 15 years, but again none was adopted.[10] So why did computer users – and, more particularly, companies which were being offered significant savings if they switched to a more efficient keyboard – not make the change? Classical economists would insist that if users were faced with an opportunity to cut costs and increase profits, they should have ditched QWERTY without a moment's sentimentality. David points out, with obvious relish, that QWERTY dominated despite the fact that there were no government regulations requiring anyone to use it, and so attachment to inefficiency could not be blamed on the usual scapegoat: government interference with the 'free market'.

David notes that there were no strong reasons why QWERTY should survive. The Remington company, the first maker of typewriters, chose this keyboard layout not for efficiency, but because it wanted the top row to contain all the letters a sales representative would need to impress customers by quickly typing the words 'type writer'.[11] In the early years of the typewriter, other companies produced machines with different letter arrangements on their keyboards. But none established a foothold. Part of the reason, David argues, is that within a decade or so of their introduction, typewriters were 'beginning to take their place as an element of a larger, rather complex system of production that was technically interrelated'.[12] Besides the makers and buyers, this included typists and organisations which trained them. Although David does not say so explicitly, all these interests had a stake in QWERTY's survival.

The role of these other interests and activities proved critical when 'touch typing', the method which still dominates, replaced earlier, less efficient methods. From its beginning, touch typing was adapted to QWERTY rather than to other keyboards, which meant that instructors used it when they taught typists. At that stage typewriters were typically bought by businesses, and so there was no incentive for typists to insist on a more efficient method (since they would not expect to be paid more if they typed faster). David argues that there was also no incentive for companies to insist on a more efficient keyboard because they would have to pay to train typists to use it, and they saw no reason why they should pay to enhance a skill a typist could easily take to another employer. The fact that an employer used a QWERTY keyboard would also be an incentive to typists to join that firm because they had been trained to use it. So, businesses bought QWERTY keyboards and typists were trained in them. They, their employers and the trainers had no incentive to change keyboards. A cycle was established in which 'each ... decision in favour of QWERTY would raise the probability ... that the next selector would favour QWERTY'.[13]

David's analysis shows that a technology was chosen not because it did the job best, but because it suited the purpose of those who had the power to retain or change it. Because not only Remington but also the typists, those who trained them and the businesses which employed them derived benefits from the arrangement or would incur costs from changing it, the makers of new, better technologies had no power to shift this arrangement to a more economically efficient alternative. The more entrenched the technology became, the more difficult it was to remove. The path dependence which entrenched a less efficient keyboard was not a product of irrationality. All the parties who ensured the dominance of an inferior technology made rational calculations of their interests, given the circumstances each faced. Arthur and David mention the increasing returns to those who benefit from less efficient technologies: they choose these technologies not because they are deluded but because they benefit from them. The more this continued, the more unlikely did it become that this technology would be replaced. Each party's rational understanding of their interests ensured a decision which, according to mainstream economic theory, was irrational.

North acknowledges differences between this analysis of technological change and change in institutions.[14] While technologies are 'locked in' by the strategies of economic actors only, institutions are path dependent because of the workings of the political system and economy, the decisions of many actors who have different bargaining strengths, and 'the role of cultural inheritance'. Despite this, he argues that there are strong parallels, and that Arthur's and David's logic can help explain why societies become 'locked in' to paths which stunt growth. He suggests that once those paths are entrenched, there is a limit to how much they can be changed as long as institutions remain unchanged: 'Individual, specific changes in formal or informal constraints certainly may change history but for the most part do not reverse its direction.'[15]

North notes that although Arthur and David present their work as a discussion of how technologies are chosen ahead of rival options, 'the competition is only indirectly between technologies. Directly it is between organisations embodying the competing technologies.'[16] He does not develop this point. But this does imply that competition is only indirectly between technologies because social actors with bargaining power are making choices: it is the choices, not the technologies, which are at the heart of the story. This establishes the link with North's understanding of institutions. The choice of technologies, like that of institutions, is the product of the rational action of those who choose them even when they produce economically inefficient outcomes. Institutions which do not produce the best economic outcomes remain, not because the societies in which they survive are irrational, but because they offer continuing benefits to those who wield power.

North continues his attempt to show that analyses of technological path dependence can be applied to institutions by drawing attention to an issue Arthur and David do not explicitly address but which he derived from their work: 'imperfect markets characterized by significant transaction costs'.[17] If markets are incomplete (if the people who operate within them do not have the perfect information and full freedom of choice textbooks say they should have), 'the information feedback is fragmentary at best' and transaction costs are significant. In these cases, the 'subjective models of actors' and 'ideology' will 'shape the path'.[18] Choices are shaped not by calculations of economic cost and benefit but by 'the historically derived perceptions' of the actors. North adds: 'The imperfect and fumbling efforts of the actors reflect the difficulties of deciphering a complex environment with the available mental constructs – ideas, theories and ideologies.'[19] So when markets do not work in the way theory says they should (which is always), economic actors will fall back on what they know best: the ideas and values – the belief systems – with which they are familiar.

To illustrate, North uses an example he discussed in greater length elsewhere – medieval and early modern Western Europe. He argues that a radical decline of the population increased the bargaining power of peasants in relation to lords and led to 'incremental alterations over time in the implicit contracts between them'.[20] Because there were fewer people, there were fewer peasants, and lords could not as easily replace peasants who demanded more from them. But the changes were far less significant than economic rationality would suggest. Both sides operated within a 'historically derived model' which assumed a master–servant relationship and did not allow for enhanced power for peasants. This prevented peasants and lords from adjusting their relationship to reflect the new economic reality. 'If … subjective perceptions were always corrected to true models, then presumably the actors would immediately have recontracted to a far more efficient joint solution.' Instead, there was a slow and incremental process of change which was retarded by the 'very slowly changing mental constructs of both parties'. This example, North is quick to point out, did end in more efficient outcomes: 'We tell it as a success story entitled *The Rise of the Western World*.' But he implies that this was more by chance than design. 'Throughout most of history the experience of agents and the ideologies of actors do not combine to lead to more efficient outcomes.'[21]

This passage is key to North's understanding of path dependence. Significantly, it also challenges notions of 'progress' which then shaped mainstream economic thinking. Instead of portraying Western economic success as the triumph of rationality over ignorance, North implies that it was a historical accident, the product of Arthur's 'chance'. So societies which develop productive growth paths are not superior; they are luckier. He implies that path-dependent societies are not rare – they are the vast majority. Where path dependence restricts growth, societies do not share the good fortune of the few who are able to shake off the patterns of the past or to harness them in ways which ensure economic success. At one point,

North also rejects the view that every society has a set of institutions which uniformly impede or promote growth: 'All economies have institutional frameworks that create both productive and unproductive opportunities for organisations' and so 'the history of any economy will show mixed results'.[22] This is an important warning against a frequent tendency to divide the world neatly into economies with 'high-growth' and 'low-growth' institutions. Some of the 'backward' countries may be better endowed to perform some economic tasks than those whose institutions seem ideal for growth.

Further evidence that North believes 'path dependence' to be more normal than might be imagined is that he does not necessarily use the term to describe a negative reality in which societies are prevented from achieving economic goals by the burden of the past. His reliance on Arthur and David would suggest that path dependence is always an obstacle, since both are interested in ways in which unproductive patterns become entrenched. But North seems to see it as a potential boon as well. He uses the example of the Northwest Ordinance, adopted by the US Congress in the 1780s (while the constitution was being negotiated) to provide rules for politically incorporating new territories in America's Midwest. It 'provided a clear, path-dependent pattern of institutional evolution'.[23] In this case, the path dependence, in his view, 'locked in' institutions which encouraged growth.

But the nature of path dependence does not depend on chance alone. Which path becomes entrenched depends on which delivers benefits to 'organizations and interest groups'.[24] Given North's remark that power determines the choice of institutions, this presumably means all those organisations and interests which wield power. Where the powerful actors benefit from institutions which do not encourage production and growth, path dependence will obstruct growth, and vice versa. The importance of power is further underscored by North's argument that productive development paths are likely to emerge out of contests between interests: 'competitive political forces' are one reason why the Northwest Ordinance produced institutions conducive to growth. While he does not develop this point, the logical implication is that interests with a stake in unproductive institutions are challenged by equally powerful interests which do not benefit from them. The result is compromise between the two, which creates the preconditions for growth.[25]

The speed of economic change, North notes elsewhere, is a product of learning: the more people learn from their experiences in the economy, the more likely they are to make changes to remedy problems which prevent them from achieving their goals. But he does not think that learning is a product of machine-like reasoning. To understand learning – and therefore economic change – we must 'dismantle the rationality assumption underlying economic theory'. History shows 'that ideas, ideologies, myths, dogmas and prejudices matter', and knowing how they evolve is crucial to understanding how societies change. The rational-choice framework, which assumes that people know what is in their (economic) interest and act accordingly, 'is patently false in making choices under conditions of uncertainty – the conditions that have characterized the political and economic choices that shaped (and continue to shape) historical change'.[26]

North allows for the possibility that in 'highly developed modern economies' the rationality assumption – the view that economic decisions are cost–benefit calculations – might apply because, where economic rules are settled, economic actors are more likely to base their behaviour on these calculations. But he seems unsure, citing research suggesting that choices in these societies might not be more 'rational'. He is sure that in times of change, in which the rules that govern economics are uncertain, economic actors will opt for that which aligns with their belief systems, not that which can be shown to be more likely to yield greater economic returns. And, although he does not say this directly here, it is also more likely that they will opt for what has worked for them in the past. People are not machines; in most cases, they make sense of the world by relying on learned values and 'knowledge' which may be simply the dominant thinking in their societies. People with the power to shape institutions are therefore likely to rely on what is familiar to them, and that necessarily means keeping alive the patterns of the past.

This is presumably one reason why institutions are not easily changed. Because of what North defines as formal or informal constraints, economies may not move closer to growth by adopting the formal rules of societies which have achieved high levels of growth. This challenges international financial institutions and development agencies who urge countries to 'get the institutions right', just as they once argued that the key to progress was 'getting prices right'.[27] Ironically, their shift from prices to institutions was inspired by North's work.[28] But North implies that formal institutions which enhance economic performance cannot be created by development technicians, partly because these institutions may have no effect on informal rules, values and habits. Even if technicians created 'state-of-the-art' formal rules, informal understandings would produce economic paths different from those for which technicians hope.

Enthusiasm for changing institutions is also common in debates in societies (like South Africa) in which growth levels disappoint elites who hope to emulate rich countries. It is often argued that shifting to the laws and systems of high-growth countries will turn the country into an economic powerhouse. But North warns that formal rules are less important than suggested by some of his argument (his stress on the influence of formal rules in the US, for example). He notes that many Latin American countries adopted versions of the US constitution and that 'many of the property laws of successful Western countries have been adopted by Third World countries'.[29] But this did not prompt high growth, because although the formal rules are the same, 'the enforcement mechanisms, the way enforcement occurs, the norms of behaviour, and the subject models of the actors are not'. Path dependence, North insists, is far more deeply rooted than those who favour shopping around the world for laws and rules which will stimulate growth would have us believe.

He goes further, asserting that path dependence can survive revolutions, such as those which replaced Britain and Spain as colonial powers in North and South America in the eighteenth and nineteenth centuries. The development path of North and South were very different, partly because 'the institutional patterns from the mother country' were deeply rooted and were continued, in modified form, after independence.[30] Here again, he suggests that historical accident was important. English colonies were formed 'in the very century in which the struggle between Parliament and the Crown was coming to a head': this prompted a religious and political diversity which influenced the institutions developed in these colonies. By contrast, Spain became a colonial power when the forces in that society which benefited from diversity were in decline, and so 'the conquerors imposed a uniform bureaucratic administration'.[31] The US constitution embodied an existing (informal) interest in diversity, inspired by England, which was absent in Latin America because of circumstances in Spain at the time. And so the adoption of similar formal rules led to very different outcomes. The crucial point in this analysis is that 'institutional constraints' survive 'tenaciously' in the face of 'radical alterations to the rules of the game'.[32]

North's understanding of path dependence is enormously influential and is often quoted. Indeed, it has passed into common speech among academics and policy analysts and is often used by people unfamiliar with his work. Despite this, his work on the topic left much unsaid, as North himself acknowledged: 'But we are just beginning the serious task of exploring the implications of path dependence.'[33] His writing is mainly concerned to show that history matters if we want to understand why economies perform or underperform. This leaves important gaps. It is important to point out that much may remain the same even when societies experience great change, but what exactly is it that remains the same? North gives some broad outlines, but they are not specific enough to allow us to pinpoint the patterns which remain path dependent.

One of his interpreters has sought to fill this gap in a manner which enhances our understanding. Scott Page suggests that what remain unchanged in path-dependent societies are 'behavioral routines, social connections, or cog-nitive structures'.[34] The first refers to the way in which economic or social life is conducted – what sort of behaviour is considered economically productive or socially useful and which is not. The last, cognitive structures, are what is valued and what is not. The middle component, social connections, should be clear: the relationships which decide who benefits. Path dependence, then, means retaining the same ways of doing things, the same set of economic and social values, and the same connections even when societies experience great change in their formal rules.

In sum, North's theory tells us that the past matters far more to the (eco-nomic) present than standard economic theory assumes. The precise way in which it matters is that institutions – the formal and informal rules which govern the economy and the society – may become so deeply entrenched that they can with-stand great changes, including replacing one set of political rules by another. This explains the roots in history of many patterns which seem entirely unrelated to the past, and why some realities remain even when we assume they have been funda-mentally changed. But how useful is his theory and how applicable is it to South Africa?

## MAKING SENSE OF NORTH

Two key questions are raised by North's work.

First, does it support the assumption that Western economies (in particular the US economy) and the free markets which are said to underpin them are superior to those of other societies, and that all economies should be judged by the extent to which they emulate them? This assumption is the economic equiva-lent of the democratic 'consolidation paradigm', which assumes that democra-cies in North America and Western Europe are the finished product and that all others are judged by how close they come to imitating them.[35] It is an expression of prejudice, not a description of reality. One of its key economic vehicles was the Washington Consensus, which imposed on economies in the global South a path which, as critics pointed out, demanded that they become far more like an idealised version of Northern economies than those economies themselves. (This is another feature it shares with the consolidation paradigm, which demands that Southern countries adopt features which are assumed to exist in Northern democracies but often do not.) Does North think that African, Asian and Latin American economies are inferior to those in Western Europe and North America because their institutions are inferior? In that case, his theory would do more to reinforce cultural biases which underpin path dependence in South Africa than to point to an alternative.

Second, is North's work on path dependence arguing for a determinism in which countries whose institutions did not develop in a way which makes strong economic performance possible are doomed to stay much as they are? If so, claims of path dependence could be the economic equivalent of the political science work of Robert Putnam, who suggests that societies with a long history – dating back centuries – of congregating in voluntary associations are more likely to become fully democratic.[36] In that case, instead of offering lower-growing societies a way to prosperity, it would simply confirm the view of Western economists (for whom North wrote and whom he sought to influence) that their societies are always fated to be rich and others fated to be poor. And it would, of course, offer no way out of path dependence because South Africa would be doomed to suffer it forever.

Interpreting North's work is not easy. His refusal to discuss the details of path dependence is only one feature of his writing which can make interpretation difficult. His work is 'not immediately accessible, as it is dispersed in numerous publications spanning a period of several decades'. And, while he often repeats key points, he modified his positions over the years. But by far the biggest obstacle is that 'on some crucial points, his position was sometimes vague, often evasive or not fully developed … Although, in general, he presented his ideas clearly, his writing was perhaps too succinct. As a result, his readers frequently find themselves wishing he had offered a fuller explanation.'[37] One discussion of North's work suggests that he wanted to produce a theory which would appeal to scholars who hold a range of views,[38] implying that he was vague and added qualifications to his claims because he wished to avoid offending particular schools of thought. North was very critical of the 'rationality assumption' but allows for the possibility that it might work in 'modern, developed' economies – and then adds a footnote to hint that it might not apply in these cases either. Since the thrust of his argument seems to contradict the idea that people make economic calculations which are unaffected by their cultural biases, the concessions seem designed more to appease some colleagues than to express a firmly held opinion.

But despite these difficulties, it is possible to use North's work to distil key elements of a usable theory. And as we shall see, North's failure to develop his analyses, and his habit of taking positions which leave open more than one interpretation, enable us to fill in the gaps in ways which help us to understand South African realities. This makes his work a useful grounding for identifying and analysing key features of the society, provided that his view is taken as a trigger to further thought rather than the last word on the subject.

## Colonial Thinking or a Key to Freedom?

There can be no greater confirmation that North's work is open to various interpretations than the fact that his understanding of path dependence in particular is used by scholars on the left who are critical of current economic arrangements[39] *and* that he has also been associated with the Washington Consensus – and has been labelled by some critics as a source for its attempt to impose a particular sort of market economics on poorer countries.

As one interpreter of North's work points out, the identification with the Washington Consensus is misplaced. North 'was a sharp critic of the simplistic advice promoted by World Bank economists, who believe that all that is needed to resolve the problem of growth is to get the prices right.' His theory of institutions 'was precisely designed to show that this approach was misguided'. North is probably identified with the Bank's position because, 'for reasons that even North might not have entirely comprehended',[40] it embraced some of his ideas selectively as they seemed to explain why its previous approach was not working. This selective interpretation of his writing seemed designed to allow the Bank to abandon one way of imposing its will on poorer economies for another. Instead of insisting that the prices of money, wages and goods be pitched at a level which the Bank's economists claimed would produce growth (often at great human cost), it insisted that they 'get the institutions right'. Yet the fact is that North's writing aimed not to show that miraculous growth could be achieved by tweaking institutions, but to warn against a simplistic stress on prices. The Bank was determined to make North's words mean what it wanted them to mean. It was able to do this partly because, whatever his intentions, his work can be read to suggest that the West – and the US in particular – is better than the rest, and that economies should be judged by criteria which make the Washington Consensus much more likely.

One of North's key terms, 'economic performance', is barely defined. The 'standard' measure of whether an economy is doing well – growth in the sum of goods and services produced – has been challenged by critics who point out that it says nothing about inequality (which could ensure that most people hardly benefit at all from what is produced) or the environment.[41] Belatedly, environmental impacts have come to be seen as an important measure of how well an economy is performing. High levels of growth which destroy the resources needed to sustain economies might be considered poor performance. An allied concern is that growth on its own does not necessarily tell us that people are living better lives. The United Nations Development Programme developed the Human Development Index (HDI), which measures not only income but also basic health and education.

In the years in which the index has been used, no automatic fit between high growth and higher levels of well-being has been shown.[42]

Therefore, if North's understanding of performance is growth numbers alone, he is ignoring the fairness with which the fruits of performance are distributed, its impact on most people and its cost to the environment. In a 1996 paper, he made a rare attempt to define performance and rejected a narrow understanding: 'I shall simply assert that by economic performance I include not only the standard quantitative measures ... but also other less measurable but important characteristics of well-being such as the quality of the physical and social environment.'[43] This seems to be an attempt to have his cake and eat it too – North allows for traditional growth measures and those which give a more rounded picture. And yet, despite this gesture, much of his analysis of path dependence seems to concentrate on growth alone. His discussion of the Northwest Ordinance, mentioned earlier, simply assumes that the US is a success story. In terms of growth alone this is accurate, but during the 1990s and 2000s, for example, the US was rated between 26th and 35th on the HDI,[44] suggesting, of course, that the country's performance on meeting human needs was significantly less impressive than its growth rate.

The sort of growth the Northwest Ordinance allowed did not rely on distributing resources more equally. On the contrary, it was only more than a century and a half later, when urban poverty triggered unionisation of workers and pressures for more equality, that the US began to address this issue at all. And, despite the New Deal in the 1930s and Lyndon Johnson's 'Great Society' in the 1960s which attempted to address poverty, it could be argued that the US has never fully come to grips with income redistribution.[45] Similarly, North's account of US development ignores power relations between economic actors – including slavery, which the architects of the Northwest Ordinance embraced but which he mentions only once in passing.[46] Key to his understanding of institutions and growth is property rights,[47] which are essential to investment and growth but not necessarily to greater equality (slaves were, of course, property). Property rights need not mean owners' unqualified right to do what they like with property regardless of the impact on others. These rights could be limited in ways which seek to ensure that owners meet obligations to society. But by simply stressing property without discussing its use, North encourages the judgement that, for him, 'performance' is another way of saying 'growth'. The definition presented in the 1996 paper did not become a central plank in his analysis.

None of this necessarily means that North dismissed unfairness and inequality as problems. But it does explain why his work could be read that way. Nor does it mean that his understanding of path dependence is useful only if we believe that growth alone matters regardless of the human cost. Nordic economists, eager to explain their country's stress on redistribution, could undertake a similar analysis of North's discussion of the Northwest Ordinance to show how the Nordic country's institutions 'locked in' the welfare state. All this argues for an approach to North's work which does not take it at face value, but extracts from it what helps to explain South African realities and discards what does not. The same point can be made about the other ambiguities in his writing.

What does seem beyond dispute is North's assumption that the institutions of the West in general, and England and the US in particular, are the 'end model' all societies would need to adopt if they want superior economic performance.[48] This underpins his work, including his understanding of path dependence, which could be read to argue that it is a feature of all societies, but that the trajectory into which England and some other parts of the West were locked was positive for growth, and those of other societies were not. This theme is one of the few features of his work which he does not qualify. There are no passages suggesting that non-Western societies developed institutions conducive to high performance, even though the success of Japan and the East Asian 'Tigers' was a settled feature of the economic landscape when he wrote – and China was emerging as a world economic power during this period too. In a later work, he claims that Muslim societies have not matched the performance of the West because their culture is a barrier.[49] He illustrates this with a comparison between eleventh-century Maghribi (Muslim, North African) and Genoese (Christian, Italian) traders. The Maghribis, he claims, built mechanisms which enabled them to transact effectively until trade expanded and became more impersonal. Their habits could not then cope with the change. The Genoese, on the other hand, were individualist and therefore made the adjustment.[50] North also tries to show that England developed institutions better suited to high economic performance than did Southern Europe. In addition, he attempts to explain why the US, as a British colony, developed institutions more conducive to economic performance than Latin American countries did.

These claims are, of course, heavily laden with prejudice. Besides the fact that societies outside the West have achieved high levels of prosperity, North (as well as many other Western scholars who simply assume the superiority of their societies) rejects the possibility that Western economic success is a product of power and force rather than institutions. He dismisses this counter-argument, made by Latin American scholars, as evidence that they fail to recognise that it is their inferior institutions, not US power, which have held them back.[51] Ironically, while North is praised for his (partial) break with neoclassical economics, it could be argued that the conventional view is less prejudiced than his alternative. The neoclassical view holds that any economy which 'gets its prices' right' (by, for example, cutting taxes and workers' wages) will grow. While this view is widely challenged, it assumes, at least in principle, that policy, not culture, decides whether societies prosper. North insists that capacity for growth is shaped by culture. He offers an economic equivalent of the work of Seymour Martin Lipset, who insisted that democracy is possible only in societies which adopt Western culture and economic values.[52] It is an indication of how deep-rooted this prejudice is in North's thinking that this is one area of his theory which he never felt the need to qualify, alter – or defend.

North's approach discriminates within societies as well as between them, which is illustrated by his treatment of property rights, one of the core elements of his theory. He insists that some property rights are more important than others. 'Efficient' property rights, according to North, must be protected; inefficient ones should be discarded because only efficient rights can ensure sustained economic growth.[53] Examples of inefficient rights, he suggests, are those which are the product of 'high tariff barriers' or 'selectively generous tax concessions'. Tariffs or taxes are surely policies, not rights. But even if they are seen as rights, North seems here to be an economic historian remarkably unaware of economic history: if the property rights of firms which benefited from tariff barriers and tax concessions were not protected, there might be very few corporate property rights left.

Critics also note that North seems to assume that some holders of property rights matter more than others. He insists that seventeenth-century Britain laid the foundation for growth by securing property rights, but 'property rights of the clans in Scotland or landowners in Ireland were no more secure than the rights of marginal groups in some developing countries today'.[54] So 'property rights' seems, for North, to be code for safeguarding the interests of formal companies. While he criticises the mainstream view of international financial institutions and donor agencies, his treatment of this issue reflects their thinking.[55] In their view too, only some property rights matter – those of foreign investors. The property rights of the poor are entirely ignored. The political theorist Adam Przeworski notes that attempts to provide a 'scientific' metric of the quality of governance in Southern countries measure these rights solely on the strength of foreign investors' perceptions of the risk of losing their property.[56]

These aspects of North's theory show that it is undermined by biases which assume Western superiority. But that does not mean that path dependence is necessarily a concept which judges societies inadequate unless they abandon their traditions and embrace those of the West. Despite North's biases, it is possible to develop his theory in ways which point in other directions. First, however, we need to examine whether path dependence necessarily dooms some societies to poverty and assures prosperity for others. If that is true, there is no point in aspiring to escape our present path, because an alternative is not possible. But it is not necessarily true.

## DOOMED TO DEPENDENCE?

The warning issued at the outset of this discussion – that it is not always easy to determine what North really meant – applies particularly to his treatment of whether path dependence is inescapable or whether societies can change course.

North is not at all clear on how institutions come to be and who creates them. This is crucial, for our understanding of what creates a reality shapes how we believe it might change. In one passage, he insists that individuals make choices which establish or alter institutions.[57] The assertion is not entirely unexpected, since the intellectual tradition within which he works sees individuals, not groups, as the core social reality.[58] If individuals did shape institutions, path dependence would be very easily changed, since other individuals could decide that their habits and attitudes are not in their best interests and change them. But if this were so, much of North's theory dissolves. Central to his argument is the claim that human beings are captives of institutions even when these are clearly not in their interests; at best he is prepared to allow that changes in relative prices may gradually alter the attitudes which underpin institutions.[59] None of this is possible if individuals make and change institutions. But he is unclear on what does make and change them.

North's writing on the origins of institutions often refers to 'mental models', ideologies and culture, but provides very little on how these came to be. Despite his claim that individuals make institutions, his treatment of the topic is consistent with the views of conservative thinkers such as Emile Durkheim[60] who see culture and tradition as the almost natural product not of individuals but of 'communities'. These 'communities' are assumed to think and feel as one (despite the fact that they are divided by differences in power, interests and values). If 'communities' adopt ways of seeing the world, it is because their powerful members believe these to be necessary. To understand whether they can be changed, it is important to know who in the 'community' adopted them and in what circumstances. While North offers some hints that interest differences shaped path dependence in English and Spanish colonies, he does not develop this analysis. Nor does he identify which interests developed the culture of the Muslim Maghribis or the Christian Genoese.

Despite his influence on international financial institutions, North refused to do what they prefer academics to do: to suggest ways to change institutions and attitudes to make growth more likely. He relies on humility to duck the issue. 'The extent to which culture is "malleable" via deliberate modification is,' he writes, 'still very imperfectly understood.'[61] Instead of offering a proposal for change, he advises growth-oriented reformers to understand and respect culture and to ensure that their policies are sensitive to it. He insists that path dependence does not mean that no change is possible: 'If, however, the foregoing story sounds like an inevitable, foreordained, account, it should not. At every step of the way, there were choices – political and economic – that provided real alternatives. Path dependence ... is not a story of inevitability in which the past neatly predicts the future.'[62] But he does not say what change is possible and how it might happen.

What North may well have had in mind is offered not by his own work but by a book which uses it, Brian Levy's *Working with the Grain*.[63] It argues against development strategies which assume that Southern countries can grow only if they are encouraged by development technicians to adopt a set of ambitious reforms that try to turn them instantly into free-market democracies. Rather, development practitioners should try to work within the realities of these societies and 'prioritize those policy reforms that seem both worthwhile and feasible, given country-specific institutional realities'.[64] These changes can produce wider reforms and begin 'virtuous circles of cumulative change'.[65] Whether this is what North originally had in mind, it is clearly consistent with his thinking since the book contains a warm endorsement from North! Levy's view that change is possible but that reformers should tread carefully, recognising institutional constraints, does offer a coherent strategy consistent with North's approach.

Whatever North's intent, it is possible to use his writings to develop a theory of change which fits South African realities. In a passage which allows a very different interpretation of his work, North declares: 'Institutions are not necessarily or even usually created to be socially efficient; rather they, or at least the formal rules, are created to serve the interests of those with the bargaining power to create new rules.'[66] In this view, it is not anonymous individuals or 'communities' which make the rules – it is the powerful. North applies this only to the formal rules, but if the powerful can impose the formal rules, why not the informal ones too? North refers repeatedly to bargaining power as a motor of change.[67] Nor does he always suggest that institutions which obstruct growth are simply products of cultural understandings. On several occasions, he argues that they survive because they offer 'massive increasing returns'[68] to some. Those who benefit must be the powerful, who are able to ensure that the patterns and values of social life are those which best serve them.

Armed with this insight, we can see that North's understanding of path dependence does not necessarily suggest that anything is inevitable. If the institutions in which path dependence locks societies are created by power holders, they can change if the power balance changes. Insisting that path dependence is about power changes it from an always limiting product of centuries of conditioning into a changeable social reality. Those who benefit from it and those whom it excludes can be identified, and we can identify the political and social processes which might challenge this power. Path dependence becomes not a culturally loaded theory which tells societies that they are doomed to live with understandings and realities that hold them back. Rather, it becomes a warning that power which was thought to have waned is still alive, forcing society into straitjackets which prevent it from growing.

## SPEAKING TO US

Aspects of North's understanding of path dependence do, therefore, help us understand a South Africa in which core aspects of power relations in the economy and society have survived the political change of 1994. But that does not mean that we need to rely on North alone for our understanding of South African path dependence.

Even if North had never observed that power is an element of path dependence – and even if everything he wrote argued only that the societies of the West (and the US in particular) alone can fashion the institutions which allow growth, leaving most of the world to live on the scraps rich states throw their way – path dependence would be a crucial tool in our attempt to understand the first quarter-century of South African democracy. Theories which help us understand the world do not stand or fall by the biases of those who develop them: if there is more to the theory than those prejudices, it helps to explain reality. There is much more to the notion of path dependency than North's implied belief that Western societies are superior or his suggestion that it might be very difficult to change an economic path.

Essential to path dependence is the idea that changing constitutions, laws and regulations does not automatically end the informal patterns which prevailed when the old rules applied. Students of politics often assume that the nature of societies is shaped by the written rules which govern them. It is, for example, often claimed that a change in South Africa's electoral system will magically reduce corruption and empower citizens.[69] Path dependence challenges this, warning that much else has to change if new formal rules are to produce a new society – and that changing rules may alter little if the underlying patterns stay the same.

As we have seen, North is not helpful in explaining what those underlying patterns are. We need to turn to Page's understanding of what remains unchanged when political change produces not a break with the past but a continuation of its essential patterns. If the way people behave in the marketplace or society does not change, if what they see as important and unimportant remains intact, and if core features of the social and economic relationships which prevailed in the old order survive into the new, then change from one set of political rules to another has not produced equivalent change in the patterns which underpin the economy or society.

Why does this happen? North does not offer a convincing or coherent answer. But building on his observations about power, we can propose an answer: path dependence occurs when, after political change, the elites which shape the economy and society see a value in preserving the patterns of the past and are powerful enough to ensure this. This can happen because, despite political change, the elites do not change – those who controlled the economy and society still hold the reins. But it may also occur because the new elite which takes over control believes it is best served by continuing the patterns set by the old. It may also be a combination of the two. So, path dependence can be changed if either the elites' perception of their interests changes (because pressure forces a change or because existing patterns do not offer the benefits they once did) or if the elite which favours the existing arrangements is replaced by one which does not.

One further point is important. Theoretical work on path dependence also suggests that it does not always hold societies back; it could ensure that they 'lock in' patterns which may be in the interests of many outside the elite. North's discussion of the Northwest Ordinance or his account of the way in which realities in English society produced patterns which differed from those in Spain may express, or be consistent with, his prejudices. But they do highlight an important reality: patterns developed in a now rejected political order can serve its successor well if they are adapted to fit new realities.

Another insight important to South African realities is that path dependence may survive more than one change of power and political system. This may happen in one of two ways. Patterns established in a political regime may be carried through into its successor and then into the order which replaces it: since path dependence is said to survive changes in political regimes, it follows that it could survive more than one change in political rules. The second possibility is extremely relevant to South Africa. Behaviours or values may be rejected by a new regime, only to return when its reign ends. The previous chapter described how post-1994 South Africa has returned to some assumptions which underpinned British colonialism but were discarded by the apartheid state. And so political change brings not something new but a return to a modified form of something much older.

These essential elements define the approach to path dependence adopted here: patterns of behaviour, views of what is valuable and what is not, and relationships between key actors may survive even if a society experiences significant changes. This survival occurs when those who held power before political change are powerful enough to ensure that the rules which benefited them still prevail, or when the elite which replaces the former power holders sees a value in maintaining these patterns, or when the two combine. It is a core argument of this book that this approach to path dependence describes South African society in the first quarter-century of democracy more accurately and fully than any other explanation.

## SOUTH AFRICAN APPLICATIONS

Developments and realities of contemporary South Africa can best be explained by noting the extent to which pre-1994 behaviour patterns, values and relationships carried over into the new order. The assumption of both the old economic elite and the new political one that a democratic South Africa should extend to everyone what the white minority enjoyed under apartheid entrenches all three of Page's elements of path dependence. The behavioural routines which are considered acceptable are those that underpinned life under minority rule. They include the emphasis on the formal economy rather than the lived economic reality of the majority, as well as the assumption in higher education – at least until student protests challenged these understandings – that teaching and learning should continue their existing patterns rather than adapt to new realities. We will return to these themes in Chapter 5.

The 'cognitive structures' or values which underpin thinking about the economy and society are also prisoners of the past. The refusal to recognise the energy and expertise of people making their living in backyards or on the streets, or the assumption that the genuinely valuable knowledge is generated in North America or Western Europe, preserves into post-1994 South Africa thinking which reigned before majority rule. There is also evidence, drawn from studies of post-1994 South African business, that cognitive patterns established under minority rule survived into the new order, and that this may have stunted growth. A 1995 study found that managers' understanding of the international marketplace was heavily influenced by traditional bonds to Europe and was therefore 'fixated' on European markets. The study also found a strongly inward-looking culture and an aversion to risk.[70] While it attributed these attitudes to the effect of international boycotts, they could equally well be ascribed to decades of protection and privilege, and a widespread sense among white managers that South Africa was, or should be, an extension of the countries which colonised it. While attitudes to international markets later changed (South African firms did move into the rest of Africa, often with great success), the legacy of minority rule identified by the study may still shape business attitudes in ways which inhibit growth: for example, the tendency to look only to Europe and North America for models. The relationships between private money and public politics in democratic South Africa mirror those under white rule, when apparent conflict between business and government was accompanied by cooperation[71] and corporate executives believed they had little use for business associations to convey their views to the government because they could call Cabinet ministers directly to achieve the same purpose.[72] Page's three elements are, therefore, central to understanding post-1994 South Africa.

These patterns survive because elites wish to preserve them: they reflect the preferences or assumptions of those who wield public and private power. But the ways in which this power originates and the ways in which it is wielded are subtle. The new political elite was not bullied into path dependence – it chose it. Some critics insist that the new elite did this in order to prosper at the expense of the majority, on whose behalf the battle against minority rule had been fought. But if that was the elite's only motive, other paths were available to it. The new elite could have followed post-colonial elites by trumpeting its anti-colonial credentials as it enriched itself.[73] But it chose path dependence because this fitted its understanding of racial change.

This is of great importance to understanding what might change path dependence. If path dependence is a product of bargaining power, it can be changed by shifts in that power. But what do we mean when we argue that power must change if path dependence is to end? To some, this must mean that those who do not benefit must overthrow those who do and chart a new path. But this poses two related problems. First, North is right to imply that there is no guarantee that a change in power relations ends path dependence. Even change which seems revolutionary can leave the essential patterns of a society intact.[74] This is the essential message of the theory of path dependence. Second, replacing one set of power holders by another is not the only way power can shift. The framework through which elites see problems and solutions can change, and this can break the patterns of path dependence. In principle, this does not necessitate any change in who holds government power – all that is required is that those who favour a new course are able to move society in their preferred direction. Path dependence could be challenged by responses which change opinion rather than by imposing a new order. But whatever strategies the opponents of path dependence use, the implication of insisting that it is a product of power relations (even if these operate more subtly than we might expect) is that it is open to challenge.

If we accept path dependence's core assumption – that the past influences the present even if the political rules change – we can, as suggested earlier, recognise that the roots of path dependence here are older than the birth of apartheid. Formal democracy's advent in 1994 was not the first time that a movement representing a dominated identity gained control of the state. In 1948, Afrikaner nationalists won state power in a white election which enabled them to challenge English-speaking control of the economy.[75] There is no moral similarity between, on the one hand, the victory of one identity group over another within a minority group which dominates the majority and, on the other, the achievement of formal rights for all. But the National Party victory of 1948 did react to the past which it replaced, and in ways which make the first quarter-century of democracy easier to understand.

Afrikaner nationalism claimed to be a rebellion against British colonialism, which, although it extended political rights to all whites, also entrenched the economic power of English speakers. After taking power in 1948, the National Party largely succeeded in achieving its prime goal: to use the state to accelerate the economic and social development of white Afrikaners. It did this largely at the expense of the black majority, but it also used control of government to favour Afrikaans speakers. Beyond that, the National Party did as much to fit into as to change patterns established by the colonial power against which they rebelled. While the government proclaimed South Africa a republic, which meant that formally the country was no longer attached to Britain, it did not fundamentally change political institutions. Regular white elections continued and Parliament remained intact. Even the notorious disenfranchisement of 'coloured' voters simply repeated patterns established beforehand.[76] The structure of the economy did not change – Afrikaners simply entered the upper echelons of the system once controlled by English speakers.[77]

While apartheid accepted no legal restraints in its dealings with the black majority, it tried to keep white legality alive by ensuring that repression observed the legal niceties. 'Even the most dire apartheid measures were carried through with punctilious legal formalism, and the actions of civil servants were scrutinised by their superiors with this in mind.'[78] Repressive laws were introduced to curb black political expression. However, one of the oddities of apartheid was that while the substance of the rule of law was eroded, the form was almost obsessively maintained. Rights were removed by law enacted in Parliament, backed by regulations published in the Government Gazette. Resistance movement leaders were jailed without trial and tortured, but once the police believed they had enough evidence to secure a conviction, political prisoners were usually (although not always) tried and convicted in courts observing all the form (albeit little of the substance) of due process. And so the post-1948 white state bore a striking institutional resemblance to its predecessor, which had also denied rights to the black majority.

The fight between Afrikaner nationalism and British colonialism was not about what South Africa should be. Both assumed that whites should rule; they shared notions of 'white civilisation'[79] which required them to preserve the appearance of procedure and process so that they could maintain a veneer of civility to whites within the country and outside it. A preoccupation of apartheid-era white elites was their image in 'the outside world', meaning Western Europe and North America. While much was said about the claimed hypocrisy of the Western powers, the fact that so much time and energy was devoted to complaining about it – and so much effort spent trying to win over these powers – showed that these societies were models of civilisation for white South Africa. Despite the occasional use by Afrikaner nationalism of anti-capitalist rhetoric, it did not challenge private ownership and corporate concentration; it wanted to share in both.[80] And so the racial affinities between English- and Afrikaans-speaking whites ensured a high degree of path dependence between 1948 and 1994, despite the fact that apartheid ideology differed in important ways from that of British colonialism.

By the early 1990s, apartheid had been largely discredited. But the ideas which underpinned British colonisation had not. Apartheid assumed that black people could never attain the 'level of civilisation' its architects believed whites had achieved.[81] As Richard Turner pointed out, while British colonisation agreed on the superiority of white norms, it also believed that at least some black people could be 'educated' to adopt them. Turner quoted approvingly the view of the South African Students' Organisation, the Black Consciousness organisation founded by Steve Biko and his colleagues, that white liberals seek 'an assimilation of Blacks into an already established set of norms drawn up and motivated by White society'. He added that the liberal norm is that 'to behave like whites is the ideal'.[82] These ideas were foreign to apartheid's view that blacks could never be like whites. But they were essential to colonialism, past and present.

Since post-1994 South Africa is formally a non-racial democracy, it was not respectable to insist explicitly that black people model themselves on whites. But far less changed than surface appearances would suggest. What did return, in a dominant position, was the idea that 'Western' behaviour patterns, values and norms were superior and that the country ought to aspire to emulate the West. 'Westernness' is often poorly defined, but it is pervasive. An indication of how deep path dependence runs is that among black South Africans, admiration of the US, in particular African Americans, dates back not only to the 1950s, when fashion, music and (if people could afford them) motor cars were considered superior if they were American. That admiration could be tracked back to the 1920s, when the activist Wellington Butelezi organised a grassroots movement by convincing his adherents that Americans (and Russians) would appear in aircraft to free black South Africans from white rule.[83] Precisely because this concern for Western opinion is so deep-rooted, it provides a far more credible framework for the staying power of the assumptions of minority rule after 1994 than do apartheid's assumptions.

## The (Mixed) Political Benefits of Path Dependence

One further feature of South African path dependence is crucial: while much of it holds the society back, other aspects arguably equip it to preserve some democratic gains.

North, as we have seen, did not see path dependence as an unmixed burden. Some of its forms could enable societies to grow. Socially and economically, the assumption that all South Africans should enjoy what whites had under apartheid is a fetter on growth and inclusion. But politically it plays a role in safeguarding freedoms. Whites not only benefited from economic privilege under apartheid; they also participated in a (largely) functioning democracy. Its features included regular competitive elections (effective enough to enable the Afrikaner nationalist alliance to win state power and to use it to dilute the power of English business and professional interests); relative freedom of speech (opposition newspapers were allowed as long as they did not step too far outside the white consensus); and judicial procedure which coexisted alongside measures to suppress black political expression. These realities may have created a form of benign path dependence built on the assumption that the freedoms whites possessed under apartheid should be extended to all, and that to diminish them would force the majority to live with less than the minority enjoyed under apartheid.

This may partly (or largely) explain why the first quarter-century of democracy has been marked by meticulous respect for democratic form. Elections whose results are accepted as accurate by all but a small but persistent band of conspiracy theorists have been held at the appointed time. When the governing party has lost power in provinces and municipalities, it has relinquished it without a murmur. Among the minority who dominate the debate, freedom of speech and other civil liberties are respected. Reverence for legal procedure continues in a respect for the courts which is sometimes excessive (since the law is often used to fight battles appropriately assigned to democratic politics,[84] and judgments which seem to do more to enhance elite cultural assumptions than to protect citizens' rights are widely accepted by the mainstream[85]). Respect for legal procedure ensures that disputes among the minority are resolved by law.

This feature of path dependence has also ensured continued respect for and compliance with the restraints imposed on the government by the constitution. When the then Public Protector's report on the presidential homestead in Nkandla held senior ANC figures including the president culpable, the senior leadership of the party not only refrained from attacking the office (rather than the report) but rebuked its youth and student wings when they did so.[86] Workers also have reason to welcome aspects of path dependence. The 1995 Labour Relations Act may be an example of path dependence, but it does entrench important bargaining rights.

These advantages of path dependence are not unmixed blessings. Free elections, civil liberties, the rule of law and worker bargaining rights are important guarantees of freedom and provide possibilities for citizens who wish to challenge inequities – they may be used to challenge the assumptions which underpin path dependence. But their benefit is limited by the negative effects of path dependence. Elections have been free and fair but not very competitive. The fact that identities – primarily race and language – shape votes is not in itself evidence of path dependence. Contrary to the prejudice which claims that voters in North America and Western Europe vote on governing party performance, identity voting is common in democracies around the world.[87] What is path dependent is the survival of residential segregation which ensures that the ANC dominates the townships, the opposition the suburbs. This reduces voters' options and bargaining power.

Civil liberties and respect for the courts are eroded by patterns described earlier which ensure that they are enjoyed in much less vigorous form by outsiders. Most people cannot afford to use courts unless they are lucky enough to make contact with a donor-funded public interest law organisation. This contributes to another form of path dependence: the degree to which citizens continue to use street protests to express themselves. And, in a further indication of path dependence, the protests tend to be reported in mainstream media only when they disturb the lives of the middle class. Little attempt is made to understand the demands of the protesters. Their actions are labelled 'service delivery protests', a catch-all phrase which claims, without evidence, that protesters are demanding that local authorities provide them with better technical service[88] rather than insisting that, as democratic citizens, they have a right to be heard. Protest as a reaction to and symptom of voicelessness is a virtually unbroken feature of South African politics over four decades, a rather stark example of path dependence.

Edward Webster's analysis also points to the limits imposed by path dependence on the bargaining rights it has bequeathed workers and trade unions. He argues that the pressure which decades-old labour patterns placed on unions and workers eroded bargaining so that strikers were bypassing the established institutions and employers were 'hostile to the institutions of collective bargaining'. The core of the labour market, where organised workers earn regular wages and enjoy union rights, was, he asserted, 'increasingly under threat from those workers who are either outsourced into precarious and lower-paid jobs, or who are retrenched and become desperate job seekers'.[89] The bargaining power of workers in the formal system was being eroded by the pressure of unemployment and poverty, prompting heightened conflict.[90] The path-dependent value placed on conspicuous consumption fuelled this turmoil.

A particularly salient sign of workplace path dependence is the persistence of what Karl von Holdt calls the 'apartheid workplace regime'. He coined the term to show how, under apartheid, relations between mostly white managers and owners and black workers mirrored those between the races in the wider society. Some of its elements included an authoritarian managerial style, low levels of trust, and 'workers' near-total non-identification with the goals of the firm'. He argues that this 'regime' has survived the political transition:[91] workers and employers continue, in the main, to relate to each other as they did under apartheid. This damages the economy, reducing productivity and obstructing negotiated solutions to workplace conflicts. The persistent 'regime' ensures that industrial relations are marked by far more conflict and violence than might be expected and explains constant complaints from media and commentators that workers are too militant.[92] These realities may explain why the workplace forums proposed by the 1995 Act have not been used. The path-dependent bargaining system designed to offer workers a say in decisions, and to ensure relative peace in the workplace, is undermined by the persistence of patterns which limit its ability to do either.

Path dependence, then, has a pervasive effect on South Africa's politics, economy and society. Some are obvious, others far less so. Not all the effects are negative, and the fact that the society retains the instruments which may enable citizens to challenge the limiting aspects of path dependence is itself, ironically, a consequence of the deep-rootedness of long-established patterns. But even these benefits are mixed. The opportunities which 'beneficial' path dependence offers the society are always diluted by the persistence of 'malign' patterns which make it much more difficult to realise their promise in practice.

# 3

# The Roots of Patronage: Path Dependence, 'State Capture' and Corruption

For some commentators, post-1994 corruption in South Africa confirms one of the truisms of politics: African states are always corrupt.

The belief that majority rule in Africa always collapses into corruption as the governing elite turns the state into its property is deeply embedded in journalistic understandings of the continent. This view began influencing coverage of South Africa almost immediately after democracy's advent. It also shapes much scholarship on Africa – 'neopatrimonialism', the term used by scholars to describe corrupt governance, has spawned a very active school of academic writing which influences African scholars as well as those in the West. This is so despite the fact that the term fails to explain anything and is more a prejudice about post-colonial Africa than a means of analysing it.[1] This way of thinking about post-apartheid South Africa underpins the view that this country negotiated a new order which closed the book on a troubled past and opened the way for harmony and prosperity until politicians, driven by greed, used public office to enrich themselves and so to ensure that South Africa went the way of all African countries.

This view implies, of course, that corruption and 'state capture' are new, a product of the moral failings of politicians thrown up by democracy in Africa. This misunderstands the dynamics of which the Zuma period was a product because it fails to see this malfeasance as a symptom of the survival of the past. Path dependence alone did not cause corruption. But corruption continues a South African pattern which is centuries old; path dependence has made it more likely and probably more of a problem than it would have been if a different path had been followed.

## A TRADITIONAL WAY OF LIFE?

Corruption – the 'unsanctioned or unscheduled use of public resources for private ends'[2] – in South Africa dates back to the beginning of white settlement in the mid-seventeenth century.

Jan van Riebeeck, the Dutch East India Company official who began white settlement, was sent to the Cape to redeem himself after he was found to have engaged in 'private trading' in a previous posting.[3] There is no evidence that he resumed his self-enrichment scheme at the Cape. But this early phase of colonial rule was marked by significant corruption. A study concludes that the public finances of the Dutch period at the Cape were in a poor state 'due to poor tax collection, tax evasion and corrupt officials'.[4]

The British colonial period, beginning in the Cape in the early nineteenth century, continued the tradition and provided the first example of 'state capture'. The 1820 settlers, who arrived from Britain and became merchants and farmers, campaigned against the corruption of various colonial governors.[5] A study of the period finds that 'state institutions were distorted to serve private interests ... In state capture the benefits accrue to the private interests ... Evidence ... from both quantitative and qualitative sources suggest[s] that the ruling elite influenced the public expenditures of the Cape Colony.'[6] One guilty party was the best-known representative of late-nineteenth-century British colonialism, Cecil John Rhodes, who was forced to resign as Cape prime minister when a close associate and Cabinet minister gave a contract to a friend allowing him to operate an 18-year monopoly on catering for the government-run railways.[7]

Coloniser corruption crossed the battle lines between British and Afrikaner settlers: the Transvaal Republic of President Paul Kruger, which Rhodes sought to destabilise and on which Britain waged war, was also a site of corruption. Its extent may have been exaggerated by the British – the Kruger republic, which resisted British colonisation, attracted much international sympathy and the British government, in its concern to justify its overthrow, vilified it. But 'anecdotal evidence certainly indicates a great deal of nepotism and financial laxity in the civil service'.[8] Another study is more emphatic, finding that the republic operated largely to the benefit of a small group of 'notables' who enriched themselves at the expense of their fellow citizens:

> The Transvaal in the late nineteenth century was a feudal society in which the Voortrekkers each 'received' a farm for which they had to pay regular tax. However, when they defaulted on their tax payments, the farms were put up for sale. With the connivance of the local Landrost [magistrate]

the 'Notables' were often the first to be informed of such sales and so they became landlords with many farms in their possession.[9]

Nepotism, often associated in scholarship and journalism with rule by black Africans, was also a strong feature of the republic. A study reports that one of the president's sons was his private secretary, and his son-in-law, FC Eloff, 'was a businessman who was granted several [government] concessions, namely business monopolies of one kind or another'.[10]

After the British defeated the republic, they did, according to one analysis, attempt to replace fairly arbitrary rule with a state governed by rules and procedures.[11] But this administration was, in this view, also friendly to 'state capture'. British colonial rule 'facilitated the rent-seeking activities of the Anglophone mine owners' who had arrived from Britain to take advantage of the discovery of gold and diamonds. 'Rent seeking' means here the search for profits which exceed those available in a competitive market: 'Rents include not just monopoly profits, but also subsidies and transfers organised through the political mechanism.'[12] So the mine owners, with the support of the British administration, used political muscle to secure advantages and profits which would not have been available without those political connections.

Why corruption was so repeatedly a feature of the colonial orders is not entirely clear. A common explanation is that colonisation is, by definition, corrupt – it assumes that a state (or, in the Cape, a company) may use force and deceit to gain the land and assets of people who are militarily weaker. This creates a sense that the country 'belongs to its colonisers and so they can use its resources for any purpose they choose'.[13] But while this explains colonisers' belief that they can use public power to extract anything they wish from the colonised, it does not explain coloniser leaders' apparent belief that they were entitled to the property of their fellow colonisers. One possibility is that colonisation is always justified by a sense that might is right: the powerful are superior beings and so the colonisers with more power deserve to exploit those with less. Whatever the reason, public officials who abuse trust and businesses which buy public power are a very long-standing South African reality.

These examples happened far too long ago to influence directly the behaviour of post-1994 officials, politicians and businesses. What may well have influenced them is that, in the last years of apartheid in particular, corruption became endemic, far surpassing any other period. Views on the impact of apartheid corruption on post-1994 government differ. Some scholarly literature argues that while there were significant similarities between apartheid-era and post-1994 corruption, there were also important differences. Another view argues that the corruption which became entrenched before democracy's advent simply continued in the new order in other forms. Before exploring these views, we need to discuss briefly the literature on apartheid-era corruption.

## Corruption under Apartheid

A common view is that corruption was low at the beginning of apartheid but later became endemic. If this is true, it applies far more to the experience of white voters than to those of the black majority. Tom Lodge notes that as late as the mid-1970s, JN Cloete, director of the South African Institute for Public Administration, 'could maintain that the controls in the civil service were so stringent that bureaucrats had "little opportunity to use patronage and the conferment of financial benefits for the achievement of improper objectives".[14] But he adds that 'there is plenty of evidence ... that by the 1980s, political corruption ... was quite common in certain government departments as well as in homeland administrations'.[15] More specific-ally, 'the case of the Department of Development Aid, the successor to the Native Affairs Department, suggests a pattern of very generalized misbehaviour. Other official enquiries suggest that land transfers administered by the South African Development Trust [a body under the authority of the Department of Native Affairs and its successors] had for decades been managed dishonestly ... Several homeland governments ... supplied documentation of political corruption on a major scale.'[16] Corruption in departments which dealt with black people seems to have begun in the system's very early years. The anthropologist Mia Brandel Syrier found in 1959 that 'clerks in the administrative offices of the township in which she conducted fieldwork charged a fixed "under the counter" fee for advice, referrals and appointments'.[17]

From the very beginnings of apartheid, then, the arms of state which dealt with black people were corrupt. Black and white officials would have been able to exploit black people because they were disenfranchised and denied rights; govern-ment functionaries could expect impunity. Aspects of the system made corruption almost inevitable. The requirement that black people carry passes if they wanted to live and work in the cities gave officials power which they could use for gain: 'In the 1970s, black policemen were commonly believed to refrain from charging pass offenders in exchange for bribes.'[18] None of this should be surprising. It would be odd if officials who could wield arbitrary power over rightless people never used this to enrich themselves. 'The more powerless ordinary people were, the more officials abused their position; for this reason homeland governments were especially dishonest as were the central government departments ... which worked most closely with them.'[19]

But even from an early stage, while black South Africans were directly in the corruption firing line, officials also used public office to serve private interests in their dealings with white society. A study of apartheid-era corruption reports: 'At one point in the 1960s it was suspected that a large part of the top echelon of [the power utility] Eskom, together with ... [senior members of the ruling establishment] used their political leverage to secure contracts for large multinational corporations.'[20] The company 'lost "hundreds of millions of Rands in secret overseas deals" by the mid-1980s, according to former accountant Dr Gert Rademeyer. In just one nuclear energy deal that turned sour, Escom [now Eskom] lost R67 million.'[21]

A study of the apartheid state adds that Prime Minister John Vorster, who took office in 1966, was 'alleged to have started some of his cabinet meetings by sending out details of recent land bankruptcies ... to inform Ministers about the availability of farms in the market',[22] thus keeping alive the tradition begun by the 'notables' in the Transvaal Republic. A key source of this corruption was the Afrikaner Broederbond, a secret society to which virtually all government ministers and many senior officials belonged (and was said to play a key role in deciding who occupied government posts). Members 'were likely to be among the first to know of forthcoming large government procurements and of where universities and harbours were to be built (an advantage for property speculators)'.[23] Dr Nico Diederichs, who was appointed to the Cabinet in 1958 and became finance minister in 1967 (and state president in 1975), was alleged to have 'agreed to moving the base for South Africa's gold sales from London to Zurich in the 1970s on condition that a small amount ... would be transferred into a private account' for each ounce sold. In 1980, a retired judge told a newspaper of a R28 million secret bank account held in Switzerland which was said to be 'linked to Diedrichs [sic]'.[24]

That the state under apartheid was viewed by the ruling elite as a source of personal enrichment is also suggested by another study, which links aspects of this behaviour to the first National Party government led by DF Malan, who took office in 1948: 'Malan and his successors pursued blatant strategies of promoting Afrikaner rent-seeking, although generally within the bounds of legality ... Corruption was somewhat constrained by the legal fetishism that was characteristic of Afrikaner nationalist ideology in this period.'[25] So 'rent seeking' was encouraged by the first apartheid government despite the public concern for legality. This was no doubt facilitated by the fact that the initial National Party project was pursuing not only white welfare at the expense of the black majority, but also the economic empowerment of white Afrikaans speakers who had been kept at the margins by English-speaking economic power holders. This may have created the sense among the political leadership of white Afrikaners that they were entitled to grow rich because they were breaking the English-speaking monopoly on wealth. So the notion that politicians and officials engaged in a political project to propel a group into the economic mainstream further this goal by enriching themselves – a view sometimes used to justify post-apartheid self-enrichment by 'notables' – is deeply ingrained in the country's history.

While there is evidence of corruption from apartheid's beginning, there is wide agreement that it increased dramatically, in size and scope, in its later years. In one sense, this was a product of success: 'By the 1970s the very success of Afrikaner nationalism had created a large new middle class and a substantial capitalist class, who were enjoying an unprecedented prosperity. These highly educated, consumerist and increasingly well-travelled groupings could no longer be contained within the horizons of organisations built around the poor and struggling of the 1930s and 1940s.'[26] In another sense, corruption reached heights under apartheid – with significant consequences for the post-1994 society – as a response to its failures.

As pressure built on apartheid, and the government began changing policy in an often seemingly incoherent way, it lost credibility among white Afrikaans speakers. 'With the Afrikaner establishment unable to discipline its followers, a scramble for personal enrichment began.'[27] Towards the end of apartheid's life, the growing sense that its days were numbered prompted those who could to take as much as possible before the opportunity to take ended. Another factor that created direct ground for corruption was the growth of the international sanctions campaign, which sought to isolate apartheid: 'A further contributing factor to the efflorescence of corruption was the government's response to the development of the international campaign for sanctions during the 1970s and 1980s.'[28] The government's 'sanctions-busting' campaign used secret and illegal connections and arrangements. It also sought to counter international opposition to apartheid through secret propaganda campaigns. In both cases, 'those involved in activities directed to these ends were shielded from normal public service or parliamentary scrutiny'.[29] Breaking sanctions and conducting covert propaganda wars were an open invitation to corruption – one accepted enthusiastically by those who fought to sustain apartheid. The journalist Ken Owen may have overstated the case when he claimed that the apartheid government was forced to negotiate by 'the bankruptcy of a nation that had been looted until it could no longer honour its debts'.[30]

But his remark does indicate the degree to which corruption became rooted in apartheid's last years.

In the view of Hennie van Vuuren, defending apartheid required a particular way of governing and a particular relationship between the government and business: 'When the struggle for South Africa's freedom was at its fiercest, economic crime not only festered but became state policy. Corruption, money laundering, sanctions busting and organised crime had become a necessity for the survival of the state.'[31] Van Vuuren and his research team showed how elaborate this operation was. Because the scheme was costly, it required a bank, Kredietbank, and a network of relationships with corporations, oil and arms dealers, governments and intelligence agencies. The domestic conflict between the apartheid government and activists working to defeat it also stimulated corruption and for much the same reason. Defending apartheid required large amounts of government money, used to buy support or subvert opponents, much of it in special funds largely hidden from public scrutiny. Jonathan Hyslop observes: 'Navy and conventional force army seem to have stayed relatively "clean", while intelligence, special forces and mercenary units seem to have been rotten to the core.'[32]

Crucially, Van Vuuren argues that the criminal networks formed within the apartheid state did not die in 1994. In his view, they form the foundation for post-1994 corruption:

> Many of the actors that were corrupt under apartheid rapidly ingratiated themselves into the new order. This created a new elite pact based on criminality and corruption. The arms deal is the most potent example of the devastating impact this new criminal class had on the country's democratic institutions. The old and the new were quickly intertwined and found in each other partners and protectors.[33]

The 'arms deal' is the 1999 acquisition of 'strategic' arms by the South African government. The procurement is widely seen by analysts, activists and much of the public as a vehicle for corruption. Van Vuuren notes that companies which illegally supplied the apartheid state with arms became bidders for the sale of submarines to a new democratic administration, allegedly paying bribes along the way.[34] A French company which, his research indicates, flouted sanctions and then benefited from deals with the new political elite was Thomson-CSF – now renamed Thales. The company has been accused of bribing former president Jacob Zuma, who was head of ANC intelligence during its fight against apartheid; the trial was pending towards the end of 2020. Declassified military documents 'reveal that Thomson-CSF was one of the most consistent suppliers of military equipment to the apartheid regime'.[35] It was 'intimately tied to the illicit ... supply of weapons to apartheid for three decades'.[36]

Thomson/Thales's alleged role was not the only example of cooperation in allegedly corrupt activity between old and new elites. Nor are Van Vuuren and his colleagues the only sources to draw attention to these arrangements. Hyslop agrees that the arms deal 'demonstrates the emergence of a confluence of interest between new and old elites, in this case between the military-industrial complex of the old regime and the leaders of their former guerrilla opponents'. He notes that BKS, a firm 'that enjoyed major civilian and military engineering contracts under [apartheid-era president] P.W. Botha, and ADS, the leading military electronics firm of the Botha era', were sold to Thales. Hyslop adds that Mac Maharaj, an ANC activist and later transport minister in the first ANC government, joined the board of FirstRand Bank after he left office in 1999. During his term as minister, 'a contract for a major national road' was awarded to a consortium which included a FirstRand subsidiary, as well as BKS and Nkobi Holdings, a company connected to one of Zuma's financial benefactors, Chippy Shaik. When the defence minister Joe Modise left office in 2000, 'he would become chair of BKS'.[37]

## Corruption Then, Corruption Now

In these cases, the demarcation between public and private is not the only fuzzy line. So is that between reality before and after 1994. Patterns established in the last years of apartheid continued into the new as figures from the new order joined those from the old in the networks:

> Individuals who entered the public and private sector after 1994 and were motivated by greed to act corruptly were likely to welcome the opportunity to work through, and with, influential people, often well networked, who had escaped criminal prosecution under apartheid for similar activity ... Corruption is seldom understood as a system that straddles the old and new order – a number of individuals who were alleged to abuse power for private benefit under apartheid are seen either courting power (most often as business people) or holding public office [after 1994].[38]

Some continuities between past and present were seemingly trivial. For instance, wine farmers who, under apartheid, would provide members of Parliament with an annual quota of wine continued the practice 'in the immediate post-1994 period'.[39] While this is a minor example, it does show how networks which offered private interests special access to public office holders, and assured material rewards for them in return, simply extended from the pre-1994 period to the then new democracy.

To these examples of corruption and 'state capture' must be added another reality. Cooperation between business and government, a reality since South Africa began industrialising, is an inevitable feature of all market economies.[40] But the relationship became far closer in the last years of apartheid. Businesses shared an interest with the government in minimising the impact of sanctions, while the apartheid state's final attempt to preserve itself required goods, services and skills from private business. Business was unhappy with the economic impact of government policy, and it became common for major companies to call for political change. But there was, at the same time, significant cooperation between them and the government. For some critics, this cooperation corrupted business and government. Van Vuuren quotes the academic Sampie Terreblanche: 'The structural corruption that took hold in the public sector and in the dealings between the public and private sector in the 15 years before 1994 was far more serious than was appreciated at the time and the long-term effects were extremely damaging.'[41] Another academic, André Thomashausen, makes a similar point: 'There is a tradition of corruption in South Africa and it's a white tradition ... [The] co-operation between business and the apartheid regime was a common conspiracy ... Corruption has become ingrained in the practice of our politics and business.'[42]

These critics may be exaggerating the degree to which corruption infected all of business. But the post-1994 government did take office after a period in which the divide between private and public had become deeply blurred. The most obvious dimension was that using public office for private gain had become entrenched. For some years this had been largely the product of a reality in which the government's core objective – staying in power – rested on secretive collusion between private and public actors to commit illegal acts or, as in the case of domestic business, cooperation on projects which were shielded by law from public sight. These arrangements did not save the apartheid state, but they did give many people, inside the government and outside it, a stake in ensuring that arrangements which had enriched them continued. They turned to members of the new governing elite.

Willingness to 'cooperate' provided attractive options to some who had operated underground or in exile living on small stipends from the political movement and who had been prohibited by apartheid from a role in the market economy – and were now expected to maintain a lifestyle 'befitting' people who held political positions. It was noted in Chapter 1 that when the ANC returned from exile, the only way its leaders could acquire the trappings of status was through private benefactors. The ANC also needed resources and saw private business as a key source of income. Some of those on whom the ANC relied were liberals who may have seen 'helping out' ANC leaders as a contribution to a stable, non-racial (and market-friendly) democracy. Others were engaged in 'ingratiation'. Whatever the motive, the effect was to maintain the private–public connection.

An example is the experience of former president Thabo Mbeki when he returned from exile as the key ANC negotiator. One of his early goals was to 'win the corporate sector over to the ANC's vision for a future South Africa and, equally important, to hit it for much-needed financial support for the movement'.[43] He needed somewhere to live and, for some time, stayed in the upmarket Carlton Court hotel, courtesy of Anglo American Corporation. Frederik van Zyl Slabbert, a key figure in mediating a constitutional settlement who was close to Mbeki, suggested to him that living at Anglo's expense was inappropriate. He introduced him to his friend Jürgen Kögl, a businessman sympathetic to the ANC, who allowed Mbeki to live in a furnished apartment he owned and soon became his confidant and adviser. Anglo and, more particularly, Slabbert and Kögl did this because they hoped the ANC would build a particular sort of society. This is unlikely to have been the motive of Sol Kerzner, whose hotel empire had flourished partly on the back of the 'independent' Bantustans apartheid created. Casino gambling was banned in South Africa but not in these 'states', and so Kerzner could build Sun City and other casinos in these areas, offering white South Africans an option previously available only if they travelled far. He was a 'generous [supporter] of the apartheid government'. Mbeki's biographer Mark Gevisser names him as one of the ANC's 'brasher benefactors, some of whom underwent dramatic Damascene conversions'. Kerzner is said to have paid for a lavish 50th birthday party for Mbeki and to have donated R2 million to the ANC's election effort.[44]

This experience reflected a widespread pattern in which ANC leaders, whom businesses expected to be the next government, were, like the ANC itself, the recipients of business largesse offered out of a combination of well-meaning and self-serving motives. Later, since businesses also needed black partners, for some former activists this largesse entailed shares in large companies and seats on their boards. Whatever the intention, the blurring of public and private continued, under a different guise, the patterns of late apartheid and is, therefore, an obvious form of path dependence. Mbeki accepted these gifts without falling prey to corruption. It is widely agreed that, like Nelson Mandela, he did not use his office to enrich himself, and, after the ANC recalled him as president, he did not accept attachments to businesses which would have enabled him to benefit from his government role. But others did not keep their distance, and what had been before 1994 networks of businesses and government officials cooperating to save apartheid now absorbed some of the 'liberation' leaders these networks had fought against. Not all these arrangements were corrupt. But they probably all fitted the notion of 'rent seeking' mentioned earlier, and ensured that the networks would continue.

The democratic order's first Speaker of Parliament, Frene Ginwala, believes that, by 1994, corruption was ingrained in the system of governance:

> We inherited an intrinsically corrupt system of governance … To survive, it created a legal framework that was based on and facilitated corruption. It has taken years in Parliament to repeal old laws and introduce even the basic legal framework that would enable us to deal with corrupt bureaucrats, politicians and police. The private sector also operated in a closed society and profited by it. There were partnerships with international criminals, and the corruption that was built into the system is very difficult to overcome.[45]

The rules were changed, but the patterns they had made possible continued – further evidence that new rules do not necessarily change the way people close to power conduct themselves.

There was another, more obvious way in which corruption was carried from the old order into the new. The 'homeland' administrations, which were particularly corrupt, were in theory dissolved and replaced by provinces. But the bureaucracies – and bureaucrats – which served them did not disappear. One of the 'sunset clauses', or temporary agreements, resulting from constitutional talks protected the jobs of public servants. This protection, and the new government's desire not to alienate former Bantustan leaders or officials, ensured that they were absorbed into the administrations of provinces which had housed 'homelands'. The result was predictable: 'The incorporation into regional administrations of homeland civil services may merely have transferred the bureaucratic location of corrupt behaviour and made regional governments vulnerable to the patrimonial politics which affected certain homeland administrations.'[46]

Since these networks thrived in areas where black citizens lived, the racial majority remain the chief victims of these practices: corruption is more prevalent in provinces which housed 'homelands'. Lodge, noting that Gauteng, in which there were no 'homelands', still experienced corruption, added that 'compared to some of its neighbours … Gauteng is an island of probity'[47] because its administration did not absorb a 'homeland' bureaucracy. Hyslop makes the point more forcefully:

> The incompetence and corruption of the old statelets was simply carried over into the new era, with the difference that civil servants now often enjoyed

the patronage and protection of ANC leaders. The most extreme corruption has appeared in the three provinces where the regional civil service was most extensively and exclusively drawn from the old Bantustan structures.[48]

Lodge points out that most politicians who were named in corruption scandals in the early years of democracy were 'stalwarts' of the fight against apartheid, not 'homeland' leaders.[49] But while the remnants of the 'homelands' may not have been responsible for grand corruption, their former bureaucrats and networks did compromise the institutions which served black citizens in former 'homeland' areas and ensured the survival of less noticed, local, abuses of public trust and resources which damaged the already limited prospects of black citizens in these areas. The next chapter discusses collaboration between provincial governments and traditional leaders in these provinces to sell land to private developers, which arguably continues the patterns of 'homeland' governance.

Some corruption was inevitable even if the transition had taken a different form. It was not realistic to expect that when anti-apartheid activists gravitated into senior positions, without any of the assets which third- or fourth-generation middle-class or affluent people brought to these roles, none would use their status to acquire some of the riches enjoyed by the minority whom apartheid had protected. Lodge notes that 'relatively low levels of official corruption in, for example, Botswana, are attributable to the existence of an indigenous ruling class which acquired its wealth before it became ascendant in national politics.'[50] The political class which took over government in 1994 had no such advantage.

Some patterns in the fight against the system also made corruption more likely. The stark divisions between 'them' and 'us' which underpinned conflicts convince some that winning means that they are now entitled to resources which 'the other side' enjoyed. The manner in which the fight against apartheid had to be funded also instilled habits which were to make corruption more likely: 'Foreign donors put large amounts of money into South Africa in order to finance oppositional activity. Because of the security difficulties entailed in doing this, a system developed where well-regarded resistance figures were entrusted with substantial quantities of cash to dish out on an ad hoc basis; proper records were not kept.'[51] This 'struggle accounting' was a response to the constraints of the time, but it created opportunities for abuse. Moreover, the fact that corruption was the product of long-standing patterns does not excuse those who did continue it – Mbeki and Mandela were by no means the only leaders to refuse the temptation and others could have done this too. But the particular form which post-1994 corruption took has continued the patterns of the past and is more evidence of path dependence.

## THE COST OF EXCLUSION

The legacy of apartheid-era corruption is not the only reason dishonest and fraudulent conduct has been so severe a problem in democracy's first quarter-century. To gain a fuller understanding of corruption's dimensions, we must examine the impact of economic exclusion.

Two interlinked realities help explain why public office is frequently used for private gain. Much of what happens in local government is not fully understood unless we recognise that, in those parts of the country where poverty levels are high, positions in local government are not only – indeed not mainly – about public service. For people with little or no prospect of upward mobility, a seat on a council is the only available route into the middle class: 'The mayor who has not completed building an expensive new home before she is deposed is unlikely to be able to do so afterwards.'[52] An example is provided by an organiser who was delegated by the National Union of Metalworkers of South Africa (Numsa) to establish a 'movement for socialism'. Although the union's leadership believed this would become a political party,[53] in the initial stages the organiser's mandate was to establish a citizens' movement. He reported that when he arrived in townships to introduce the idea to residents, he was always approached by people who wanted to know when the party list was to be drafted and how they could secure a place on it.[54] Election is the difference between a middle-class lifestyle and poverty, which is why those who lose their seats are reluctant to vacate them.[55]

The second reality flows from the first. Because local politics is a route into the middle class for the few able to make use of the opportunities, people whose path upwards is blocked by their outsider status gravitate towards political party branches in the hope that this will do for them what the market is meant to do. Their hope is that by attaching themselves to political parties and politicians, they will gain access to the resources which are beyond their reach in the marketplace. This creates fertile ground for patronage, the distribution of material benefits to buy political support. Public office can enable not only a middle-class lifestyle but also the possibility of building a support base by distributing money and favours. A further 'benefit' of office is that it may attract the attention of business people who can gain favoured government treatment by offering inducements to officials and politicians.

Predictably, these realities have particularly damaged the ANC, since its status as governing party opens doors to public resources and attracts the attention of private wealth. The problem is not new; it began appearing in ANC reports before the end of the party's first decade in government. Its celebrated document on leadership, *Through the Eye of a Needle?*, which is frequently quoted by ANC activists worried about moral decline, identified the problem in 2001:

> Some individuals ... compete for ANC leadership positions in order to get into government. Many ... view positions in government as a source of material riches for themselves. Thus resources, prestige and authority of government positions become the driving force in competition for leadership positions in the ANC.
>
> Government positions also go hand-in-hand with the possibility to issue contracts to commercial companies. Some of these companies identify ANC members that they can promote in ANC structures and into government, so that they can get contracts by hook or by crook. This is done through media networks to discredit other leaders, or even by buying membership cards to set up branches that are ANC only in name.[56]

The report adds that positions in government also offer opportunities to appoint others:

> Some members make promises to friends, that once elected ... they would return the favour ... Cliques and factions then emerge within the movement, around personal loyalties driven by corrupt intentions. Members become voting fodder to serve individuals' self-interest.[57]

This diagnosis is repeated in ANC documents over the next two decades. A 2010 investigation into whether the concerns in the 2001 report had been addressed[58] quoted ANC publications, beginning with an organisational report to its 1997 conference, complaining that 'leadership in the ANC is seen as stepping-stones to positions of power and material reward in government and business'; 'disturbing trends of "careerism, corruption and opportunism", alien to a revolutionary movement, [are] taking roots at various levels, eating at our soul and with potential to denude our society of an agent of real change'; and 'divisive leadership battles over access to resources and patronage [are] becoming the norm [with] allegations about corruption and business interests of leadership and deployed cadres abounding'. Members were used as 'voting cattle' and recruitment was about finding delegates who would vote for particular candidates. The consequence was internal decay, evidenced by 'gate-keeping, ghost members, commercialization of membership and other forms of fraudulent practice'.[59]

By 2017, so deep had this rot become that as the ANC headed towards its conference at which Cyril Ramaphosa and Nkosazana Dlamini-Zuma and their factions were to contest party leadership, it seemed highly unlikely that the ANC could hold competitive elections in which one faction won at the expense of the other. The battle for power and resources in which money and the prospect of position were used to assemble votes had so eroded internal structures that it had become common for electoral contests to trigger legal disputes[60] or chaos at conferences in which both sides questioned the credentials of the other's delegates and complained that procedures had been breached, disputes which sometimes prompted violence between delegates.[61] A hotly contested election which produced a decisive victory for either side would almost certainly ensure that the results would be overturned by the courts (internal decay is so pronounced that claims that correct procedure had not been followed are usually upheld by judges) or that the conference would descend into squabbles which would prevent the election of a new leadership, or split the ANC.

Circumstantial evidence suggests that ANC leaders settled the contest in the only way which would prevent these damaging possibilities – by reaching a deal between the factions. One aspect of the horse-trading was reported: David Mabuza, Mpumalanga premier and ANC provincial chair, was said to have promised Zuma that he would deliver the province's sizeable vote (it has the second-largest ANC membership of all the provinces) to Dlamini-Zuma. But he told his delegates to vote as they pleased and this enabled Ramaphosa's victory. Mabuza himself was elected deputy president.[62] This may have been the product of a deal between Mabuza and Ramaphosa. At the same time, the top six ANC positions, and the 80 elected members of its national executive committee, were divided evenly between the factions. The realities of ANC politics suggest that this could only have been achieved by a bargain. ANC conferences are dominated by 'slate voting', which allows the largest faction to win all the positions even if it enjoys only a slim majority. The only way to achieve an even split in 86 positions is to tell faction members to divide their votes between slates, which would happen only if the two sides had agreed to split the positions between them (possibly after agreeing that the presidency would be contested).

The realities described here seem to have so damaged the ANC's structures and processes that they made it impossible for the party to hold a fully contested election. This ensured that ANC leadership for the ensuing five years would be hampered by an uneasy balance of power between rival factions. The same fate would probably await any party which became the national party of government. Its primary cause is not the design of ANC elections but the reality that at stake is who will enter or remain within the middle class. Because the stakes are so personal for so many, cut-throat competition between factions which can be avoided only when they strike a bargain is almost inevitable. So are the abuses which are likely when the stakes are this high.

But these realities also explain why corruption is about more than the simplistic tale of bad people who misuse democratic government. Karl von Holdt points out that the 'narratives presented in the media and the public domain' usually portray corruption and attempts to curb it

> as a struggle between a state-capturing network of politicians, officials, brokers and businessmen bent on looting and self-enrichment, and a band of righteous politicians and citizens, drawing together the 'old' ANC, activists, 'good' business and citizens in general, intent on rebuilding institutions and good governance, the rule of law, international credibility and fostering growth and development.

However, 'a much deeper set of social forces and processes underlies and shapes the struggles within the ANC'. More broadly, corruption 'is a mechanism of class formation, rather than primarily a moral or criminal issue'.[63]

Von Holdt explains 'class formation' thus: The formal economic sectors 'are dominated by established business and corporations, opportunities are few, the demand is high and competition is fierce'. Ambitious new entrants – who are, inevitably, black since it is they who have been excluded – are unable to gain access in most cases. Because the market is not accessible, 'the state is the location of jobs, revenue, contracts, tenders and licensing and is an obvious resource in the formation of a new elite'. The centrality of the state as the means to create a new black economic elite (and so to end minority rule in the upper rungs of the economy) has 'given rise to a pervasive informal political-economic system that pre-existed Zuma's accession to the Presidency and which is much more extensive than the Zuma-Gupta project'. It 'is shaped by the intersection of patronage and factionalism, as patronage networks form political factions in order to gain power in the state'. Because the networks and factions were there before the Guptas arrived and Zuma became president, 'the purging of the Zuma-Gupta network ... and even their jailing, will not lead to the demise of this system'.[64]

Von Holdt argues that the patterns which enabled Zuma and the Guptas began early in the post-1994 order: 'during the Mbeki period as well as the presidency of Mandela'. Rejecting a much publicised study which sees 'state capture' as the invention of Zuma and the Guptas,[65] he argues: 'There must have been a significantly wider set of tender-based beneficiaries, each able in turn to distribute opportunities and largesse more broadly ... to account for the political longevity of and broad support for Zuma.'[66] He also challenges the notion[67] that the 'informal system' which made corruption possible was 'centralised by the Gupta-Zuma nexus; it was rather a decentralised system in which various party barons were licensed to conduct their own operations as long as they provided political support or cover for the Presidential faction. Hence looting proceeded at an accelerated pace across the system.'[68] This network appeared at national, provincial and local levels; it relied on 'state officials, ambitious entrepreneurs as well as smalltime operators' who were 'rigging tenders or engaging in other kinds of fraud so as to use revenue flows from the state to sustain or establish businesses, or simply to finance self-enrichment'.[69] Zuma's tenure extended it but did not create it. The network is not an aberration created by a head of government and his business patrons; it is deep-rooted and thus far more tenacious than the account which blames only the Guptas and Zuma would have us believe.

The key to this system is the inequality 'between black business and white business, as well as between black and white middle-classes more broadly'.[70] The post-1994 government's means of addressing this is Black Economic Empowerment (BEE), which seeks 'the transfer of assets from existing corporations to new black business partners'. But BEE 'share transfers are financed through a range of mechanisms which entail substantial debt financing for new black owners'. It relegates black capitalists to 'junior partners' while offering 'a new source of profit for (white) financial capital'.[71] This is why black managers and business people complained that 'the rules of the game were rigged against black business, making it virtually impossible to penetrate the private sector because of long established relationships'.[72]

This subordinate status cannot satisfy an emerging black economic elite which wants control of politics to also bring economic power – as it did for white English and then Afrikaans speakers. Von Holdt sees 'the fierce struggle of indigenous elites to come into existence and lay hold of the sources of wealth in Africa' as a predictable consequence of political freedom. The anti-colonial theorist Frantz Fanon thoroughly disliked the process but recognised its importance.[73] It provides the motor for corruption and explains why Zuma and his supporters insist they are fighting 'white monopoly capital' (even if they are not).

This development may be inevitable but it does not take the economy or society forward. Within the ANC, it was once common to urge the creation of a 'patriotic bourgeoisie' which would be committed to the country as well as profit.[74] This view drew from theories of society ranging from Marxism to modernisation theory which saw the formation of a business class, whatever its motives, as a means to develop the economy and society by unleashing new productive forces. In South Africa, that the development of a black business class could also benefit society has been argued by, among others, the intellectual and former ANC Cabinet minister Pallo Jordan, who, at the turn of the century, proposed engagement between the ANC and an emerging black business class:

> Such engagement could involve the elaboration of standards of conduct and a business ethic that will speed job creation, the fostering of skills development, the empowerment of women, the strengthening of the popular organs of civil society, and active involvement in the fight to end poverty ... Rather than merely pursuing money and hefty profits, the Black bourgeoisie should give the lead within the business community regarding responsible corporate behaviour.[75]

Despite this hope, Von Holdt notes that the 'class formation' described here does not contribute to development. In theory, 'the Zuma-Gupta project (was) committed to ... facilitating the emergence of an embedded black capitalist class ... more amenable [to] ... growing the South African economy and benefiting its people'. In reality, it redirected 'state funds towards personal enrichment, political faction building, the extraordinary profit-making of a foreign family, and the enrichment of the president's own family ... We have little evidence of this project aiding the formation of an indigenous capitalist class invested in long-term growth and expanded accumulation'.[76]

One reason why class formation in South Africa does not produce an 'indigenous' business class committed to expanding the economy is a form of path dependence discussed earlier: enrichment is often 'directed towards conspicuous consumption rather than productive investment'.[77] As apartheid enriched whites, spending lavishly on consumption became ingrained in the habits of the elite. Flaunting wealth became a measure of success and status, a message amplified by the media and popular culture. Since this was the measure of worth set by those the new elite hoped to emulate, it is no surprise that showing off wealth should be a priority. This is perhaps an inevitable consequence of the attempt by a section of the black elite to ensure that it is enriched and empowered by democracy in the same way as the white elite was enriched and empowered by colonisation and apartheid.

Because the marketplace is not accessible, 'elite factions' battle for resources within the state. This includes 'the struggle for positions of power ... over the deployment of cadres, the allocation of tenders and other opportunities for fraud, the opportunities for preferred status in BEE deals with private sector corporations, and the distribution of employment opportunities'. State tenders are 'critical to the future of many emerging black-owned businesses'. This ensures fierce competition 'and collusion between state officials and contenders for contracts in order to rig the tender process and inflate contracts'.[78] It creates pressure on the rule of law and political institutions since they are expected to bear the weight of intense conflicts for resources.[79] While these conflicts are usually blamed on black politicians and business people, Von Holdt notes that 'white capital' can be a party to them too: 'An important consideration in the choice of BEE partners is their degree of political connectedness'.[80] This reinforces competition between political factions who are vying not only for public resources but also for the largesse of businesses, some of whom, as Van Vuuren's work shows, have been accused of participating in 'tender rigging' themselves.

Von Holdt argues:

> The state constitutes the primary agency for redistribution and class forma-tion, not only in the sense that it makes and implements policy for society, but also that it controls the biggest revenues, budgets, assets and payroll … as well as access to mining rights, broadcast rights, and other lucrative opportunities. This makes the state itself the key site for black economic empowerment.[81]

A sign of the damage this cut-throat competition does is the assassination of ANC officials and politicians. The trend began in Mpumalanga[82] and has since moved largely to KwaZulu-Natal. While this is sometimes attributed to factional battles – which implies that people are murdered because they support particular leaders – the evidence suggests that the murders are aimed at people who opposed, or threatened to report, corruption.[83] This, of course, suggests that the murders are a consequence of the patterns described here.

Von Holdt cites studies, including his own, into the 'intersection between community protests and ANC politics' which 'revealed how, already in 2008–9, local government had become a source of intense struggles over access to tenders, budgets and jobs between different factions of the ANC in many towns and townships'. A 2011 study of grassroots protest by a research team headed by Von Holdt found that 'salaries from high-level jobs in the local town council, the power to distribute both high- and low-level council jobs, as well as the opportunities for business with council, and the patronage networks that link the two, are key mechanisms in the formation of the elite, especially in small towns with limited employment opportunities'.[84] After 1994, one reason for continued township protest was the desire of local political figures for these posts: 'Outsider factions positioned themselves as leaders in community protests against the incumbent factions, with the aim of accessing the resources at the disposal of local government and ... constituting new patronage networks to reward their followers.'[85] While some protest leaders were 'genuinely concerned to struggle against corruption and incompetence', others saw protest as 'an opportunity to oust their opponents in the town council ... so as to gain, or regain, positions of power and access to lucrative council business'.[86] A local councillor claims that '90% of the so-called service delivery protests [in an informal settlement] are due to people who feel left out of the jobs that Council generates'.[87]

So, while protests are often portrayed purely as battles between 'the people' and unresponsive leaders, many were mobilised by aspirant elites who sought government positions and their attendant benefits. This does not mean the grievances are manufactured or that protesters are 'useful idiots', manipulated by aspirant members of the new property-owning class. Protesters know what motivates the elite: 'People are just fighting for tenders, but using the community to do so,' a protester told researchers. Another agreed: 'Some of the leaders were angry that they were no longer getting tenders and then they decided to mobilise the community against the municipality.'[88] People participate despite this because they do not believe they are heard by authorities and the protests offer an opportunity for voice: 'In a sense, the crowds were using these leaders to articulate their grievances within the ANC, just as these leaders were mobilising popular grievances in their own campaign [for leadership positions].'[89]

Local divisions within the ANC are largely explained by these dynamics. In the 2011 study headed by Von Holdt, they were an important feature across case studies.[90] The local partnership of the ANC, the South African Communist Party and the South African National Civic Organisation (which is close to the ANC but not formally allied to it) provided the 'infrastructure' through which these battles were fought. The reason is obvious: the ANC dominates electoral politics in most townships and shack settlements and so it is the source of access to the state and the resources it brings. The factionalism which is so central a feature of national ANC politics is, therefore, also evident in local politics. This does not mean that the divide is the same. National divisions are an insider contest which reflects the wider economic divide between 'insiders' and 'outsiders', while local factionalism is largely a contest between 'outsiders' for access to the state which might make them 'insiders'. The common thread is the impact of the economic consequences of path dependence on politics – and on the governing party in particular.

## THE MORE THINGS CHANGE ...

The work of Von Holdt and his colleagues has been discussed at length here because it is firmly rooted in studies of grassroots dynamics and offers a convincing explanation of these realities.

But Von Holdt provides a more complete account of local dynamics than of their national equivalent. The chief flaw of his analysis of the latter is that it does not offer a coherent depiction of the Ramaphosa faction. Is it simply another alliance dedicated to gaining access to resources? Or does something else motivate it? The analysis proposed here – that the Ramaphosa contingent expresses the interests of people who have been incorporated into the market economy in ways which enable them to benefit from it – does not contradict Von Holdt's analysis. But a weakness in his account may be its tendency to assume that no black business people – or other black South Africans – are integrated into the market on terms which would prompt them to defend it. This leaves much unexplained. Why would Ramaphosa and his allies want to restore elements of pre-2009 arrangements if all this does is make them vassals of white business? Surely they want this because they have a stake in the system? By ignoring the possibility that a section of black South Africa has acquired an interest in preserving the post-1994 market economy (although they may wish to reform it to make it more inclusive), Von Holdt's analysis reflects only a part of the reality.

That said, the insights are crucial to our understanding of path dependence, its role in forms of corruption and 'state capture', and its impacts on politics. Post-apartheid corruption continues patterns which are deeply embedded in South African history and, in particular, apartheid's closing period. But this explains only a part of the reality. The networks discussed here explain another crucial part. They would exist even if the apartheid state's fight against sanctions and domestic resistance had not created criminal webs which survived into the new order. They are explained, rather, by the impact of economic path dependence on the thwarted ambitions of black South Africans who want to do what the theory of the market economy says they are meant to do: use their energies to rise to the top.

Von Holdt's work enables us to analyse more precisely the form of exclusion which produces the corrupt networks. The key motor is not the exclusion of outsiders living in poverty, although at times this may aid the networks by fuelling grassroots anger which enables some local elites to mobilise citizens. Far from enabling corrupt networks, the excluded at the grassroots often resist them. The networks did not prevent millions of ANC voters from withholding their support in the 2016 local elections. Research shows that the victims of economic exclusion reject local corruption and the politicians who engage in it.[91] Patronage's role in amassing support for the politicians who use it is important (but not decisive) in internal ANC politics. It is far less effective outside it. The probable reason is that the dispensers of patronage are 'dependent patrons':[92] they depend on links with private economic power holders. This limits what they have to distribute and the numbers to whom they can distribute it.

Corrupt networks, therefore, may well be, as Von Holt argues, less about grassroots exclusion and more a reaction to the barriers which make it very difficult for new black entrants to access the upper echelons of business. Their motor is elite exclusion – the obstacles which stand in the way of black aspirant elites frustrated by the fact that political change has not fundamentally changed the racial patterns in formal business and who see the state and politics as the route to advancement which the market is meant to provide. But whatever the precise nuances of post-1994 corruption, an analysis of the networks which enable it at the grassroots confirms that corruption, the ill most frequently associated with the post-1994 order, is a continuation of both past patterns and the consequence of their survival in the formal economy.

# 4

# The Bifurcated Society: Mahmood Mamdani, Rural Power and State Capture

The realities which face a path-dependent South Africa were, in the view of many scholars, identified in a book written in the mid-1990s by a celebrated Ugandan-born academic: Mahmood Mamdani's *Citizen and Subject*.[1] While the book discussed post-colonial African states in general, it devoted much attention to South Africa in particular (its author was based at the University of Cape Town during the early years of democracy).

The book seems to describe contemporary South Africa in uncanny detail. It insists that the present is shaped by the past. It argues that essential to the continuity between past and present is a society in which some enjoy much fuller citizenship than others; that many are excluded from the 'civil society' in which citizens use their rights to make the government hear their voice and so from the national debate; and that the divide between urban and rural which was a core feature of colonisation was perpetuated by government after minority rule's end. These are all realities in South Africa today: the book's relevance to the issues facing the society is confirmed by daily news bulletins. But while this testifies to the importance of Mamdani's book, it does not mean that its argument for why all this came to be explains reality.

For Mamdani, realities under minority rule have survived its end in South Africa, as elsewhere on the continent, because the 'bifurcated state'[2] built by colonialism, including apartheid, lives on. Mamdani argues that the colonial state (which very much includes South Africa's apartheid state) rested on a 'dualism of power', which was exercised very differently in the towns and rural areas. In urban areas, the colonial power ruled directly. In the countryside, it relied on 'decentralised despotism': it handed authority to 'traditional leaders' (who were not always entirely traditional since some were appointed by the colonising power) who ruled on the colonial state's behalf by imposing order on the leader's subjects, ensuring that they would not disturb minority rule.

In South Africa, this was a core feature of apartheid: black people were assigned citizenship in 'ethnic homelands' ruled by 'traditional leaders' chosen by the state, not because they were authentically traditional, but because they would cooperate in imposing order. At independence throughout Africa, rule was, Mamdani believes, deracialised, but 'decentralised despotism' stayed. While the people who were subjected to this control were now, in theory, citizens with rights, in practice they remained subjects of unaccountable power: hence the book's title. So the patterns in today's South Africa are a consequence of the survival of this form of state, even though the ethnic 'homeland' system has been abolished.

Mamdani's book has significantly influenced thinking on South Africa. According to one commentator, the country is paying the price for not heeding *Citizen and Subject*'s warning. Jonny Steinberg, reflecting on attempts by the South African state to 'distort' rural land ownership, writes: 'Here is the warning Mamdani issued in 1996: in their struggle to deracialise the civilised laws of Europe in the cities, South Africans will be blindsided to the continuation of despotic rule in the countryside. And the consequences will not be confined to out-of-sight rural ghettos but will come to shape SA's collective fate.'[3]

Mamdani's warning was not as emphatic as Steinberg thought. But failing to see this is perhaps understandable, given how closely events in South Africa seem to confirm Mamdani's diagnosis of a divide between urban and rural people, and between those who enjoy citizenship and those who remain subjects. Nevertheless, important similarities between the argument of *Citizen and Subject* and current reality do not necessarily mean that the problem is a particular form of the state. Nor does it mean that the urban–rural divide of which Steinberg writes is a cause rather than a symptom of other patterns which ensure that citizenship is not enjoyed equally by all. This chapter argues that while the path-dependent realities of post-1994 South Africa seem to confirm Mamdani's thesis, the cause is the survival not of a form of state, but of a form of society which the state has been unwilling or unable to change.

Mamdani was prescient in insisting that achieving formal democracy and removing legally imposed racial barriers would not necessarily close the divide between the included and the excluded, a very early recognition of the crucial role of path dependence. But the source of the problem is not, as he argued, the continuation of a form of state which uses 'extra-economic' coercion[4] to exclude some people from real, rather than formal, citizenship. The problem stems from the survival of patterns of domination and power in the society which the state might at times reflect but does not shape. A clear urban–rural divide is a key feature of current South African politics and society, but it is a consequence of the society's particular form of path dependence, not the form of the state. To elucidate this argument, a brief discussion of *Citizen and Subject*'s analysis is necessary.

## THE DESPOTISM WHICH DOES NOT DIE

The chief concern of *Citizen and Subject* is to challenge accounts of post-independence Africa which imply that governance failures and democratic deficits are a product of African 'culture'.

This view of Africa – which often uses terms such as 'patrimonialism'[5] to describe governance failures and other political ills – is, as noted earlier, extremely popular among scholars, particularly in the West. It expresses deep-rooted prejudices, implying that Africans are unfit to govern or hostile to democracy or both. Mamdani wants to show that the authoritarianism which plagued many African countries after independence is not a break with the colonial past but its product. African governing elites are not replacing the efficiency and rationality of colonial regimes with 'African' despotism but are continuing the coloniser's despotic rule. While he does not use the term, Mamdani too is arguing that South Africa, along with other post-colonial African states, is trapped in path dependence. The colonial state, he argues, relied on direct rule in the cities, indirect rule in the countryside. In the former, it directly imposed racialised rule on Africans. In the latter, ethnic-ally defined traditional authorities – either genuinely traditional or selected by the coloniser – ruled despotically on behalf of the colonial power, largely relieving it of the burden of keeping the colonised in check.

On independence, Mamdani argues, 'the bifurcated state that was created with colonialism was deracialized but it was not democratized'.[6] African states embarked on a 'conservative' or 'radical' path. The conservative variety retained the ethnic 'native administrations' which imposed despotic rule on rural citizens. This was justified on the grounds that they were authentically African. Again, the state ruled directly in the cities, indirectly in the countryside. The radical states rejected the ethnic divisions of 'tribalism' and the traditional authorities which reinforced them as relics of colonialism and embarked on a programme of deracialisation and detribalisation. But they did this not by democratising society. Rather, they relied on centralised administrative control and direction from the top, just as the colon-iser had done.

Radical states, mimicking the coloniser they denounced, '[enforced] adminis-trative imperatives through extra-economic coercion – in the name not of custom but revolution'. The identity of the rulers changed but not the despotism: 'Even if there was a change in the title of functionaries, from chiefs to cadres, there was little change in the nature of power.' This centralisation of authority kept rural despotism alive not by preserving chiefs, but by replacing them with equally unaccountable rule from the centre. Again, rural citizens were reduced to subjects, now by an implied sense that the rural was inferior to the urban. Radical and conservative states 'reproduced one part of the legacy of the bifurcated state and created their own distinct version of despotism'.[7]

Mamdani proposes a way forward for African democrats who, when *Citizen and Subject* was written, were pressing for a 'second independence', not from the colon-iser but from the elites who replaced it. He warns that unless democratic reform is accompanied by local rural democracy, the bifurcation and despotism will continue. The freedom of city dwellers able to take advantage of national democracy would contrast with continued rural bondage: 'An electoral reform … which leaves rural areas out of consideration … is precisely about the re-emergence of a decentralized despotism.'[8] Equally importantly, reformers needed to break with the assumption which underpinned the post-independence bifurcated state – that the urban, where individual citizens enjoyed rights and activity in civil society, was superior to the rural: 'Key to reform is linking urban to rural, linking binary opposites such as rights and custom, representation and participation, centralization and decentral-ization, civil society and community.'[9] This would require an end to a form of path-dependent thinking which sees cities as centres of modernity, the countryside as a place of backwardness.

This analysis applies generally to post-colonial African states. But *Citizen and Subject* is particularly interested in South Africa because Mamdani also rejects 'South African exceptionalism', the claim that, because of its larger and more sophisticated economy, it is different from the rest of the continent. The book appeared just after South Africa had become a democracy, so it was not an ana-lysis of the post-1994 order but an attempt to warn those who would shape it that apartheid was not a unique form of colonisation. Moreover, they could not assume that a democratic South Africa would find it easier to shake off the yoke of the past because it was (or thought that it was) more 'modern' than the rest of the continent.

Mamdani insists that his analysis of the colonial state applies to South Africa under apartheid too, despite the attempts of much scholarship to treat it as a unique form of domination. He does acknowledge differences between South Africa and the other African states he analyses. He notes that the labour movement is far more substantial and, more generally, 'the specificity of the South African experience lies in the strength of its civil society, both black and white'.[10] Both of these realities were products of urbanisation and a much larger formal economy. But apartheid, he argues, was not unique. It tried to impose a bifurcated state on an urbanising society because it saw in black urbanisation the threat of urban revolt. Apartheid tried to defuse this threat by imposing ethnicity to 'fragment' the African population and freeze its movement: 'The bifurcated state tried to keep apart forcibly that which socio-economic processes tended to bring together freely – the urban and rural, one ethnicity to another.'[11]

A key pillar of this attempt to control urbanisation was migrant labour. Laws preventing most black people from living permanently in cities sought not only to keep urban areas as white as possible, but also to tightly control those black people who were allowed to work in them, who could be expelled if they disobeyed. Even the end of influx control in 1986 was, in Mamdani's view, designed to achieve the same end – 'it was as if the government hoped that by allowing rural people to flood into the cities, it would drown the urban revolt'. Apartheid South Africa's industrial workforce may have been much larger than that in other African countries. But if focus shifts from 'the labour question to the native question', apartheid becomes a bifurcated form of colonial rule like all others. For Mamdani, it is the form of state, not the economy, which enables the past to survive. 'Economistic' explanations of apartheid stress 'the mode of exploitation, not of rule'.[12] South Africa was much more industrialised than other African states, but it too was governed in a way which drove a wedge between town and countryside by imposing different forms of rule on them. Mamdani knows that if apartheid was trying to prevent urban resistance, it failed spectacularly: the cities were key sites of mobilisation against the system. But he insists that the form which the 'struggle' took shows that a damaging division between rural and urban had been created by imposing two forms of rule. His evidence is the intense and often violent conflict between migrant workers and permanent urban residents which was a key feature of the fight against apartheid in the 1970s and 1980s.

The wave of resistance which defeated apartheid began with the Durban strikes of 1973; Mamdani notes that migrant workers were key to resisting apartheid. But when the site of resistance shifted to Soweto in 1976, migrants in urban hostels became marginal to the urban revolt and then blocked it, prompting violent conflict between city dwellers fighting apartheid and migrants seeking to protect the rural order. This conflict was a product of the failure of urban movements to develop 'an agenda for democratizing customary power gelled in indirect rule authorities'.[13] In this view, although the anti-apartheid resistance rejected the ethnic Bantustans which apartheid created to control rural areas, it did not build a democratic resistance in these areas; it assumed that they would be freed by urban resistance. This repeated the pattern set by radical post-independence elites elsewhere on the continent because it privileged the urban and reduced rural people to spectators (or 'sell-outs' who opposed the fight against apartheid). It also abandoned rural people to the authority of rural despots.

This prompts Mamdani to alert us to the dangers of preserving the bifurcated state in the post-apartheid order. *Citizen and Subject* does not predict this will happen; rather, it highlights the need to democratise the countryside to ensure it does not. If the post-apartheid state were to leave indirect rule intact, Mamdani cautions, South Africa would not escape the path of other post-independence African countries: 'With free movement between town and country, but with Native Authorities in charge of an ethnically governed rural population, it will reproduce one legacy of apartheid but in a non-racial form.'[14] Either the gulf between urban and rural, between democracy in the cities and despotism in the countryside, would be closed by the democratisation of the countryside, Mamdani warned, or the democratic project would be obstructed, presumably by conflicts between countryside and city like those which plagued the fight against apartheid.

## A PROPHETIC WARNING? SOUTH AFRICAN SOCIETY TODAY

Have Mamdani's fears been realised? Path dependence supports his view that the post-1994 society retains important features of reality under apartheid.

Suburban residents are, in Mamdani's terms, citizens, not subjects. Although they do not vote for the governing party (and many are hostile to majority rule), they use political rights to ensure a higher standard of public service and more responsive government than that associated with townships, shack settlements and rural areas. People who live in townships and shack settlements cannot be neatly slotted into either category. Their citizenship is weakened by local power holders and poverty; they often protest in the streets because they insist this is the only way to persuade authorities to listen.[15] But they are not always subjects either. Some exercise their citizenship rights in social movements, local civic associations or political party branches, and they do use their vote to send signals to the governing party. But a reality in which suburban residents enjoy substantive rights, high living standards and adequate services while just about everyone else does not is a clear case of path dependence.

## From Town to Countryside

There is also a contrast between town and countryside which seems to show that Mamdani's warning was not heard.

A key feature of apartheid was the elevation of traditional leaders willing to do the bidding of the white state to positions of authority in ethnic 'homelands', some of which received notional 'independence'. Where chiefs would not impose control on the state's behalf, they were replaced by others who would. This 'Bantustan' system was accurately identified by the ANC and other 'liberation' movements as a resource for white power: those who occupied positions of authority in this system were seen as agents of the state. The constitution which ended apartheid therefore abolished Bantustans and extended equal citizenship rights to their residents.[16] But the government's response to traditional authority was ambivalent. It did not strengthen it, and at times it claimed to be seeking ways of democratising it. Chiefs do not wield formal political authority. But many of the features of the pre-1994 order persist.[17]

Traditional leadership is recognised by the constitution, but after 1994 the government seemed unclear on what to do about it. Despite campaigning against Bantustans before 1994, the ANC, after it was again a legal organisation, courted chiefs, including some who ran Bantustans. The claimed reason was that traditional authority was authentically African and had been distorted by apartheid – the real reason will be discussed shortly. But some within the ANC insisted that traditional authorities be subject to democratic rules. The result was an attempt at balance. The Traditional Leadership and Governance Framework Act (No. 41 of 2003) (TLGFA) renamed tribal authorities 'traditional councils': one-third of council members are meant to be women and 40 per cent must be elected. The stated purpose was to align traditional authority with a democratic constitution. But traditional leaders and men remained in charge. 'Although the draft legislation presents serious critiques of colonial and apartheid legislation on traditional leadership and governance, by maintaining the tribal authority boundaries the TLGFA reproduces many of the violences and material inequalities … its predecessors set in place.'[18] Mazibuko Jara is more emphatic, stating that traditional councils were 'spaces of tribal governance reproducing almost, as it were, the apartheid homeland maps'.[19] Jara suggested that the councils also reproduced Bantustans' manner of governing. But even these halting reforms were resisted by chiefs – the law was amended in 2011 to deal with the reality that, eight years after it had been passed, most ignored it.[20]

Land rights, identified by Mamdani (and many others) as the core of traditional power,[21] received similar treatment: moves to democratise access to rural land did not remove control from traditional authorities. Land is the key resource in traditional areas and so control over it is power. Whether rural dwellers are forced to depend on traditional authorities for access to land decides 'whether [they] continue to be subjects under the political rule of unelected traditional authorities or will enjoy the citizenship rights, including the right to choose leaders and representatives, that the … Constitution confers on all South Africans'.[22] So land rights are the key to whether people are citizens or subjects. The vehicle for addressing land was the Communal Land Rights Act (No. 11 of 2004). While it did offer people living under tribal authority greater say in land decisions, the law was criticised for retaining traditional authorities' control:

> Some critiques … suggest that the Act entrenches particular versions of 'customary' land tenure that resulted from colonial and apartheid policies, and that this will have the effect of undermining rather than securing land rights … The [Act] shifts the balance of power away from individuals and households towards the group and its authority structures … and towards the Minister.[23]

One account reports that the law was skewed towards traditional leaders after they 'threatened in 2003 to boycott the forthcoming national elections because the new Traditional Leadership and Governance Framework Bill did not give them enough power'. The government 'backed down when the Communal Land Rights Bill (CLRB) was amended at the eleventh hour to give traditional councils the power to represent rural communities as the "owner of the land". The amendment sparked an immediate outcry from rural women and land rights organisations.'[24] This suggests that the ANC believed that chiefs were able to influence the votes of people living under their authority.

But while the government conceded to the demands of traditional leaders, the courts did not: in 2009, they ruled the CLRB unconstitutional.[25] This was not the last time courts struck down laws or practices which strengthened traditional leadership on the grounds that they violated the constitutional rights of people in traditional areas. Since the courts are as much a part of the state as the government, this means that some parts of the state were more eager than others to hold traditional authorities to democratic norms, a point which is of some importance to Mamdani's analysis.

### Forward to the Past: Revitalising Traditional Authority

For some scholars and observers, the government trajectory described here, in particular its handling of land, endorses traditional authority: 'Since 2003 … law and policy have come down squarely in favour of transferring title of communal land to traditional leaders and institutions, as opposed to the people who live on and work it.'[26]

It would be more accurate to see government actions as an unsuccessful attempt to balance 'customary land tenure and democratic rights'.[27] Lungisile Ntsebeza sums up the process: 'The Department of Land Affairs intended to subject traditional authorities to a system that would make them more representative and account-able to their communities. However ... establishing democratic and accountable structures while recognising an undemocratic and unaccountable institution of traditional leadership, especially in the form that has been inherited from the apart-heid past, is a fundamental contradiction.'[28] So the problem was not that traditional power was strengthened by the new state, but that the government's attempts to democratise that power have been half-hearted: 'After fifteen years of debate, law making and legal action, post-apartheid South Africa is no nearer to addressing the key issue of the uncertain legal status of the land rights of millions of people living under communal tenure, mostly in the former reserves.'[29] The government did not set out to bolster the power of traditional authorities. But nor would it take decisive steps to democratise them.

If policy really had entrenched traditional leadership, there would have been no need for the ANC faction led by then president Jacob Zuma to seek, from 2008, to strengthen the power of chiefs at the expense of their subjects. In some areas, trad-itional authorities' lack of formal power did not prevent them from delivering the votes of their 'subjects' to political parties. The ANC's initial failure to achieve an electoral majority in KwaZulu-Natal was partly a consequence of the influence of the Inkatha Freedom Party (IFP) on traditional leaders and, through them, their subjects. Before the 2009 general election, Zuma, who is steeped in the politics of the province's 'traditional' areas, persuaded many chiefs to cross to the ANC – this won the party the province since traditional leaders there enjoyed enough power over their subjects to influence their votes. A Bill boosting the power of traditional authorities was introduced in 2008, presumably in an attempt to pre-sent the ANC, not the IFP, as the guardian of chiefly interests – and to create an incentive for similar alliances with traditional leaders elsewhere. Later, political developments made strengthening the power of chiefs a priority for Zuma and his allies. In 2014, when the ANC largely lost the votes of the urban black middle class, its factions' reaction depended on their place in the political economy. The urban insiders in Gauteng sought to regain middle-class support, while a patronage faction based in the rural provinces, assuming that urban middle-class voters were lost to the ANC, sought to compensate by ensuring a block rural vote. Building on the KwaZulu-Natal experience, they hoped to do this by strengthening traditional authority in the expectation that chiefs in other areas would be as willing and able to persuade their subjects to vote for the ANC as those in KwaZulu-Natal.[30]

Their first vehicle was the 2008 Traditional Courts Bill. It responded to demands by chiefs that these courts, instruments of their authority, be given enhanced powers and that 'provisions for people to opt in or out of the system' be removed. These demands 'exactly mirrored apartheid-era legislation and the official customary law defined under colonialism' which traditional leadership now wanted 'formalised and protected in law'. When the Bill was tabled, 'by its own admission, the Department of Justice consulted only traditional leaders and a few stakeholders'.[31] It did as the chiefs asked: it strengthened the powers of traditional courts and forced everyone living in an area controlled by a chief to submit themselves to traditional law. During Zuma's term as president, passage of this law was frustrated repeatedly by activist campaigns and the opposition of urban ANC politicians.

After the 2014 election, the Zuma faction's attempt to strengthen traditional authority turned to the role of chiefs in land restitution. The then president encouraged chiefs to engage actively in the restitution process, which is meant to restore land to people deprived of it by apartheid. The more chiefs did this, it was assumed, the more they would be able to control land and those who live on it. A 'last-minute' addition to a Traditional and Khoi-San Leadership Bill, which Parliament passed in 2016, gave traditional councils 'unfettered power to transact on community land without consulting the people living on [it]'.[32] In 2016, Zuma exhorted chiefs to take the lead in land restitution.[33] An amendment to the Restitution of Land Rights Act, passed in 2014, gave them a vehicle: 'We have seen traditional leaders launching restitution claims to vast swathes of "historical tribal land" in response to the recent enactment of the [Act], and President Zuma's encouragement to do so.'[34]

The strategy was, predictably, justified as an anti-colonial campaign to return land to indigenous people. But it triggered a rural conflict in which an alliance between traditional leaders, provincial governments and companies seeks to wrest land from farmers organised into communal property associations, usually to sell it to private developers. The Constitutional Court has come to the aid of the communal farmers,[35] but the battle continues. Since the urban bias Mamdani criticised is very much alive in post-1994 South Africa, these dynamics have been largely ignored by public discussion of 'state capture'. But a process in which the regional state is used as a vehicle by traditional authorities and private companies to acquire resources at the expense of the public is no less an example of 'state capture' than its urban equivalent. The impact of this 'rural state capture' on the lives of those it affects is every bit as serious as the damage wrought by the urban version.

From the 2014 election to Ramaphosa's election as ANC president in late 2017, it was Zuma's faction of the ANC which sought to ensure that traditional leaders enjoyed the power to control their subjects, ensuring that they did not become citizens. Since the opposing faction was defined by its dependence on the market, there seemed to be no reason why it should support traditional power. So when Zuma was replaced by Ramaphosa, it seemed inevitable that laws imposing the power of traditional authorities on their 'subjects' would be dropped. But the Ramaphosa-led ANC has done what Zuma and his faction could not: it has secured the passage of the Traditional Courts Bill, complete with the clauses forcing citizens (subjects?) in traditional areas to use these courts.[36] This was not as surprising as it seems since Ramaphosa had, since his election as ANC president, assiduously courted traditional leaders.[37] His response continued, as we will soon see, a long-standing but often ignored ANC tradition. It may also explain why urban politicians who had opposed the Bill when Zuma was president now let it pass once the dictates of factional politics did not require them to oppose it. The result was that the ANC seemed, in 2019, to have followed Mamdani's conservative path, passing a law reducing millions of rural citizens to subjects.

These trends show why parallels are drawn between *Citizen and Subject* and contemporary South African reality. Steinberg, writing on earlier attempts to strengthen traditional authority's power, sees the parallel thus:

> The government is dressing an apartheid legacy as a claim to be erasing apartheid legacies ... The degradation of citizenship is happening under the aegis of land restitution. And so, opponents of the government's project are caught in a bind; the moment they voice their protest they are accused of being against people retrieving stolen land. They have to explain that they are in fact the ones in favour of restitution – the restitution of the rights of ordinary people.[38]

For him, the link to Mamdani's book is clear:

> Apartheid thinking had so deeply infected South African thinking, Mamdani worried, that we would not understand the implications of what was happening. Caught up in the quest to deracialise the cities, we would not understand the significance of the countryside. He was quite right. Urban politics in SA is suffused with anger ... the call for apartheid legacies to go is deafening. And yet this urban movement is quite oblivious to what is happening in the countryside.[39]

There is, arguably, one aspect of contemporary South African reality which does not fit *Citizen and Subject*'s prognosis: the tenacity of racial hierarchies in the economy and society. In the other societies which Mamdani discusses, racial domination is not a post-independence problem, either because European colonisers never settled in the colonised country, or because those who did were neither numerous nor influential enough to influence the post-independence society. But, with this exception, South Africa after more than two decades of democracy seems to be bifurcated in the way Mamdani feared that it might be.

However, this does not mean Mamdani is right that this is a consequence of the persistence of the apartheid-era state form. The patterns he identifies are the product not of the form of the post-1994 state, but of continuities between apartheid society and current reality. It is the society, not the state, which shows strong continuities with the pre-1994 past.

## THE ALL-CONQUERING STATE? URBAN–RURAL CONFLICT IN LATE APARTHEID

To examine *Citizen and Subject*'s applicability to current realities, we must briefly analyse its understanding of apartheid.

Mamdani's complaint that urban resistance to the system failed to develop a strategy for democratising customary power is well founded. While in the 1950s rural dwellers in Pondoland did rebel against traditional leaders,[40] this did not prompt a sustained attempt by the ANC to organise rural people. Ambivalence to traditional leaders may be explained by the fact that during the fight against apartheid, the ANC judged these leaders not by whether their relationship with those subject to their authority was democratic, but by whether they were for or against the version of 'the struggle' favoured by the ANC. While many chiefs defended an apartheid status quo which was the source of their authority, some – in the Eastern Cape and Sekhukhuneland – sided with the anti-apartheid resistance. If they did, the ANC asked no questions about how they ruled.[41] During the transition period and after, this ensured that chiefs were welcomed into the ranks of the ANC if they expressed loyalty to it. Despite the role of the Bantustans in shoring up apartheid, again the fault line was where traditional power stood on the leadership role of the ANC. This may also partly explain why migrant workers who opposed the urban 'struggle' (not only those from KwaZulu-Natal but also those who travelled to the Western Cape from the Eastern Cape) were seen as despised pre-modern obstacles. The divide between town and countryside was evident in the strategies of anti-apartheid resistance.

But was this divide created or sustained by 'decentralised despots'? The migrant labour system was largely responsible for the urban–rural divide and the tensions it produced. Migrant labour is not necessarily a feature of societies in which chiefs rule in the countryside: many countries had chiefly power but no system of labour migrancy. Nor did migrancy in South Africa need traditional authority. It was at times helped by it, as in the 1950s, when chiefs were expected to force women to carry passes (and were replaced by 'chiefs' who would do this if their predecessors refused).[42] Some used force to recruit labour for the mines and factories. But in the main it was enforced directly by the apartheid state's agencies and could have survived even if there were no chiefs. In 1973, when migrants formed the core of the Durban strikes, 'decentralised despotism' was on their side: a representative of the KwaZulu Bantustan, Barney Dladla, provided invaluable support to the strikers.[43]

Since migrant labour is not a necessary product of the colonial state, and traditional authority was not essential to it in South Africa, we need to look beyond the nature of the state for explanations. This is particularly so because in Mamdani's discussion of the role of migrant labour, he seems to want to have his cake and eat it too. How can the state defuse urban protest both by restricting black access to cities and by 'swamping' them? The most credible accounts of migrancy see it as a product of what Mamdani calls the 'mode of exploitation', not 'the mode of rule', as the consequence of the way in which white colonisers extracted cheap labour from black people rather than a strategy to quell political resistance.[44]

*Citizen and Subject* exaggerates the power of the state. Evidence does not support the view that the end of influx control was a new state strategy designed to prevent urban revolt. The system was abolished because the state felt it was left with no option by the resistance of black people who refused to comply, either as an organised act of defiance or because economic necessity made it impossible for people to obey the law.[45] Asked why the state did not crush the resistance to influx control by force, an apartheid government official responded, with some anguish, that it had spent years trying. Its efforts included using floodlights to demolish shacks by night as well as day, 'but they kept coming back like black ants'.[46] The system collapsed, not because the state was powerful enough to end it, but because it was powerless, in the face of social reality, to maintain it. This attempt to keep apart what social reality brought together failed because social and economic reality proved stronger than the state. This is not an isolated example. Almost from its inception, apartheid's attempt to stem the tide of change was in retreat, forced repeatedly to change tack in the face of social pressures.[47] What *Citizen and Subject* sees as the consequence of the form of state is, rather, a product of the nature of society.

A similar point applies to Mamdani's perceptive warning that rebellion against control over the movement of black people tended to descend into authoritarianism. He notes that many shack settlements established by people defying influx control 'began with an emphasis on participation and ended up with a shacklord',[48] a despot who lorded it over residents and used force to repel rivals. The most notorious example was the fate of the action which began the end of influx control, the movement of residents of men's migrant hostels into shacks in the Crossroads camp in the Western Cape. This protest movement descended into a war between vigilantes controlled by 'shacklords' and urban activists fighting apartheid.[49]

*Citizen and Subject* explains this as evidence of the influence of the rural state form in the cities. Shack leaders, in this view, become shacklords because the despotism of the rural authorities of the areas from whence they come shaped the way they rule the shack settlement. But while the migrants who opposed urban protesters in Soweto were linked to a rural state structure – the KwaZulu Bantustan – the Crossroads vigilantes' despotism stemmed from urban reality, one which is not peculiarly South African. Authoritarian power structures in areas which have been occupied by land invasions are common across the global South and are not necessarily linked to traditional authority. It seems more appropriate to see them as a symptom of the constraints which face democratic organisation where residents depend for their continued residence not on a guaranteed right but on the power of a local leader. Given the origins of Crossroads, it is more appropriate to see authoritarianism as a symptom of the breakdown of state control than as its product.

*Citizen and Subject* teaches us much about the clash between urban organisation on the one hand, and migrant labourers and people in informal housing on the other. This was an important contribution because, after 1994, the triumphalism of a successful fight against apartheid often obscured these realities behind romantic visions of a united people confronting oppression. But it does not show that the distinction between those who are permanently in the cities and those on their peripheries is the product of a form of state, rather than of patterns in society. The same can be said of the post-apartheid path dependence discussed here.

## VICTIM OR VILLAIN? THE STATE AND ECONOMY AFTER APARTHEID

The separation of South African society into 'insiders' and 'outsiders', discussed in the Introduction, is not a neat urban–rural division.

The divide between suburbs and townships is much more significant than that between town and country. Within the urban economy, the key divide is between core and periphery. As Edward Webster has shown, while migrancy is a reality for some outsiders,[50] who are often excluded because the physical spaces in which they live are far from economic activity,[51] the divide is manifest in cities. Township and shack-settlement residents are, we have seen, often subject to arbitrary power much like that which Mamdani discusses. But this is not a product of importing rural authority into the city. Patterns of politics in towns which were once part of the Bantustans and governed by decentralised despots are much the same as those in urban townships.[52] The division is less between urban and rural than between inclusion in and exclusion from mainstream economic and social institutions.

Urban insiders and outsiders are not products of different forms of state. In the cities, black people were, under apartheid, ostensibly governed by 'black local authorities' which were intended as instruments of indirect rule.[53] But they were never this in practice. The central government, in keeping with *Citizen and Subject*'s hypothesis, relied on direct rule in the cities, and so was unwilling to extend to these authorities the powers which would have allowed them to play their intended role. They were firmly controlled by Administration Boards which were extensions of the central state and were labelled toothless 'toy telephones', not instruments of effective control. They were never a distinctive state form, since it was always clear that the white government controlled the townships. The divide between township and suburb is not between different forms of state but between contrasting social realities within a common form of state. As in urban townships, the politics of exclusion and inclusion in former Bantustan towns has far more to do with relationships to local power structures, usually associated with the ANC and its allies, than with traditional authority structures.[54] Whether we see inclusion and exclusion as economic, political or cultural – or all three – they are products of patterns in society, not of differing forms of state.

Nor is the divide between citizen and subject as clear-cut as Mamdani assumes. A critique of *Citizen and Subject* by Steven Robins argues: 'In its quest for symmetry and conceptual clarity, [it] sacrifices the more ambiguous and "messy" forms of everyday life … Most people in South Africa act as both citizens and subjects, and they strategically and situationally engage with "rights talk" and the political discourses of liberal democracy.'[55] The citizen living under a traditional authority retains rights derived from the constitution which they may be able to use to exercise citizenship – as communal farmers did when they used courts to challenge the chiefs and the North West government. The resident of an urban township or shack settlement living under elected local government may, as we have seen, contend with local power structures which treat them as subjects, not citizens. Rural dwellers may be subjected to chiefly power, but they can use their vote to express their resistance. People act as citizens when they deprive the governing party of votes in Nkandla or Marikana; they become subjects when they hope to be heard by the policy debate but are ignored. The complex nature of citizenship and subjection in contemporary South Africa shows convergences we would not find if they were products of the bifurcated state.

The bifurcation Mamdani saw does live on in contemporary South Africa. But the form of state is not its cause. He is right that the 'native question' has greater explanatory power than the 'labour question': race is still the society's prime fault line. But since 1994, the 'native question' is not a product of a form of state. It stems from the complex ways in which racial power survives in a society whose law has seemingly abolished it, and in the distinctly racial flavour of social and economic exclusion. The racial hierarchies endure because social power is stronger than that of the state, or because those who control government are unwilling to challenge deep-rooted patterns, not because the state continues to impose them on society. Again, it is the form of society and the state's limited capacity to change it which is decisive.

The attempt to impose traditional authorities on rural areas may seem at first glance to refute this, but it actually strengthens the argument. There would be no need to give chiefs powers which make them despots if they already enjoyed this status. It is precisely because apartheid-style chiefly control over rural areas has eroded that laws are needed to revive it. Before apartheid ended, the links between rural residents and the urban economy frustrated an attempt by Mangosuthu Buthelezi, then head of KwaZulu, to maintain the apartheid form of state by seceding.[56] Migrant workers, many of them supporters of Buthelezi's IFP, feared this would cut them off from work opportunities outside the province. Even then, economic need and social reality proved stronger than 'decentralised despotism'.

Current trends also question the assumption that chiefs are strong enough to shape the voting patterns of their 'subjects'. KwaZulu-Natal traditional authorities could do this, but they were an exception rather than the rule. One possible explanation is the Ingonyama Trust, established in 1994 before the democratic constitution began operating, allegedly to persuade the KwaZulu ruling elite and its political vehicle the IFP to participate in the first universal franchise election.[57] It gave the Zulu monarch powers over land not enjoyed by traditional authorities in other provinces. Whatever the reason, courting chiefs elsewhere had precisely the opposite effect: in the August 2016 local elections, the ANC lost between 9 and 16 percentage points in rural provinces where chiefs hold sway, a bigger drop than in the cities. This phenomenon is not necessarily new:

> The 1994 election results are probably the best indicator of the danger of relying on traditional leaders to deliver the rural vote. In that year, the ANC won more than 90% of the votes in Limpopo and more than 80% in the North West, Mpumalanga and the Eastern Cape – all rural provinces that had been intensely involved in antiBantustan and antichief rebellions during the build-up to the elections.[58]

Results like these suggest that voters supported the ANC in the hope of weakening chiefly power. The attempt to use laws to build a rural power base which would counteract the political influence of the cities does not seek to preserve the dominance of chiefs over rural residents. It hopes to create it precisely because chiefs are not nearly strong enough to impose political choices on their 'subjects'.

If chiefly control over rural citizens is exaggerated, then so too is the power which control of the state is said to bestow on the ANC. The post-1994 reality is arguably not the strength of the state and its influence over society, but that pre-1994 social patterns survive despite a change in the nature of the state. While the ANC's pre-1994 programme called for a 'national democratic revolution' in which control by a racial minority would be defeated, racial domination in the economy remains – a product not of the form of state, but of the governing party's unwillingness or inability to change social reality. In the townships and shack settlements, ANC dominance reflects not the continuation of a form of state, but power relationships which emerged during the fight against apartheid. It is also a product of continued economic exclusion. Those who now govern are open to the charge that they have not tried to change these patterns, but they – and the state – did not create them.

A theoretical framework for understanding the limits of the state's role is proposed by Bob Jessop,[59] who, from a Marxist perspective, argues against 'crude instrumentalism' – the idea that the state simply does the bidding of the ruling class. The importance of his argument lies in his view that states are not independent actors: they are rooted in social conflicts and processes. In this sense, they reflect reality rather than shape it. The Marxist contention that the state served only the interests of the holders of economic power was not, in Jessop's view, necessarily accurate: the state could do this only if it could direct the society's agenda.[60] The state can place its imprint on society, but this is not assured. To accomplish this, the state would need to lead efforts to change social realities within the limits of the possible. The state cannot simply impose itself on society, but it can influence it and perhaps even reshape it. It is always forced to negotiate a relationship with contesting interests in society and so can never shape it as it pleases. Whether the post-1994 state has attempted to reshape social reality is a question we will discuss later (Chapter 7). If it has tried, it has not succeeded. No attempt has been made to build rural democracy. But this is largely because no great progress has been made in building a new social reality.

In post-1994 South Africa, the form of state has changed significantly. The formal rural power structures have been integrated into the constitutional order, and the current state form provides opportunities for citizens to exercise power which did not exist before 1994.[61] Courts, which are crucial parts of the state, have intervened to overturn attempts to impose feudal power on people in the country-side – and they may do so again to overturn the law imposing traditional courts on people in traditional areas. But the state's role in changing social reality has been limited, and pre-1994 power relationships remain stubbornly resistant to the change in state form. It is South African society which remains bifurcated in ways which sometimes mirror realities before apartheid ended. It is this social and economic reality which the altered, and no longer bifurcated, form of state has been unable or unwilling to change.[62]

# 5

# A Cycle of Crisis and Compromise: Path Dependence, Race and Policy Conflicts

nclusion and exclusion are core features of South African path dependence. But inclusion in post-1994 South Africa is more complicated than it might seem because there are important distinctions within the included. The conflict these distinctions ensure is a significant feature of post-1994 politics – indeed, it may well be its most important feature. Since the excluded remain unheard, politics is always insider politics, and conflicts which seem to be waged between those who have been absorbed into the economy and those who have not are really battles between insider groups.

There are important economic distinctions within the insider group. Anyone who earns a weekly or monthly wage or salary is an insider because many who aspire to a regular income from employment are denied it. But the factory worker or street sweeper does not enjoy the power and privileges of the chief executive. This has consequences. For example, one reason for the declining effectiveness of trade unions is the tendency for union leadership to become a route into the middle class,[1] often at the expense of members who are wage-earning insiders but do not enjoy the leaders' opportunities. This does not reduce worker militancy, since many remain on the wrong end of the economic divisions within the insider group. The economic divisions are, therefore, a key reason for strikes.[2]

It has also been argued that demonstrations in townships and shack settlements are a 'rebellion of the poor'.[3] Whether this is so is the subject of a complicated debate, but one that does not belong in a discussion of insider politics, because the 'rebellion' participants are almost all outsiders. The divisions between insiders trigger conflicts over policy: even the Congress of South African Trade Unions (Cosatu), an ally of the ANC regarded as far less committed to economic change than its rival the South African Federation of Trade Unions (Saftu), is likely to take a very different view on policy from that of business.[4] Equally importantly, insider divisions ensure conflict within unions. 'Social distance' between leaders and members, a reality because leaders enjoy a lifestyle which is barred to members, causes tension within unions: 'Workers are losing faith in some trade unions. They regard some union leaders as unreliable, unaccountable, selfish and greedy individuals who seek to use them.'[5] One of the starkest symptoms of path dependence is its effect on the union movement, which has lost its ability to mobilise protest (rallies or demonstrations are sometimes called but few people participate) and is also often unable to strategically guide its members, largely as a consequence of the realities mentioned here. But, as real as these divisions are, economic relationships within the insider group are marked by cooperation and compromise as well as conflict and even, at times, by alliances: the coalition which resisted former minister Nene's dismissal illustrates this. It could be argued that, given inequality within the insider group, the level of internal conflict is surprisingly mild.

This may well be because the most important divide between insiders – in its effect on politics and policy debates – is race. The racial divisions within the insider group are far deeper than we might predict given the growth of a black professional and business class. In regular and social media, issues which we might expect to be deeply divisive in a country with inequality levels said to be the highest in the world[6] – radical economic change, for example – do not elicit anything like the polarisation prompted by the mention of race. While supporters of the racial status quo claim that only small, politicised groups are unhappy because survey evidence shows that race relations are fairly harmonious,[7] these claims misunderstand the nature of racial difference and the tensions it produces.

Contrary to some fears on the right, South Africa is not a society in which widespread racial violence is likely. An implicit recognition of interdependence means there is little support on either side of the divide for eliminating the other group. But, as in other societies with a history of state-imposed racial domination, while people are resigned to coexisting, they have not discarded either the sense of superiority among the dominant group or the sense of injustice among the dominated.[8] The surveys report that when asked to choose policy priorities, very few respondents (2 per cent) identify getting the government to fight racism. But as we will see, policy demands are really about racism, and the concerns which interviewees express may be coded demands for racial change (even if the survey method is valid, which is contested). Observed reality suggests that, despite contrary claims, racial divisions ensure that black middle-class South Africans are the angriest group in the society. This greatly influences politics.

## THE ROOTS OF DIVISION

Available data show that although black participation in the professions and business is growing, the pace of change is slow and whites continue to dominate the economy's upper echelons.

Chapter 1 discussed the very limited progress towards racial equality at the end of the Mbeki presidency. Black economic conditions did not deteriorate, but the racial hierarchy remained. Nor have the ensuing ten years altered this reality, despite the claims of Zuma and his supporters that his administration was responsible for 'radical economic transformation', which, in South Africa's insider politics, means an attempt to reduce racial inequities in business.[9] Consistent with the understanding of path dependence proposed here, shifts in racial patterns in the professions and business show that there has been significant change in a quarter-century, while the underlying pattern – white dominance – remains intact.

But in the view of many black professionals, the data are symptoms of a much deeper problem. Despite the end of formal race discrimination, racial equality of opportunity remains elusive. Middle-class black people, a study found, 'are angry at their exclusion from mainstream economic activity, where "boardroom racism" and a racial ceiling are clearly at work'.[10] In this view, which the data and other evidence tend to support, the impact of race on middle-class black people is a textbook case of path dependence – in particular of the features identified by Scott Page (discussed in Chapter 2). The abolition of racial laws and the adoption by the post-1994 government of policies which favour black businesses and professionals might be expected to prompt a rapid shift away from apartheid-era patterns. But behaviour patterns, beliefs and values, and social connections combine to ensure that despite the growing number of black participants in the upper reaches of the economy, the essential feature of minority dominance is maintained.

Cognitive patterns may be a prime reason. If a ruling group uses force to ensure that executive positions and professional qualifications are monopolised by people of a particular race, people assume that only the dominant group can play these roles – hence Richard Turner's observation that white liberals, opposed in theory to racial hierarchy, assumed white superiority.[11] Because, for more than a century, only whites in South Africa managed large companies and performed skilled work, the natural order seems to be one in which these roles are their preserve – it would take a very conscious rejection of racial bias for whites (and some blacks too) to be operated on by a black surgeon. Decisions on who to hire, who to promote to decision-making posts or who to choose as a partner in a project are influenced by prejudices which may be so deep-rooted that the person taking the decision would be horrified to learn that he or she harbours them. One oft-mentioned effect in white-owned companies is that black people are invited onto boards or promoted to executive roles primarily in the hope that their connections will enable them to represent the company's interests to (black) trade unionists and politicians – this shaped Cyril Ramaphosa's response at Marikana. Inevitably, this has limited racial change in business[12] and has demoralised and angered black professionals and managers.

These assumptions entrench ways of ordering professional and business life which suit the needs and experiences of those who ran organisations before the change of political system, but may be alien to those who were excluded from them. Two US scholars and activists cite expressions of organisational cultures which privilege whites: 'the belief that traditional standards and values are objective and unbiased; the emphasis on a sense of urgency and quantity over quality, which can be summarized by the phrase "the ends justify the means"; perfectionism that leaves little room for mistakes; and binary thinking'.[13] Whatever the merits of these examples, the key point is that people who are used to controlling organisations will associate the way they operate with competence even if doing things in other ways would be just as effective. The required habits are not those of the Muslim Sudanese business people described in an important work by Abdou Maliqalim Simone.[14] Despite their habits – or, no doubt, because of them – they built a profitable network of international businesses. The way organisations are run and the way they deal with each other could ensure that business and the professions are dominated not by those who are most competent, but by those who are best at doing things in the approved way. Again, this places obstacles in the way of black participants who were excluded by racial laws when these ways of doing things developed. And again, this creates unsurprising anger.

Connections can also be a powerful way of keeping hierarchies alive. Social networks are as important as ability in deciding whether people succeed in professions and management, which is partly why Simone's business people succeeded. If the networks which open opportunities are not accessible to black participants, while opportunity is seemingly equal, those who have the connections keep the upper hand. The point is illustrated by a report in a British newspaper showing how students from working-class backgrounds who are admitted to that country's elite universities are severely disadvantaged by the social networks to which they have no access.[15] A key source of recruitment into prestige jobs is holiday internships in large companies or elite professional practices. They enable the student to demonstrate ability and to make contacts which may ensure a job offer on graduation. Working-class (and black) students lack the social connections to secure the internships; most don't even know they exist and are essential to recruitment. And so they are frozen out of the job market even if they perform better academically than their connected fellow students. These networks operate in South Africa and, for obvious reasons, open doors to white students which may be shut to their black colleagues. Within the workplace too, social connections matter – black professionals in large organisations were once at a disadvantage because they did not play golf. Now many do, but they may still lack the connections required to advance as far and fast as their white counterparts. Again, this thwarts ambitions.

Middle-class people are far better able to make themselves heard than people living in poverty, and so it is their concerns which shape political debate. The frustrations discussed here explain why they enter debate on the side of those challenging current policies and practices, ensuring that disputes which seem to express tensions between insiders and outsiders are really battles within the insider group prompted by racial path dependence. Key policy disputes emerge when black middle-class citizens identify with a demand which appears to advocate radical change, not because their immediate economic interests are served by it, but because they see it as a means to express frustration with the survival of pre-1994 racial pecking orders.[16]

## THE DYNAMIC OF CONTENTION

How might people with access to the public debate and the skills and qualifications needed to participate in it respond to a sense that, although they enjoy qualifications and opportunities denied their parents and grandparents, they encounter the same racial attitudes and their concerns are not taken seriously by public or private power holders?

They might conclude that they are unlikely to be taken seriously unless power holders are jolted from their complacency by a sense of crisis – the realisation that present arrangements are costly and that new ways are needed. They may also conclude that mobilising in support of their immediate concerns is not advisable, both because their relative affluence may brand them as spoiled and because they believe their experiences are a symptom of a deeper problem: the survival of racial patterns in a democracy which is meant to have ended them.

No one would need to devise a conscious strategy which followed this line of reasoning. If it broadly describes reality for many middle-class black people, it would emerge organically out of people's understanding of their situation. In a society in which race remains the core divide, divisions within groups (between black people able to gain access to the benefits of the market and those who cannot, for example) are usually less important than differences between them. And so, middle-class black people enthusiastically support demands which appear to assist outsiders because they want change, not necessarily because the issue is important to them. The assumption that nothing will change unless there is a crisis is accurate: we have seen that a defining feature of path dependence is that there is a distinct limit to the change in elite thinking which is possible in a path-dependent society. Where set ways of thinking and acting have become entrenched, change is likely only if events induce a sense of crisis.

## Fees, the Land and ... ?

Two highly publicised policy disputes follow the pattern described here. The first is the Fees Must Fall movement, in which university students demanded an end to tuition fees.

A first wave of protests, in 2015, demanded that an increase in fees be frozen. The demand was widely supported by students and was conceded,[17] but demonstrations began again in 2016. The new protests elicited another concession: the government exempted students whose household income was less than R600 000 a year (a high ceiling which included most students) from fee increases.[18] This concession substantially reduced the numbers who supported the protests since the original demands of most had been met. But some students continued the protests, which became a campaign for free tertiary education for all. This call, supported by a range of voices in the public debate, was presented by both the protesters and their supporters as a push for radical redistribution. It was described as an attempt to realise a demand of the Freedom Charter, adopted by the ANC and its allies in the mid-1950s, that 'the doors of learning and culture shall be open to all'.[19] The demand for free higher education was repeatedly portrayed as a blow to privilege.[20] But despite this egalitarian rhetoric, the end of fees would impose burdens on working and poor people.

To be sure, paying any fees at all is a burden to many students. Financial need among black students in particular is acute – research has revealed that almost a third of students do not receive adequate nutrition.[21] But the fact that the protests which followed the concession were supported by far fewer students suggests that

the concession did persuade many that their financial needs had been met suf-
ficiently to remove the need for further protests. Nor is there evidence that the
fees demand attracted much working-class and poor support. Worker support was
enthusiastically bestowed on one student demand: an end to 'outsourcing', a practice
in which university services such as cleaning and security are performed by profit-
making contractors. Directly employed workers enjoy better pay and conditions
and more job security.[22] But this did not mean support for free tuition. Exempting
the affluent from fees offered nothing to low-income workers and to people living
in poverty. As we shall soon see, when then president Zuma partially implemented
the demand, the poor paid the price.

Given this, it would seem logical to dismiss the Fees Must Fall protests as a cynical attempt by the sons and daughters of executives to extract free education at the
expense of the poor. The more affluent the protesters (and many were affluent),
the more likely in this view was it that they were using radical rhetoric for financial gain. But the vehemence of the protesters, some of whose parents could clearly
afford to pay far more for their tuition, suggests the contrary: that the protests were
fuelled by a strongly felt sense of injustice. To understand what triggered it, it is
important to recall that the protests of 2015 began early in the year at the University
of Cape Town (UCT), where protesters mobilised not against fees but behind the
demand that 'Rhodes Must Fall'. This referred to a campus statue of Cecil John
Rhodes, the removal of which the students demanded. The protests were about
far more than a statue – the protesters were rebelling against the university's 'colonial nature'.[23] Formerly white universities such as UCT, the protesters argued, were
still underpinned by assumptions of white and European supremacy in their hiring
practices, teaching and organisational culture.

The protests reacted to a stark form of path dependence in higher education. It
was analysed and anticipated by, among others, the social theorist Harold Wolpe,
who devoted the late 1980s and early 1990s to researching and writing on education,
higher education in particular. Racial change at universities was new when Wolpe
criticised the approach to black students of elite universities which had been open
to whites only. He and his colleagues were responding to claims – particularly those
of another key figure in South African academic life, Charles van Onselen – that,
unlike historically black institutions, white English-speaking universities had grown
'organically' to serve the core economy and were therefore attuned to its needs. Van
Onselen argued they should be developed as centres of excellence because only they
could produce the human resources and research the economy and society needed.
A majority government should not demand changes in the way these universities
operated because this would compromise their contribution to the society.[24]

Arguing that formerly white universities were as much products of apartheid as the black universities established by the system, Wolpe and his colleague Zenariah Barends added that if universities were allowed to assume that they were centres of excellence, they would have no incentive to make the changes needed to cater for the needs of students disadvantaged by apartheid. They cited an observation by the educationist James Moulder that historically white universities offered black students academic support programmes, designed to help them fit into the university, because they assumed that '[the students] have to change so that it [the university] does not have to change'.[25] But the universities needed to change so that they could 'teach the majority of students who come from a specific historical and socio-economic milieu'.[26] Drawing on evidence from South Africa and Britain, Wolpe and Barends suggested that some standards imposed by these universities imposed cultural prejudices on black students.

Wolpe and Barends were warning of a path dependence which would define universities for the first two decades of democracy. It was this, not fees, which sustained the second round of protests. Although the racial composition of the formerly white universities changed dramatically, little else changed. This prompted an inevitable sense of alienation among black students who felt that they were expected to adapt to an institution designed by and for others.[27] The 'Rhodes Must Fall' protests were an explicit response, and the later 'Fees Must Fall' demonstrations were a variation on the same theme. While the protests did influence the fee structure of higher education, they also triggered discussions in universities on 'decolonising' higher education, a term which expresses a sense that universities are still instruments of the minority.[28] The fact that debate on decolonisation outlived the stress on fees suggests that it was the real message of the demonstrations.

The student protests were less an attempt to change the finances of tertiary education than a challenge to racial path dependence in the universities. Until the protests, black students felt that they were still seen as intruders. The demand for an end to fees provided a vehicle to challenge this.

## The Land: Soil or Symbol?

A similar pattern is at work in the second example: the campaign for land expropriation without compensation.

At its national conference in December 2017, the African National Congress passed a resolution declaring that the expropriation of land without compensation 'should be among the key mechanisms available to government to give effect to land reform and redistribution'. It should be implemented in a way which does 'not undermine future investment in the economy, or damage agricultural production and food security' and 'must not cause harm to other sectors of the economy'.[29]

ANC resolutions, like those of many other governing parties, are often not implemented for years, if at all. Governing parties represent only some of the people, while governments must govern everyone, and so there is often a gap between what delegates at a party conference would like the government to do and what it actually does, once the interests of all key parties are considered. But this resolution seemed to acquire immediate momentum. Ramaphosa, in his address closing the conference after his election as ANC president, singled out the land issue for special mention, committing the ANC to implementing the resolution amid loud applause.[30] The issue seemed to rapidly become a core concern for him and his administration once he became state president in early 2018.

'Seemed to' because the politics which produced the resolution and the government response to it were complicated. Ramaphosa and his allies did not initiate the expropriation demand: given their interest in the market economy, they were not enthusiastic about measures which could damage investor confidence. But path dependence made it very difficult for them to oppose it. Apartheid had deprived most people of access to land, and while the post-1994 government had committed itself to land reform, its efforts fell far short of its goals.[31] To insist that nothing need be done about black landlessness, one of apartheid's central features, was untenable for politicians who were meant to speak for most citizens. So Ramaphosa and his faction did not dismiss the resolution – they insisted that it be implemented. But they sought to manage the process to ensure that it did not threaten property rights and frighten off investors. The clause which stipulated that change not harm the economy enabled them to do this. After the conference, this balancing act shaped government policy. On the one hand, the government insisted it was committed to expropriation without compensation, and would change the constitution if this was needed. On the other, it sought to ensure a compromise which would enable it to insist that it had implemented the resolution but also reassured property owners and investors.

While landlessness is a significant problem, the government was not responding to the demands of the landless. The push for change came from people in the middle class. Two pressures placed the expropriation demand on the agenda. The most immediate came from within the ANC. While many delegates at the 2017 conference who pressed for the resolution no doubt supported the demand on principle, Zuma's faction saw it as a way to pressure Ramaphosa and his allies. If they did not agree to implement it, they could be accused of ignoring the wishes of their own party in their eagerness to obey 'white monopoly capital'. The second influence – although its role is often overestimated – was the Economic Freedom Fighters (EFF), the country's third-largest party, which made expropriation without compensation one of its key slogans. While the EFF portrays itself, and is usually portrayed, as a party of the poor and marginalised, its base is middle class: EFF supporters on average hold more formal qualifications and enjoy higher incomes than ANC voters.[32] It also became clear that there was widespread support for expropriation without compensation from middle-class black people. Landless people remained silent; both supporters and opponents of a change to the constitution were so sure they were doing what the landless wanted that they saw no reason to ask them.

It seems likely that many middle-class supporters of expropriation are home-owners and, therefore, landowners – and that few want a career in farming. So they were not inspired by a desire for land. They fervently support the demand for much the same reason that affluent students supported the demand for an end to fees: because support for it expressed frustration with the impact of racial path dependence on the black middle class. The land dispute is a particularly graphic illustration of this reality. In South African political history, demands for 'the return of the land to the people' did not express a preference for farming. When supporters of the Pan Africanist Congress repeat its slogan 'Izwe lethu', or 'The land is ours', they are talking not about agrarian concerns but about control of the country and its institutions.[33] The same can be said of other references to land during the fight against minority rule. It is therefore hardly surprising that demands for the return of the land to the majority would be seen as a demand for racial change, not an agricultural policy proposal. The land demand rebelled against the absorption of black people into business and the professions on terms which retained the hierarchies of the past. It was far more a response to the survival of racial bias than an expression of support for a policy.[34]

## CRISIS AND COMPROMISE

These two examples highlight some effects of path dependence on political and policy discussion.

The claim made earlier – that all politics in democratic South Africa is insider politics – seems strange. A feature of the country's politics is a left-wing tradition which began in 1915 with the formation by European émigrés of the International Socialist League[35] and was a core feature of the culture of resistance to apartheid. Demands for radical economic change are frequent. But the voice of the poor is never heard. And so the debates between left and right are waged within the insider group:

the only participants who are not middle class or affluent are trade union members whose access to a wage makes them (junior) insiders. Outsiders such as the landless are spectators to bitter ideological battles about them which never include them.

A pattern has emerged in how these battles are waged. It may well endure if the form of path dependence which prompted it remains a reality. The pattern is best described as a cycle of crisis and compromise. Black insiders know that the behaviours, attitudes and habits which continue to entrench pre-1994 patterns are deep-rooted. They therefore assume that neither the economic nor the political elites are likely to heed demands for change unless they are shocked into doing this. And so when a demand emerges which could precipitate a crisis, it is enthusiastically supported by black insiders. The demands inevitably trigger intense alarm among much of white opinion, accompanied by predictions of imminent economic doom, confirming that the demands have touched a raw nerve among power holders, forcing them to consider an issue they would prefer to ignore. This further entrenches support for the demand, and positions harden on both sides.[36] The crisis is created by history and circumstance, not by design.

The demands are a proxy for deeper concerns, which explains why they end in compromises that fall far short of the stated goals of the campaign. Zuma's concession to the Fees Must Fall movement did not come near the protesters' demands, but there was no subsequent pressure for fee-free education. The land demand may never prompt a change in the constitution, despite constant government commitments to an amendment. Some opponents will ask the courts to rule that expropriation removes a fundamental constitutional right and therefore will need a parliamentary majority of 75 per cent,[37] which it is unlikely to receive. But even if a way around this is found, a change is sure to protect property rights – it could strengthen them by making clear that expropriation without compensation is allowed only in very particular situations. The section of the constitution scheduled for change allows no compensation to be paid if the purpose is to 'redress the results of past racial discrimination'.[38] This phrase is vague enough to make property rights uncertain because they depend on interpretation of redress, which will inevitably differ between judges. Defining circumstances in which this would be allowed would limit the courts' discretion and make the right more secure.[39]

If the amendment is not passed, or if it secures property rights, an angry reaction is unlikely. Almost two years after expropriation without compensation emerged as a demand, the government was under no great pressure to change the constitution. Attention on both sides had shifted to National Health Insurance, which may become the new battleground,[40] particularly after Covid-19. This is neither surprising nor irrational, despite the vehemence of demands for expropriation without compensation. If the demand is voiced because it expresses other frustrations, there will be less interest in whether the government gives in to it. People who can afford fees and own land (or expect to) have no immediate stake in whether free education or land expropriation is actually achieved, and so they are unlikely to be particularly angry if it isn't – or is achieved only in very diluted form.

It should be apparent why the pattern triggered by racial path dependence is a cycle of 'crisis and compromise'. A crisis emerges because a demand is voiced which appears to power holders to require radical change. But since it is voiced by people who don't need the demand to be met, and there are no other voices calling for the change, it ends in a compromise which falls well short of the demand. But there is no challenge to the compromise, because the purpose of raising the issue was to address the path dependence which maintains racial hierarchies in business and the professions. Because this is never fully addressed, the cycle continues as new issues emerge which trigger the same pattern.

This cycle is not a sham: it has become a pattern because it speaks to realities experienced by South Africans. It has become entrenched not because anyone is dishonest or irrational, but because crisis and compromise are rational responses to the realities participants experience. But the cycle does not produce progress. Issues dominate the debate not because participants feel strongly about them, but because they symbolise other divisions, which are not discussed directly. The society is a double loser: it fixates on issues which are not the real concerns of campaigners and ignores what really worries them. The economy also loses. While the threatened action never comes, few people in the marketplace understand this, and the result is a decline in investor confidence which further weakens the economy. Measures which would restrict businesses are always likely to receive negative investor reaction, but the irony for South Africa is that dips in confidence occur not because a serious attempt to redress poverty and inequality is in prospect. Rather, the cycle stokes fears but rarely produces changes which contribute to greater fairness or equality. And because compromise over one issue is followed by crisis over another, the result is protracted negativity caused not by a shift in economic power, but by the anxieties triggered by the lack of change. This aspect of path dependence holds costs but few, if any, benefits.

## THE DYNAMICS OF INSIDER DEMOCRACY

Why are outsiders inevitably excluded from this cycle?

Insiders monopolise politics because economic exclusion makes organisation very difficult. It forces outsiders to concentrate on coping with poverty rather than voicing concerns. Resources are needed to organise, which outsiders lack. Insiders have cultural capital. They know how to express themselves in terms the mainstream debate will understand and they have the confidence to do this. So they can be heard in ways not available to outsiders. This may explain the fact that although cellular phone ownership is almost universal, and smartphone penetration, which enables owners to access social media, is now estimated at 80 per cent,[41] people who use social media to participate in public debate are almost all insiders. This may be partly because outsiders cannot afford data, but equally plausible is that they are far less likely to write in English, the only language of mainstream public debate.

More is required to participate in politics than resources and leisure, as important as both are. Another essential is the assumption that you – or people like you – are likely to be heard. In unequal societies, people at the bottom of the ladder tend to assume that power holders, public and private, simply don't listen to people like them and that, if they voice their opinions and concerns, they are likely to be punished, not heeded.[42] Even if they don't expect punishment, fear of being ridiculed or ignored may keep them silent.[43] Despite the differences between the insider groups, and the conflicts which these often trigger, insiders share something: they can monopolise political debate even when it seems to be a clash between insiders and outsiders.

Outsiders do participate in demonstrations, but demonstrators can influence events only if they can force power holders to respond to their demands. Because the demonstrators are not organised, their demands are not negotiated with power holders. In most cases, the reasons for their demonstrations are ignored or explained away as 'service delivery protests', which removes any need to establish exactly why people protest. So protest, often a means by which people excluded from public debate can force their way into the conversation, becomes, perversely, another form of exclusion as the voices of the demonstrators never reach the desks of power holders. Since the protests are often stigmatised as violent even when they are not, the response to them entrenches the insider–outside divide because the 'reasoned, democratic' debate of the insiders is implicitly contrasted with the 'senseless violence' of the outsiders.

Race, which is central to political conflict, is an insider concern. This is so not because racial bias is a manufactured problem or a middle-class fetish: it is real and all classes are its victims. But precisely because outsiders are excluded from the formal economy, race and racism are not their most urgent concerns. In a deeply divided society in which attitudes enforce segregation that law once commanded, the economy is the only place in which people are likely to meet – and compete – across racial divides. So it is those who are included in the formal economy who experience racial hierarchies directly.

Insider politics is, therefore, more often than not racial politics. But in insider demands, the language is often that of the left: it highlights social and economic inequality. Giving priority to racial divisions was once derided on the left. The early socialists who arrived from Europe believed race was invented by capitalism to divide workers.[44] But later socialists usually recognised that racial domination was the core South African reality. Since 1994, the idea that apartheid's defeat ended racial divides within social classes, and that black and white business people, and black and white workers, share a common class interest, has become not a left-wing but a mainstream view,[45] amplified by those who reject talk of race in a society in which all are in theory equal. Nevertheless, it became common to use left language even when race was at issue. Decades of using this language to battle racial domination has blurred its focus, and so it is not only worried conservatives who confuse insider conflict with the battle between insiders and outsiders. Presenting one as the other is also ingrained in left thinking.

## KNOWING LEFT FROM RIGHT?

These realities help to make sense of an apparent oddity in the contemporary debate: the tendency for demands which claim to champion the poor to advocate policies that favour the middle class and affluent. This is illustrated by two campaigns: the already mentioned demand for fee-free higher education and the battle against electronic tolling of Gauteng freeways.

In both cases, closer inspection of a demand embraced by the left reveals that it serves the interests of those who have, not those who lack. The reason is the centrality of race in politics, which ensures that insider concerns are understood, by those who express them as well as those who try to make sense of them, as demands made on behalf of outsiders.

### Whose Fees Must Fall?

At first glance, few demands seem as clear an expression of the outsiders' demand for inclusion as free tertiary education.

Education, campaigners argue, is not a commodity, but a public good to which all are entitled. A society which values education will not expect people to pay for it.[46] Many are excluded from higher education because they cannot pay, and many who are accepted by tertiary institutions may not realise their potential because they face crippling financial burdens – some students can afford only one meal a day. This may be one reason why advocates of free tertiary education claim that to oppose this is to ignore the promise of the Freedom Charter, to embrace the 'neo-liberal' economics of the wealthy and the continued exclusion from educational opportunity of those who cannot afford to buy it.

But in a society marked by deep inequalities,[47] if only tertiary education is open to all, inequities will remain in pre-primary, primary and secondary education. The first is the most neglected but possibly the most important, since educational potential is shaped in the preschool years.[48] Affluent parents usually equip their children for a school education. In the households of the poor, a lack of resources and a history of educational exclusion may condemn children to meagre support at best; and so inequality is maintained and deepened. If it is to be eroded, resources would need to be devoted to ensuring that poorer children receive, through publicly funded preschool education, what their homes cannot provide. But it is the children of the affluent who enjoy preschool education while the poor are excluded: 'Many parents are deterred from enrolling their children at ECD [early childhood development] facilities because of prohibitive costs.'[49] And so the children of those left behind in the previous generation are left behind in the next.

In schools, policy says no child is excluded because they cannot pay, but the system also reproduces inequality. Not only can the affluent buy private education (there is little private tertiary education), but within the state system, school governing bodies can raise and spend money; public schools in the suburbs can offer much better education than those in poor areas.[50] While in principle these schools cannot turn away learners who cannot pay, in reality entry for the poor is restricted.[51] So inequalities are strengthened by the education system long before learners end their schooling. But while the non-governmental organisation Equal Education has campaigned against inequality in schooling, no social coalition has emerged to join the campaign. This may partly explain why there are few voices pointing out that the more money is devoted to free higher education, the less will be available to tackle unequal access to schooling, ensuring that those who can get to university, even if they were raised in poverty, are already members of a relative elite.

Free tertiary education needs public funding, which, even before Covid-19, faced huge demands to address poverty and deprivation. The costs of fee-free higher education are illustrated by the consequences when Zuma, in the last days of his ANC presidency, ignored the recommendations of a commission he appointed and announced a partial concession to the demand. Although only first-year students whose household income was under R350 000 a year qualified for free tuition, this added R40 billion to the budget, R25 billion of which was paid for by reduced spending. The director general of the Treasury, Dondo Mogajane, said this required cuts to provincial and municipal infrastructure projects.[52] People living in poverty missed out on infrastructure improvements to pay for the cut in university fees. If tertiary education fees were eliminated, the poor would have to forgo even more to ensure that the children of corporate executives receive free tuition.

Free tertiary education would benefit many who can afford to pay far more for it. This redistributes upwards, rewarding the rich at the expense of the poor. In Brazil, free tertiary education has maintained inequality. Because the state can afford only a limited number of university places, free higher education has created intense competition for admission to the better universities. Because the (overwhelmingly white) upper-middle class can afford the best school education, they move to the front of the queue, the poor are excluded, and again inequality is passed from one generation to the next. This is why protesters in 2013 demanded an end to free tertiary education – and why the then Workers' Party government said it would change it.[53]

It seems puzzling that champions of equality would want the affluent to use a public resource without paying. Equity is served not when no one pays for tertiary tuition, but when no one is denied it because they cannot afford it. This is only possible if those who can afford it are forced to pay more so that money is available for those who cannot. Advocates of free tuition respond: 'Even if a small minority of parents have the resources, that can hardly be a major criterion for national planning or obviate the necessity for free public education.'[54] It is hard to imagine an argument which more clearly violates the principle of equity. Inequality is a problem precisely because very few benefit at the expense of everyone else. Campaigns around the world for a fairer economy charge that only the '1 per cent' benefits,[55] and that equity means that this segment must share its resources. Advocates of free higher education claim only 5 per cent of the population can afford the full cost.[56] But they do not say how much this more than two million people can afford to pay. So we have no idea how much money can be raised to improve access for people in poverty by raising fees for the wealthy.

Despite this, critics of free tertiary education are routinely dismissed as 'neo-liberal' defenders of privilege. This is surely possible only because the debate excludes most citizens – who would be forced to pay the costs. It is yet another insider debate in which outsiders are talked about to strengthen an argument but are otherwise ignored. This is all the more remarkable because insiders who approach the issue in this way believe they are campaigners for equality. Something about South African reality ensures that apparent demands for a fairer society are actually a plea for another benefit for the better off.

## E-tolls: The Burden of the Middle Class

Resistance to e-tolling is an even clearer example of a policy debate in which the views of insiders are presented as those of everyone, and demands which would benefit people who are not poor are presented as attacks on poverty.

The campaign focuses on a national government decision to seek to recover the costs of improving freeways in Gauteng, the country's richest province, by levying electronic tolls on vehicle owners; buses and the minibus taxis used by people living in poverty are exempt.[57] Some critics of the toll use the arguments we would expect from a middle-class lobby campaigning against a government tax: that the money will fund corruption and fuel inflation. But others insist they are fighting for the poor and excluded by opposing the 'privatisation of a public good' which would serve the affluent and place new burdens on the poor.[58] Once again, anyone who opposes this view is branded as an enemy of the poor. So deep-rooted is this belief that the battle against e-tolling is an act of solidarity with the poor that a group of clergy, several of whom are identified with campaigns for social justice, announced plans to engage in civil disobedience to protest against the tolls.[59]

But the demand for an end to the tolls does not benefit the poor. It helps the middle class and the affluent. It is no accident that anti-e-toll campaigners found themselves on the same side as the retail motor industry and a campaign led by a (then) car-hire company executive.[60] E-tolls do not privatise freeways; the roads are publicly owned. The burden is borne not by the poor but by those who can afford to own or rent a vehicle. Some opponents of the toll claimed it would hurt the poor because companies would pass on the cost to consumers, but the favoured proposal of the toll's opponents, an increase in a fuel levy, would force the poor in all nine provinces to pay. All taxes on business could be criticised for adding to the costs to consumers. This is an argument often advanced by advocates of a 'free market', but in this case it is invoked by those who claim to reject it. Opponents have argued that the tolls do not reduce inequality because exemptions do not reach all who are entitled to them. They add that the concession to manage the toll was granted to a foreign company which, they believe, profits at the expense of South African motorists.[61] But these are criticisms of the way the toll is administered: they do not change the reality that it requires the better off to pay for a public good enjoyed by people living in poverty. To use these objections to reject e-tolling is like insisting that the social grants which are essential to the poor must go because the contract to distribute them was awarded to a private company.

Another sign that the e-toll dispute is an insider controversy is that government officials and ANC politicians, some of whom have loudly supported the tolls, have never defended them as a measure which favours the poor. Still less have they sought to counter middle-class and affluent opposition to tolls by mobilising poor people to support them. The exemptions for the poor were not initially planned; they were a concession to some of the toll's opponents.[62] For the government, e-tolls were a technical solution – they used the 'user pay' principle because this was what governance theories popular in the West at the time recommended. Public transport was exempted in the hope that it would make the technical remedy easier to implement. So neither the architects of e-tolls nor their opponents saw value in ensuring that those who can afford to own cars pay for roads on which those who cannot afford them can travel. Within the insider debate, those who champion the rights of the car owner proclaim themselves friends of the poor; those who support the poor do so by accident as they embrace fashionable public finance theories. And the champions of a more equal society loudly support the vehicle owners seeking to avoid paying for roads which poorer people use.

## THE PERSISTENCE OF RACE

This tendency to clothe campaigns which do not represent the interests of the poor as radical assaults on privilege seems to turns its back on a core theme of the struggle for freedom.[63]

Little more than a decade after the first South African socialist organisation was founded, the president of the ANC, Josiah Gumede, became an admirer of the Soviet system and favoured an alliance between the organisation and the Communist Party. His view was rejected, but left activists played a significant role in the ANC from the 1940s onward, before and after the Communist Party was banned in 1950. After the ANC was forced underground and into exile, the left's role in it grew. Radical thought was also embraced by organisations to the ANC's left. The language of the left was so common in movements fighting apartheid that it was often used by members who were not left-wing. The examples discussed here seem to suggest that today's activism has strayed from this tradition.

But this is yet another case of path dependence: today's activists are following a very old tradition. ANC president Gumede admired Communists. But he saw white domination of black people as the core issue and the Communists as useful allies in that fight. He first opposed communism because he believed it was hostile to property owners like himself.[64] This pattern was to be repeated over and over during the fight against apartheid: the left was part of the battle, but the fight was against race, not class, domination. While the left did influence the Freedom Charter and radical thinking outside the ANC, racial domination was always primary. The Charter spelled out what its authors believed was needed to end racial domination, not the rule of one class over another. This stress on racism was officially endorsed by the Communist International, which declared in the late 1920s that Communists in South Africa should fight for a 'native peasants and workers' republic'. Despite the language, this meant that the aim was black freedom, not that of workers or peasants.[65] Left activists usually tried to distinguish themselves from others by the zeal with which they fought apartheid, not by their concern for the interests of workers and the poor over other black people.

All the political traditions to the left of the ANC saw race as crucial. Neville Alexander, perhaps the most influential black Marxist to the ANC's left, was a product of the Non-European Unity Movement (NEUM), the most self-consciously Marxist of all the resistance traditions. His 1979 book, *One Azania, One Nation* (written under the name No Sizwe), argued that only the NEUM's anti-nationalist Marxism explained minority rule in South Africa. But he also saw Black Consciousness (BC) as a 'progressive' response to apartheid: 'Black solidarity has come to mean, in practice, united action by all oppressed people ... [It was] the revenge of the slave on the master.'[66] The NEUM, known for its left orthodoxy, replied to Alexander not by arguing that BC was wrong to stress blackness, but by insisting that it was imitating NEUM ideas. Its theorist IB Tabata declared: 'The Unity Movement ... set itself as one of its immediate tasks: (a) to smash the walls that divide the oppressed, African, Indian and Coloured people ... [and] (b) to fight against slave mentality.'[67] Across the spectrum, to be left-wing was to be an anti-apartheid militant more than to champion the poor.

So ingrained was the use of left language that, particularly after 1994, it was used by ANC leaders (primarily Mbeki) to justify policy positions which favoured black business. An example was its use in a 1998 paper, 'The State, Property Relations and Social Transformation', which argued for the promotion of a black business class and cooperation between business and the new government.[68] It was seen as the first salvo in an attempt to persuade the movement of the merits of privatisation of state-owned enterprises. If Marxist language can be used to justify 'free market' economics, then left demands for free rides for car owners and the children of the wealthy are a continuation of a trend, not a break from it.

This use of pro-poor language to frame proposals which advantage others could be dismissed as a cynical ploy. But something more subtle and important is at play. If people are used to using left ideas to think about a fight against racial domination (which affects everyone in the dominated group, including the well off), this becomes a deeply embedded way of viewing events in society. In a sense, we are all equipped with a set of antennae, shaped by the way we experience the world, which enables us to make sense of events. Given the importance of the fight against racial minority rule, racial antennae are in very good working order: racial bias, even when it is subtle, is noticed quickly by those at whom it is aimed because black political actors (and some whites sensitive to racism) are attuned to the many varieties of racial domination. But antennae which might detect threats to the poor may not work at all because their interests have always taken a back seat to the central problem, racial domination.

This may help explain why South Africans living in poverty are always spoken for and rarely speak.[69] Besides the reasons already given, deeply rooted in the intellectual framework of resistance to apartheid is that the core unit through which the needs of people living in poverty is viewed is the 'community', which is still used as a synonym for people living in areas apartheid once reserved for black people.[70] In this 'community' there is no difference between the affluent and the shack dweller, the taxi owner and the commuter. This view shapes the antennae through which most policy issues are viewed. Its roots lie in the culture of resistance. Faced with the apartheid state's strategy of driving wedges into black unity by forcing people into ethnic groups or offering privilege to some black people only, resistance organisations responded by denying differences within the racial majority. This shaped the ways of seeing of activists, including those on the left, making it more likely that campaigners do not distinguish between the interests of the poor and of those who can afford to contribute.

Concern with race is not a delusion. No black left thinker has ever denied the importance of race, because racial domination was and is a core component of the lived reality of most South Africans. Race has been the central South African divide since the seventeenth century, when the first white colonist, Jan van Riebeeck, planted a wild almond hedge to establish the border of the white-controlled colony.[71] Race was central from the nineteenth century, when white colonisers fought frontier wars with indigenous people as they sought to entrench racial dominance.[72] Since race was, for the next century and a half, the divide which determined who had power and privilege, it is difficult to imagine how a path-dependent transition to democracy would not have preserved, albeit in modified form, pre-1994 racial hierarchies and the tensions they produce. The Trinidadian Marxist CLR James's view that 'to neglect the racial factor as incidental is an error only slightly less grave than to make it fundamental'[73] describes South African reality.

The antennae work far better to detect racism because they are attuned to discern the form of domination which is central to South African reality. While economic domination is an important feature, it is not the society's principal cleavage and so not the one which most shapes people's reactions to events. Lumping together the owners of cars with those who cannot afford them, or the children of top-income earners with those of families struggling to get by, is not the inevitable consequence of fighting racial domination in words and thoughts usually associated with the battle between classes. But this outcome becomes far more likely when, for understandable reasons, the language of social and economic equality is used to describe a battle for something else. And so the gap between what campaigners say they are demanding and reality is not a new twist, but a continuation of a way of seeing the world shaped over decades.

# 6

# Missing the Target: The Negotiations of 1993, the Constitution and Change

For most of those who agree that the past lives on in post-1994 South Africa, there is a clear and obvious reason: the compromise of 1994 and the constitution it produced.

In this view, the hope of a fundamentally different society was betrayed by a deal between elites in which the ANC leadership, presumably in haste to participate in national government, made compromises which entrenched minority privilege. The result is said to be a constitution which blocks change. In 2011, a then government deputy minister, Ngoako Ramatlhodi, summed up this position, arguing that in the negotiations which produced the constitution, the ANC made 'fatal concessions' which ensured 'a constitution that reflects the great compromise … tilted heavily in favour of forces against change'.[1] An academic critic of the constitution noted that Ramatlhodi's comments, which seemed to argue that a majority government should be able to do as it pleased, aimed to bolster the power of the government at the expense of the people, but endorsed his view that the constitution entrenches the inequities of the past.[2]

The argument presented here rejects this view. As argued in Chapter 4, the roots of path dependence lie not in the state but in the society. It follows that the state is not an obstacle to change and that the constitution, the state's founding law, is not a barrier either. This chapter presents a detailed response to claims that South Africa is locked in the past by the constitution, and that path dependence is a product of compromises made at the negotiating table by opponents of minority rule.

Those who blame the constitution for freezing the past are reacting to a 'triumphalism'[3] or a 'fetishistic overinvestment and overreliance on constitutions'[4] which assigns to the document almost magical properties. Thus, the legal scholar Karl Klare argues in a much-quoted article that the constitution itself is a vehicle for 'transformative constitutionalism'.[5] Much of his article expressed worry that the reigning legal culture might not be up to the task of realising the constitution's potential. But he did see the document as a route to a new society if lawyers and judges rose to the challenge: 'The South African Constitution, in sharp contrast to the classical liberal documents, is social, redistributive, caring, positive, at least partly horizontal, participatory, multicultural, and self-conscious about its historical setting and transformative role and mission.'[6] Another scholar goes much further, labelling the constitution 'social democratic',[7] by which he meant that it was a charter for a fair and democratic society. Outside the academy, the notion that the constitution is 'the most progressive in the world' is so often stated – even by the only party in Parliament which voted against its adoption[8] – that it has become a cliché.

This chapter does not join the constitution's praise-singing chorus. While the rights it entrenches have enabled citizens to contest unaccountable power, it can also constrain action (when, say, courts are expected to substitute for democratic politics).[9] Rather, the aim is to contest that the constitution, and the 1994 bargain which produced it, is a cause of path dependence and a barrier to a decisive break with the past. The view argued is not that the constitution has been an agent of change, but that it is not what has prevented change. Political choices and social realities, not the rules adopted in 1996, preserve the past. The cure for path dependence is new political choices and policies which create new social realities, not a new constitution.

## THE NATURE OF THE DEBATE

The constitution and its impact have, not surprisingly, been the subject of intense debate among scholars, many of whom teach and study the law.

The criticism has a dominant theme, which is that the constitution's property clause obstructs change. Beyond that, there are two broad strands of opposition. The first, rooted in Africanist and Black Consciousness (BC) thought, attacks the document as a licence for continued colonial conquest and white control of the society which ignores African values and legal understandings. The second argues that it entrenches, or fails to challenge, social and economic inequalities. Both critiques question the process which produced the constitution, arguing that it was a bargain between elites in which citizens had no say. In this view, the constitution obstructs change partly because the people who most need a new society had no say in designing it. While the criticism focuses on the document itself, it is aimed also at the compromise settlement which produced it.

## The Right to Conquest

The Africanist scholar whose work has been most influential in this debate is the philosopher Mogobe Ramose, whose critique stems partly from an analysis of change (or its absence) in Zimbabwe and South Africa.

Ramose argues that the constitutional negotiations were marked by two 'contending paradigms': decolonisation and democratisation. The first paradigm seeks to nullify white conquest of the land by restoring 'territory and sovereignty' to the indigenous majority. The 'democratisation paradigm', because it extends rights to conquerors as well as the conquered, reflects the conqueror's view that injustices which occurred a long time ago should not be rectified. This, he argues, is not an indigenous understanding of justice. It 'conflicts with the fundamental legal doctrine of *ubuntu* constitutional law which commands that *molato ga o bole* – meaning that an injustice remains an injustice until it is rectified'.[10] It ignores the lasting effects of land conquest: 'In its determination to achieve victory over apartheid, the democratization paradigm lost sight of the fact that the land question was a basic issue long before apartheid was born.'[11] This paradigm prevailed, and so the negotiations became a 'second conquest', by consent rather than force.[12]

For Ramose, the constitution has enshrined a 'right of conquest'[13] because it protects the rights of white conquerors who dispossessed indigenous Africans by force. A constitution within the 'decolonisation paradigm' would express 'the restoration of complete, unencumbered and integral sovereignty to the conquered as at conquest … [This] entails … the return of the land to the indigenous people.'[14] He is not persuaded by the argument that negotiators had to compromise to end conflict:

> The defenders of the compromise … argue, among other things, that [it] was the best option at the time since it averted an impending 'civil war' … Since colonisation, South Africa has been practically in a state of war. A hypothetical 'civil war' in the 1990s could not justify the sacrifice at the altar of compromise of the moral and political imperative to bring about a just and peaceful end to the ensuing colonial war.[15]

Thus, the compromise did not end conflict; since 1994, it has simply taken on a new form.

So far, Ramose's argument seems to centre on the constitution's property clause and its presumed role in entrenching whites' right to land seized by conquest. It is this point which inspires other critics. But, as the previous chapter pointed out, 'land' in South Africa never means soil alone, and Ramose has far more than land redistribution in mind. While restoring the soil to the black African majority is an element of the decolonisation paradigm, he advocates a form of state very different to that which the constitution established (one which, for reasons that will become clear, is never discussed by the legal scholars who cite his work).

Decolonisation, Ramose argues, will not be achieved until the traditional authority which governed Africa before colonisation is restored. He hails KwaZulu-Natal as 'the torchbearer on the road to the federal republic of South Africa'[16] because it has, through the efforts of the Inkatha Freedom Party (IFP) and the Zulu monarchy, done more than any other actor to demand real powers for traditional authority. The constitution insists that 'African customary law' may operate only within its rules, but 'from where does the Constitution of South Africa derive the power to subordinate the law of the African king?'[17] 'The subordination of "African customary law" to the "law of the land" is without ethical and political justification.'[18] A minimum requirement for a decolonised constitution is, therefore, not only the return of the land to indigenous people, but also 'conceding parity to the legal paradigms existing in contemporary South Africa'.[19] Ramose envisages a 'decolonisation' in which the powers of the Zulu monarchy would be restored, prompting demands from other ethnic kingdoms for similar powers. The result would be a federation or confederation of kingdoms. A unitary state would need to be reconsidered because 'the multiple and disparate kingdoms that would emerge are likely to insist on their right to … territorial authority, as well as political independence'.[20]

Ramose seems to be arguing for a constitution which would subordinate everyone to traditional rule by ethnic kingdoms. But this is by no means clear because he also advocates constitutional protection for racial minorities: 'Compromise without justice is blind and empty. But justice without compromise is a recipe for future contestations … The dialogue towards the post-conquest South Africa should … [acknowledge] the cultural diversity of (its) peoples.'[21] This sounds like an argument for racial minority rights; a critic concludes that he 'advocates consociationalism and ethnic federation proposed by the Buthelezi Commission as alternatives to constitutionalism'.[22] The Buthelezi Commission, established during apartheid, recommended that racial minorities enjoy a veto over all decisions which affect them[23] – which would surely maintain the 'right to conquest' forever.

It is easy to see why radical critics of the constitution who quote Ramose approvingly might prefer not to mention proposals which seem to preserve racial minority rights. Ramose's proposal also fits neatly the 'conservative' approach to traditional authority criticised by Mahmood Mamdani: his position does seem to support the Traditional Courts Bill and other laws which subject rural citizens to traditional authority whether they like it or not. Ramose's seemingly radical rejection of path dependence appears, therefore, to endorse that dependence by seeking to return South Africa to a version of grand apartheid, in which all black people were meant to be governed in ethnic enclaves, or an arrangement in which the rights of the monarch are assumed to be those of the people too. Ramose argues that traditional arrangements are more democratic than the current constitution,[24] but they are obviously an attempt to return to the past, not to build a new society.

The next two critics, both legal scholars, endorse and develop some of Ramose's themes without supporting his desire to return to the past. Tshepo Madlingozi labels the current social order 'neo-apartheid', and argues that the constitution 'is actually complicit in the continuation of this anti-black bifurcated societal structure'.[25] It is also an attempt to displace and suppress the power of citizens acting in pursuit of common interests. In the late 1980s, the ' "people's power" civic organisations that had emerged to render South Africa "ungovernable" ... were brutally suppressed by the apartheid regime and finally demobilised by the returning ANC ... The suppression and demobilisation of these radical black community organisations went hand in hand with the emergence and valorisation of public interest litigation organisations and human rights non-governmental organisations [NGOs]'.[26] This helped preserve the past because organisations which sought a new society were forced to give way to law firms and NGOs that operate within a framework which continues the past.

Which aspects of the constitution ensure that it entrenches the past? Madlingozi singles out the Bill of Rights, quoting retired Constitutional Court judge Albie Sachs, who wrote at the beginning of the negotiation period that 'most proponents of a Bill of Rights in South Africa see it as an instrument designed to block ... significant social change'. They sought, he added, a 'hidden or democratic apartheid' achievable through the 'de facto constitutional freezing of historical injustice'.[27] The constitution also, Madlingozi notes, 'does not undo the settler-created house' and '[hinders] an extensive scheme of reparation and restitution'. More specifically, 'the transmutation of ill-gotten property into constitutionally protected property *via* a supreme constitution obviates the decolonisation project'.[28]

Madlingozi's critique does not say why the Bill of Rights freezes the past. The fact that some advocates of such a Bill thought it would preserve minority privilege does not necessarily mean that it does this. There is no magical property attached to a Bill of Rights which ensures that it always preserves the past. Whether it does depends on its wording, and Sachs, writing at the beginning of negotiations, could not have been saying anything about the wording of a Bill which had not yet been written. Sachs was an ANC constitutional negotiator who played a role in shaping the Bill as well as a long-serving Constitutional Court judge – he presumably would not have played either role if he believed the constitution froze historical injustice. Nor does Madlingozi identify those clauses which prevent 'reparation and restitution'. It is also not always clear whether he is rejecting the constitution or the way it is used (or misused) by courts and civil society organisations: 'Although the Constitution explicitly permits both horizontal and vertical application of enshrined rights, [civil society] social justice groups' gaze of social emancipation is focused vertically against the post-1994 government and away from historical beneficiaries of colonialism and apartheid'.[29] So the constitution does allow action for change, but the civil society groups do not use it to press for change. He offers only one example of a constitutional clause which blocks change: the property clause.

A more detailed and sustained critique is that of the legal scholar Joel Modiri, who relies not only on Ramose's work and that of the BC theorist Steve Biko (the subject of his doctoral thesis) but also on critical race theory, a critique of white racism which is the work of American legal scholars. Modiri's body of written work – only a fraction of which is discussed here – offers an exhaustive critique of both the constitution and the manner in which it has been interpreted by judges. Like Ramose, he sees it as an endorsement of, and a means of sustaining, white privilege, which in his view is unaltered by the settlement of 1994.

For Modiri, the constitution 'tends to assume and affirm Western liberal constitutionalism and moderate politics to the exclusion of more radical alternatives'.[30] It 'represents a Western and hence colonial order of legal knowledge that suppresses and marginalises indigenous African ways of knowing and doing law'.[31] It 'constructs a narrow, assimilationist and rights-based vision of what freedom from … racial oppression entails for Blacks and eclipses a more radical politics of decolonisation and liberation'.[32] The 'constitution in South Africa (since, as I am suggesting, it is not truly the constitution of South Africa)' is an 'act of invention': it 'clears away the history that precedes it and [imagines] the absence of an indigenous people, with laws, customs, Kings and Queens, with a history, knowledge and an autochthonous moral and ethical grounding'.[33] It 'effects a colonial superimposition, most vividly reflected in the Constitution's supremacy over the African law of the indigenous people'.[34] This critique follows Ramose's: the constitution erases black culture and ethical insights and so legitimates conquest. But Modiri steers this criticism into avenues not travelled by the other two critiques.

'The Constitution is fundamentally flawed,' Modiri writes, 'not only on account of its Eurocentricity and undemocratic imposition on the indigenous people of South Africa but also because, as the outcome of a faulty pact between Black and white political elites, it is central to the maintenance of a social order predicated on racial subordination and the … concealment and legitimation of historical injustice.'[35] It 'brought into being a new constitutional order that would paradoxically be the afterlife of colonial-apartheid'[36] – one which perpetuates the past. Modiri seeks to support this view by discussing two Constitutional Court cases, in both of which Biko happens to be an important factor.

The first, *Azapo*,[37] was brought by Biko's widow, Nontsikelelo Biko, the BC political party Azapo, and the families of four activists murdered by functionaries of the apartheid state. The case challenged the constitutionality of section 20(7) of the Promotion of National Unity and Reconciliation Act of 1995, which allowed amnesty for apartheid-era gross human rights violators. For Modiri, the Act gave reconciliation priority over justice. The Court rejected this view. He believes this was inevitable: 'The Constitutional Court and the Truth and Reconciliation Commission originate from the same source … a faulty negotiated political settlement whose very *raison d'etre* was the … legitimation of the … "post"-apartheid constitutional dispensation.'[38] No other judgment was possible, he believes, because the political settlement's quest for reconciliation rests on denying justice – as does the Constitution. Modiri sees the judgment as a product not of the biases of the presiding judges but of the settlement and the constitution.

The second case, *City of Tshwane*,[39] was brought from a very different quarter: Afriforum, an NGO which campaigns for the interests of white Afrikaners. It asked the Court to overturn a decision by the Tshwane metropolitan council to change the names of streets which honoured Afrikaner heroes – one was renamed after Steve Biko. A judgment by Chief Justice Mogoeng Mogoeng rejected the application. Modiri notes: 'Mogoeng CJ is clearly unsympathetic to Afriforum's application. For him, as a matter of both law and political morality, the preservation of colonial-apartheid era street names and the promotion of sectarian white interests through the use of legal technicalities is fundamentally irreconcilable with the constitutional project.'[40] He points out that the Court's only two white judges – Johan Froneman and Edwin Cameron – dissented, suggesting that the judgment did not respect Afrikaner cultural traditions. The Court thus split on racial lines, an extremely rare event, with black judges all supporting the chief justice.

A case in which black judges joined together to reject retaining street names which celebrated the conquest of black South Africans in the face of dissent from their white colleagues would seem to argue strongly against Modiri's view that the constitution and the Court which interprets it erase black historical experience. But he rejects the terms in which the majority reach their conclusion. Because the black judges use the language of 'reconciliation', they are little different from the white judges who want to ignore the conqueror's violence: 'All the judges remain within the same constitutional paradigm of integration, assimilation and of placing reconciliation and unity above justice.'[41]

Elsewhere, Modiri spells out why he believes that even these rulings perpetuate domination: 'Part of the blind spot in South African race discourses (which in turn undergird human rights and equality) is an insistence ... that since 1994 ... whites and blacks now equally enjoy formal legal rights (or ... that the law is no longer instrumental in ... perpetuating deep inequalities between whites and blacks). This is evidenced by the use of the phrase "*previously* disadvantaged group" to refer to ... blacks.'[42] The constitution and the Court assume that equality has already been achieved and so ignore continued white domination. He cites the *Prince*[43] case, in which the Court upheld a decision denying a Rastafarian the right to practise law because his religion required him to use marijuana. Modiri argues that the Court failed to recognise that Rastafarians suffer discrimination because they are black: 'Once again, the equality aspect was ignored and the possibility of a race-conscious approach (that takes difference and diversity seriously) was negated.'[44] For Modiri, by embracing the non-racial framework, the constitution and the Court assume that all South Africans are already equal. This hides the reality that blacks are still dominated by whites.

A further target for attack is the constitution as a vehicle for fighting discrimination, operating through the Bill of Rights. Here, Modiri notes the view of legal scholar Anton Kok that 'the people for whom the anti-discrimination legislation was intended – blacks – are not the ones to bring the claims.'[45] Cases which illustrates this are *Walker*,[46] in which 'a privileged white man brought a claim of racial discrimination' (he complained that black residents of Tshwane were being charged less for services than whites), and *Van Heerden*,[47] 'the first affirmative action claim brought, ironically, 'by "old order parliamentarians"'. Neither case ended in a triumph for white interests. In *Van Heerden*, the Court rejected the claim of a white member of Parliament that the parliamentary pension fund rules favoured black MPs. In *Walker*, the Court rejected the view that it was discriminatory to charge black residents less, although it did agree that the council could not collect charges from whites only. But Modiri argues that both decisions show that equality provisions meant to undo white supremacy could also be used by whites to preserve it. Whites were more likely to use them since they were more likely to afford lawyers: 'We still await cases brought by black South Africans enforcing the positive duty of the state to redress past and current imbalances ... as well as more claims against private entities and multinational corporations which supported and benefitted from apartheid.'[48] It is not clear whether even this use of the Bill of Rights would meet Modiri's concern, which seems partly to echo Ramose's view that a constitution which extends rights to all must empower the beneficiaries of conquest.

Thus far, Modiri appears to reject the constitution entirely. But some of his writing suggests that his position is more complicated – and contradictory: 'South African society is stuck ... somewhere between an authoritarian system based on racial oppression and inequality and a "transforming" democratic system based on dignity, freedom and equality.'[49] So the settlement and constitution have not purely preserved the past. He observes: 'The advent of a new democratic, multi-racial order under-written by a constitution that promises non-racialism ... has done little to change the uneasy relationship between race and law in the journey towards this elusive "new" South Africa.'[50] This does not mean the constitution has entrenched white supremacy, but simply that it has been unable to change it. He goes further, suggesting it might be a tool for change: 'Even though it generally operates in ... ways that marginalise poor black communities and maintain unjust systems of power ... constitutional litigation also holds *possibilities* for race-sensitive approaches to legal reasoning and judicial adjudication that could result in tangible (albeit short-term and often temporary) outcomes for the disadvantaged and indigent.'[51] How can the same constitution be 'central to the maintenance of white domination' and a potential tool for addressing the needs of the 'disadvantaged'? These passages from one of the constitution's fiercest intellectual opponents suggest that it may not, after all, be a necessary block to change.

The work of one further critic deserves discussion here, not least because it is cited by Modiri in support of some of his positions. Writing in 1997, the US-based Kenyan legal scholar Makau Mutua argued that the constitutional settlement favoured the forces of the past: 'It seems that the NP [National Party] ... was protected against the will of the majority to substantially transform the state.'[52] In this view, 'the new constitutional rights framework has frozen the hierarchies of apartheid by preserving the social and economic status quo'. His reason is that the ANC accepted a human rights–based framework. 'While rights discourse had the power to galvanize the oppressed and garner the sympathy of some segments of the middle and upper classes during the struggle against official apartheid, the Mandela government's near total dependence on rights discourse as the tool for the transformation of the legacy of apartheid is a mistake.'[53]

By a rights framework, Mutua does not mean the Bill of Rights alone; he too sees constitutionalism with its checks and balances as an endorsement of pre-1994 power: 'Is it feasible to re-create a deeply distorted society primarily by employing the human rights framework that is fundamentally anti-statist in its mission to curb arbitrary or excessive state power? Is it possible to do this without a cataclysmic social and political revolution in which the *ancien regime* [is] categorically defeated?'[54] The past can be changed only by state power, unlimited by citizen rights or other constraints. What is needed is not rights and rules but a state with all the power it needs to undo conquest. The settlement gives the new state less power than that held by its minority-ruled predecessors 'even though [it] seeks to create a fair and just society, whereas its predecessor used its power to do precisely the opposite'.[55] If apartheid had not existed and left no legacy, a rights-based constitution 'would have been largely beneficial'. Since it does leave a legacy, 'the rights approach gives no more than formal and abstract rights to blacks … For white beneficiaries of apartheid, by contrast, the rights-based state, with its independent courts and … commissions and watchdogs, is a golden opportunity to protect most of their privileges and legitimize the results of apartheid'.[56]

Mutua notes that while the constitution was drafted by an elected Parliament, it could operate only within principles agreed to in multiparty talks. This put the ANC 'in an iron box, taking away its ability to transform South Africa according to its vision'.[57] In September 1996, the Constitutional Court refused to certify the draft constitution because it did not conform fully to the principles. The Court wanted to limit the powers of government by making it more firmly accountable to the constitution and watchdogs such as the Auditor-General and Public Protector.[58] Mutua suggests that the Court also wanted enhanced powers for provinces (although the IFP complained that it did not offer them enough power). Although only one of its required changes could be said to protect business (a stipulation that employer bargaining rights be recognised), limiting the powers of the government represents a 'conservative, pro-business, anti-redistributive direction' which 'enjoys the support of most white captains of industry'.[59] Mutua too cites the property clause as a barrier to change, although he also observes that 'no radical land reform program is contemplated' by the government,[60] which suggests that the constraint to change may be government policy and strategy, not the constitution.

Mutua observes:

> Nowhere is the use of the rights language more poignant than in the … preservation of rights and privileges of the apartheid security forces, judiciary, and bureaucracy … The protection of these interests through the new

constitutional order in effect binds the ANC and robs it of any ability to carry out major reforms ... The democratic, rule of law, rights-based state has ironically turned out to be an instrument for the preservation of the privileges and the ill-gotten gains of the white minority.[61]

But these protections lapsed within a few years of the beginning of the new order – a temporary measure is denounced here as a permanent guarantor of preserved white rule.

Mutua's critique is based on a careful reading of the constitution and the law. But it can be reduced to the argument that any measure which weakened the national state and made it more accountable, or ceded some of its powers to provinces, strengthened interests which want to preserve the past. His objection is to constitutionalism itself, which obliges the post-1994 state to subject itself to rules that did not constrain the apartheid state. His quarrel is with the idea that a post-apartheid government should be constrained by any rules at all.

## A Friend of the Rich?

The second strand of criticism is concerned that the constitution and settlement have prevented action against poverty and inequality.

Sanele Sibanda's critique argues for a jurisprudence enabling 'the poor to become true political agents rather than the recipients of welfare-style handouts that will keep them and future generations "in their place"'.[62] He is more sympathetic to the constitution than the other critics. Klare's notion of 'transformative constitutionalism' has 'a clear textual basis in the Constitution' and the courts 'have sought to enforce its principles and aspirations'. But despite their best intentions, 'the prevalence of a liberal democratic constitutional paradigm' has prevented the constitution from addressing poverty because it has '[defined] the goods of constitutionalism in narrower terms than is ... necessary or desirable for ... pursuing a truly transformative project of poverty eradication'.[63] Much of his criticism is directed not at the constitutional text but at how the legal profession and judiciary have understood it.

He cites a 2010 article by Judge Dennis Davis: 'The ... democratic society promised by the Constitution which, in part at least, would have required a radical transformation of the legal concepts which underpinned the entire society was replaced by a narrow vision: the eradication of what admittedly was a significant cancer in the body of the legal system prior to 1994.'[64] Change stopped at removing formal racial discrimination. For Sibanda, 'transformative constitutionalism' has been thwarted by a 'liberal' understanding by judges which sees constitutionalism 'as essentially a limiting doctrine'. It is 'primarily understood as being designed to ensure that the exercise of governmental power is subject to ... limits'. South African constitutionalism is 'grounded on liberal tenets'[65] which are concerned with limiting government, not with ensuring that it enjoys the authority to change power relationships which keep poor those who live in poverty.

But, if change is limited by the way the constitution is understood, not by its wording, why question the document? For Sibanda, its wording gives the liberalism he opposes free rein. If 'transformative constitutionalism' depends on 'interpretation by lawyers and judges of different political persuasions ... transformation will always be at risk of being undermined'.[66] The constitution must explicitly side with the poor: 'Without the translation of the goals of transformation into explicitly entrenched constitutional provisions that demand reconstruction, redistribution and more deeply democratic popular participation that go beyond the Bill of Rights, ... transformative constitutionalism was always going to struggle to entrench itself'.[67]

The constitution does not block change, but it leaves too much to interpretation and so allows understandings which do block it. It is liberal because it does not go nearly far enough in mandating change in terms so clear that lawyers and judges would have no doubt what it means. Sibanda suggests, tentatively, that a 'transformative' constitutionalism would need greater commitment to 'mass bottom-up truly participatory democracy' which 'allows people to take an active part in the decision-making processes that concern them'; structural interventions 'targeted at delivering a more equitable ... distribution of wealth' and 'more generally striving towards a more just and fair society that rejects the ... legacies of colonialism and apartheid'.[68] A new text must make these commitments clear because a constitution founded on recognising rights, not rejecting poverty, will allow the interpretations Sibanda and Davis decry. The problem with the constitution is not what it says but what it does not say.

A less detailed critique is offered by Jane Duncan,[69] an academic and social commentator, who argues that the constitution 'mapped over' a '50 percent solution', which excludes half the population from the economy's benefits by 'cementing political agreements that left white control of the economy largely intact'. She too cites the property clause: 'In a cruel twist of fate, the ANC government took on the responsibility of paying for the property that black people had been historically dispossessed of by the white minority'. The constitution's 'socio-economic rights regime ... is not geared towards changing these structural problems' because 'litigants cannot get rights on demand; they can only persuade the court to ensure that government realises rights progressively'. There are clear similarities with Sibanda's view: because governments must realise social and economic rights only over time, what the courts award people in poverty always falls short.

Duncan lays the blame for a constitution which can 'only tinker at the margins of ... poverty and inequality' on the process used to frame it. She cites claims by Sampie Terreblanche that 'formal negotiations were accompanied by parallel, informal, economic negotiations with corporate South Africa' which 'led to concessions by the ANC on the inevitability of a neoliberal growth path ... at least for the foreseeable future'. By implication, this persuaded the ANC to accept a constitution which entrenched the interests of the powerful. The constitutional principles agreed upon by unelected negotiators meant that the constitution was 'circumscribed by the agreements arrived at during negotiations'. While the process invited public submissions and was open to the media, many contentious issues 'disappeared in expert committees at critical moments'. A constitution drafted by a democratic process would look very different: 'If constitutionalism is to survive in South Africa, and survive it must, then it must be based on a Constitution that genuinely reflects the will of the people.'

A less uncompromising criticism is offered by Karl von Holdt, whose work on corruption is discussed in Chapter 3. He argues that the settlement ensured that 'a new democratically elected government would not be able to seize the assets and property of either the white middle-classes or the owners of capital'.[70] Again, the property clause is to blame: 'In recognising and protecting property rights the constitution ratifies the outcome of over three centuries of colonial and apartheid violence.'[71] This view that the settlement shut off economic options is widely held. The economists Jonathan Michie and Vishnu Padayachee argue that 'in the process of negotiations, certain concessions were made by the ANC in respect of economic issues which, however important they may have been to the political settlement, did serve to blunt the movement's economic weapons [and] close down certain policy options'.[72]

Von Holdt argues that use of the state to accumulate wealth is a product of the settlement and constitution: 'The constitutional constraints on the redistribution of assets in the private sector have driven the struggle for asset accumulation and elite formation into the state.'[73] The black elite legitimise these practices 'as an avenue for overcoming the constitutional and policy constraints of the democratic settlement'.[74] Writing in 2013, Von Holdt warned: 'Calls for rewriting the constitution, "transforming" the judiciary, seizing land, nationalising mines and other assets, all draw on a sense among aggrieved elites and marginalised citizens that the current order of things maintains historical injustice.'[75]

But he sees the constitution as an opportunity as well as a constraint. The new order does not simply continue the past – it is 'shot through with tensions, ambiguities, contestations and contradictions'. The settlement and constitution 'represented a profound political rupture and the formation of a new symbolic order founded on democracy, the rule of law, and human rights, in which for the first time the black majority were recognised as full citizens'.[76] The constitution is 'a complex document reflecting the stalemate between the contending forces'. It protects property owners but recognises 'the legacy of black exclusion ... by permitting the expropriation of property to achieve land reform and the redress of past racial discrimination' even though it is 'limited by the requirement for fair compensation'. It also recognises the legacy of poverty and exclusion 'with far-reaching third-generation human rights clauses such as the right to housing, health, food, water and social security'.[77] The 'progressive provisions of the Constitution create space for policy innovation as well as contestation over the meaning ... of the various rights'. He cites approvingly the left analyst Hein Marais,[78] who described the settlement as 'ambiguous, constituting a dramatic political shift but leaving socio-economic inequality intact and open to further struggle'.

Von Holdt also addresses an issue largely ignored by critics of the constitution and settlement – that they might be blamed for politicians' choices. 'It is', he notes, 'an open question' whether the Constitution can 'facilitate redistribution, since the ANC in government has hardly tested the possibilities'. The government's 'conservative policy choices' have 'placed powerful constraints in the way of overcoming the legacies of apartheid'.[79] The constitution leaves inequality intact but opens the possibility of action for change. Unlike Sibanda and Duncan, Von Holdt sees the constitution as a potential enabler of change. Unlike many legal scholars, he does not assume that change depends solely or largely on events in court and so evaluates the document's likely impact on political action in society.

## THE CASE FOR THE DEFENCE

Before responding to these criticisms, three defences of the constitution help to focus on the issues: papers by a legal scholar and a social theorist discussed in an earlier chapter, and two speeches by a prominent jurist who hails from an intellectual and political tradition similar to that of the Africanist critics but reaches very different conclusions.

The first paper is written by Firoz Cachalia, a legal scholar who served as an ANC member of the Gauteng provincial legislature and in the province's executive council. He rejects a 'legalist' reading of the constitution which 'leaves nothing for the democratic communities and generations that come after the founding generation to accomplish'.[80] The constitution does not substitute for action; it enables it. He rejects the view that 'all that is required to achieve justice in a country with a history of colonialism and apartheid is to faithfully implement … the text triumphantly adopted in 1996'. Constitutions in democratic societies are 'in principle always provisional, and their meaning always open to contestation. Their legitimacy and efficacy has to be established in each generation through democratic politics. It is only in this way that they can come to endure.'[81]

The constitution does not suppress African notions of justice – it expresses them. 'Key ideas' that made their way into the constitution, such as the 'rights idea' and the idea of 'democratic self-determination', reflect the thinking of 'anticolonial nationalist intellectuals' who 'consistently proposed democracy as a response to colonial oppression and apartheid for generations before "negotiations"'.[82] The idea of a Bill of Rights was included in the ANC's African Claims document in 1943, so it can 'hardly be presented as a continuation of a "colonial project"'.[83] Nor is this tradition restricted to the ANC. In his speech to the inaugural conference of the Pan Africanist Congress (PAC), which was born of an Africanist rejection of the ANC, founding president Robert Sobukwe 'made it clear that the new party was committed to the establishment of a "political democracy as understood in the *West*"'. Subokwe said he wished 'to emphasise that freedom of the African means the freedom of all in South Africa, the *European included*', and called for 'a genuine democracy in which all men [*sic*] will be citizens and will live and be governed as individuals and not as distinctive national groups'.[84] In 1943, the Non-European Unity Movement, perhaps the most left-wing of the liberation movements, 'adopted the "Ten-point Programme", which included the demand for "full democratic rights"'.[85]

Cachalia notes that the idea of 'constitutional checks and balances' was not 'foreign to precolonial thought in Africa'. He cites the scholar Basil Davidson on the seventeenth-century West African Asante kingdom: 'Power was exercised … with constitutional checks and balances tending to prevent abuse of power … Executive power derived from the degree to which its founding principles were observed: in the rule of law, in the diffusion of executive power, and in the encasing of that power within political and legal checks upon its use.'[86] The constitution and its rights framework have deep African roots. Dismissing them as a colonial imposition ignores this history.

Arguing that the constitution does not block change, Cachalia challenges the critics' understanding of the relationship between law and social and economic reality.[87] He agrees with the legal scholar Stuart Woolman[88] that 'the gap between the constitution's norms and the way in which the society operates [is] a "collective action problem"', and adds that 'the possibilities of collective action are shaped by the continuing structural conditions ... *outside the text itself*. The constitution is neither the cause nor the cure for 'deep inequalities'[89] – they are shaped by social and economic realities. The constitution enables collective action to change these realities.

Action in society, not a legal document, turns these values into reality. If there is a huge gap between the two, this is not because the constitution creates it, but because the society (or those in society with the power to do so) allows it. For Cachalia, those with the power to act have no interest in doing so, while those with an interest in realising the goals lack the power. To blame the constitution is to duck the problem: 'The important ... question of the decolonisation of ... our postcolonial society is today sublimated in the form of a ... critique of the constitutional text.'[90] Blaming the constitution becomes a substitute for showing how a society which perpetuates the past can break free of it.

Citing the political philosopher Chantal Mouffe, Cachalia argues that the constitution 'provides an agonistic framework for dealing with these unresolved questions through democratic ... dialogue and contestation.'[91] Mouffe used 'agonistic' to describe democracy as always unfinished and open-ended. In her view, democracy never settles conflicts permanently. Rather, it provides a framework in which dissension can be pursued without violence. The constitution does not decide what change is needed. It provides a framework which allows continuing debate on this. It is 'a framework only ... It does not itself set out a settled comprehensive conception of justice ... It sets out instead a political ... conception of justice which recognises that "We the People" are normatively plural and politically self-determining.'[92] The constitution is not a recipe for the good society, but nor does it obstruct it: it recognises, and provides expression for, differing views on what that society should be. 'Democratic constitutionalism leaves such questions open-ended ... to be resolved through democratic politics.'[93] The constitution does not impose a template which prevents change, but provides a framework for democratic action and continuing debate on what South Africa should be.

The second response is offered in two speeches by former deputy chief justice Dikgang Moseneke, who was imprisoned for PAC activities and remained a member of the party after 1994.[94] In one speech, he strikes a similar note to Cachalia: 'It is true that the paper on which the Constitution is written did not give us the land back. It did not resolve the class distinction in society. It did not with one wand induct social equality. In fact the Constitution, as a written pact, cannot on its own transform society ... [Rather, it] envisaged and allows great and honest leaders to lead their people to a re-imagined social condition.'[95] For Moseneke too, the constitution makes change possible (although, in contrast to Cachalia, he places his faith in leaders, not the people). It does not impose a liberal view. The judges of the Constitutional Court 'have fashioned the notion of substantive equality that travels well beyond the liberal notion of formal equality. We have insisted that laws and policy must provide for adequate protection of children, people with disabilities, refugees as well as migrants and root out domestic violence.'[96] He adds that the Constitutional Court has taken seriously the circumstances of people living in poverty and has created an approach which comes to their aid. While the Court has not ended poverty and inequality – something it cannot do – it has pointed to a way of seeing the law which offers remedies.

Moseneke argues that the constitution's property clause is blamed for the choices of politicians. According to a report on the speech, he 'argued that, contrary to much of the bluster that often surrounds the issue of land, the Constitution does allow for expropriation and does not make land reform impossible … neither the phrase "willing buyer, willing seller", nor the logic behind it, [appears] in the Constitution'. The 'often strident misrepresentation' of the constitution on the land issue 'has two primary political functions'. One 'is to deflect responsibility for the failure to achieve meaningful land reform … away from the ruling party'. The other is to present 'the constitutional order as an impermeable barrier to … popular aspirations.'[97] Moseneke made these remarks before the controversy over expropriation without compensation. But his core point is that the constitution is not a block to land redistribution. As Mutua noted, this has not been tested, because the ANC chose not to challenge pre-1994 ownership patterns. Given different political choices, the constitution could be a means to realise change.

Both these responses – one influenced by the ANC's political tradition, the other by the PAC's Africanist vision – see the constitution as an enabler of change. For both, the vote and rights for all break with the pre-1994 past despite the survival of poverty, inequality and racial domination. For both, the constitution enables action to fight the patterns of domination which linger. For them, it is not the cause of path dependence, but one of its antidotes.

The third contribution is a 2015 article by Mamdani[98] which he later expanded into a book. It is, in effect, a response to Ramose's argument that the constitution ignores the African view that an injustice remains unjust unless and until it is remedied. His purpose is to contrast South Africa's transition to a view among activists in other parts of the world that the post–World War II Nuremburg trials, which convicted Nazis of crimes against humanity, are the appropriate 'template' for dealing with human rights abuses. He argues that Africa should not see past violence (or injustice) as criminal. It should adopt South Africa's approach, which, he believes, saw past injustices as a political problem and so 'provided the constitutional foundation to forge a post-apartheid political order'.[99]

Mamdani agrees with criticisms of the constitution discussed here. He notes that the property clause appears in the Bill of Rights while 'the clause providing the restoration of land to the majority population was placed outside the Bill' (a probable reference to the Restitution of Land Rights Act No. 22 of 1994). 'White settlers' received constitutional protection, 'black natives … no more than a formal acknowledgement in law'.[100] He identifies two measures in the interim constitution which in his view entrench white privilege. The first gave white local governments the power to veto decisions in the 'pre-interim phase' of change to a new municipal order. The second prevented new local governments from taxing white suburbs to spend more in black areas: 'Thus did CODESA [Convention for a Democratic South Africa, the forum which negotiated the constitution] entrench white privilege, both in the constitution and in the law that established the framework for local government'.[101]

Despite this, the settlement is 'farsighted' because both sides recognised 'that their preferred option was no longer within reach: neither revolution … nor military victory (for the apartheid regime) were in the cards'. This recognition was the only feasible way of moving away from the past: 'If South Africa is a model for solving intractable conflicts, it is an argument for moving from the best to the second-best alternative … political reform.' It was born of a realisation that 'if you threaten to put the leadership from either side in the dock they will have no interest in reform'. This 'led to a shift away from criminalizing or demonizing the other side to treating it as a political adversary'. This was necessary because the groups 'would have to live in the same country'.[102]

For Mamdani, radical change could not be achieved by negotiation. 'The demand that the end of apartheid should have delivered social justice ignores the political reality … The political prerequisite for attaining social justice would have been a social revolution, but there was no revolution in South Africa. If apartheid was not defeated, neither was it victorious. The most one can say is that there was a stalemate.'[103] With Cachalia and Moseneke, he believes this offers the prospect of advance. The alternative to a settlement was continued violence; Codesa recognised 'an opportunity to re-found the political community'.[104] The settlement was 'neither victors' justice nor victims' justice … The point of it all was not to avenge the dead, but to give the living a second chance.'[105] By recognising reality, the settlement did not bring about a new order, but established the possibility of creating one.

Mamdani believes the constitution's limits were needed because the choice was between continued conflict and the prospect of an inclusive society. The violence of the conqueror cannot be erased by that of the conquered: if violence is used to defeat dispossession, the cycle of violence is unlikely to end when political change is achieved. A 'second-best' transition which leaves some aspects of the old order intact is, therefore, a better option for the victims of domination even though it limits change. The settlement offers the dominated new possibilities, even if it does not end minority privilege.

## THE SOCIETY, NOT THE STATE

What does this debate tell us about the constitution and path dependence?

The critics offer eloquent and carefully crafted arguments but little evidence beyond repeated references to the constitution's property clause. Mamdani's two examples did not survive long (he seems to cite them more to analyse the negotiation process than to describe South Africa today), while Mutua anticipates administrative and judicial curbs on a majority government which never happened. The NP's attempt to ensure white political control over change failed, which is why, in mid-1996, it withdrew from the Government of National Unity mandated by the interim constitution, citing the ANC's failure (or refusal) to consult it on decisions.[106] Von Holdt says the constitution causes the patterns he identifies, but he does not show that they are a product of the document rather than realities in the society.

Modiri offers a compelling critique of a series of Constitutional Court decisions to justify his view that the constitution blocks change. But the examples do not show this. While the refusal to overturn the amnesty provision and the denial of the right to practice to a Rastafarian lawyer because he used marijuana raise important issues, and both may well show insensitivity to black experience, neither shows that the Court is blocking the structural social and economic change which would be required to end path dependence. Nor does Modiri offer evidence for his claim that the constitution could be interpreted only in the way chosen by the Constitutional Court.

Modiri devotes much attention to showing that even when they seem sensitive to it, Constitutional Court rulings are blind to the black demand for redress. And so, he criticises *City of Tshwane* despite the fact that it refuses to reinstate apartheid-era names – and united all the black justices – because of the way in which the majority judgment is framed. After praising three judges, Mokgoro, Sachs and Madala, for stressing 'the significance of traditional African jurisprudence and the value of uBuntu as introducing an alternative [to] the Eurocentric western model',[107] he observes: 'It is sad then that Sachs J later refers to these arguments as "political" … maintaining the false distinction between law and politics, which is a hallmark of … legal orthodoxies that seek to insulate law from broader social and political concerns.'[108] While he notes that the gap between critical race theory and South African jurisprudence 'relates not so much to what the court said but to what it didn't say',[109] he is often critical of what it does say – he is sometimes concerned less with what the Court ruled than how it worded its ruling. It could be argued that people seeking redress are concerned about whether they get it, not which words the judges use to give it. And the judicial attitudes he rejects could be seen not as a product of the constitution, but as symptoms of a society whose elites are unwilling to countenance radical change, whatever the constitution says.

The most successful attempt to link the attitudes of judges with the text of the constitution is Sibanda's. For him, the constitution allows free rein to judges who are unsympathetic to the poor, and so a constitution is needed which demands pro-poor rulings. Duncan's point that the constitution defers social and economic rights because they need only be gradually realised shares this concern. It seems hard to fault this argument, now influential among critics of the constitution, that a document which insists on change in clear terms is needed if path dependence is to be addressed. But stipulating in detail what courts must find may do as much to block change as to ensure it.

Like much writing by legal scholars, Sibanda's argument exaggerates the power of constitutions – and ignores the negative consequences for democracy of allowing these documents and the judges who interpret them too much power. This should concern Sibanda far more than most of his colleagues since he does recognise that the power to change rests with citizens more than constitutions: an important feature of his critique is a plea for more popular participation in decisions. During the negotiations, some scholars insisted that there was no social ill that could not be cured by inserting the right words in the constitution. One said he had discovered wording which would improve university education. Another insisted that the constitution not simply allow affirmative action but mandate it. When asked whether this could lead to abuses, he said a schedule could be drafted banning abuses. Clauses cannot improve education and schedules cannot prevent people misusing policies. Nor is there any guarantee that clauses which instruct judges to order the government to address poverty would have the desired effect – not because judges would not listen, but because social reality can be stubborn. Constitutionalists are often irritated when reminded that Irene Grootboom, a homeless person who was the chief plaintiff in a much-heralded Constitutional Court case on housing rights, died without receiving the house to which the judgment said she was entitled.[110] But this does show that courts have limited ability to change the world. If constitutional clauses no longer said the government must realise social and economic rights only 'within its available resources', it would not suddenly acquire the resources it needs to introduce the required change.

More important is the effect on democracy. As Cachalia suggests, the more the constitution decides what social policy should be, the more does power shift from politicians and the voters to whom they account to judges and lawyers who are not bound to reflect the wishes of citizens. This is illustrated by a debate between constitutional scholars on 'minimum core content'.[111] For some years, legal scholars have argued that the Constitutional Court does not do enough to tackle poverty and inequality. While these scholars welcome some of the Court's earlier judgments, such as *Grootboom*[112] and *TAC*[113] (in which the Court instructed the government to make the antiretroviral medication essential for combating HIV and AIDS available to pregnant women to prevent mother-to-child transmission),[114] they argue that the Court retreated from instructing the government to meet the needs of poor people into a 'proceduralism' in which it ordered government to negotiate solutions. This was an abdication of the Court's responsibility to fight poverty.[115] Some scholars insisted that the Court would meet its responsibilities only if it laid down a 'minimum core content': the minimum the state would need to provide citizens to realise their rights.[116] It is criticised for overturning the *Mazibuko*[117] judgment, in which a lower court ruled that the government should provide 12 kl of free water to the poor per month, not the 6 kl it was providing. The Court explicitly rejected the idea that it should adopt 'minimum core content' (of which the lower-court ruling was a prime example). It argued that its job was to decide whether government decisions were reasonable, not to make policy.[118]

But this and similar rulings strengthen democratic action. Instead of deciding what poor people are entitled to, the decisions ordered the authorities to give the poor a direct say in determining this themselves.[119] This produced gains for people who demanded social and economic rights.[120] It also shifted deciding what was fair from the Court to a process in which citizens used the Court's protection to claim a voice. It has been argued persuasively that courts which order negotiation should intervene to ensure that people living in poverty are not overwhelmed by the powerful, and that the bargain is as much one between equals as possible.[121] If courts did intervene in this way, citizens used to being told what to do by power holders (including judges) are more likely to gain a voice than people who are 'favoured' by a beneficent court ruling.

Sibanda's proposed remedy would, therefore, not empower citizens. It would allow constitution drafters and lawyers to decide for them. It would impose on society a view on what people living in poverty need which would be difficult to alter when reality changes. The judgment of drafters is far from perfect, and there is no guarantee that what they would mandate would point a way out of poverty and inequality. Ironically, Sibanda's proposed solution to path dependence might be a recipe for its continuation, entrenching the very old South African pattern in which a minority decided what is good for everyone else. Given these considerations, Cachalia's view that the constitution enables democratic decision-making offers greater prospect of a society in which the social and economic patterns of the past are changed by popular decision-making than turning the constitution into a set of instructions.

The constitution's impact on path dependence must, therefore, depend on whether it prevents social actors from making the changes needed to end it. Despite the elegance of the critiques discussed here, none of them demonstrates that it does. The post-1994 national government has never been blocked by the courts from making changes which would undo the past. Despite *Azapo*, some apartheid-era rights abusers have been jailed. For Modiri, this may fall far short of black demands. But that is a very different point from the claim that the constitution protects the power of the white-ruled past. None of the critiques shows how it does this.

But what of the property clause? The right to property is far more than the right to own land.[122] It is the foundation of the market economy because it protects private owners – hence the argument that it blocks change by allowing those who benefited from apartheid to keep what they have. Again, the land issue is really about control of the economy: 'When one takes into account that land taken in 1913 has since transmogrified into stocks and other items of value, focusing on land and improvements on it might only scratch the surface of property relations, leaving the property regime unchanged.'[123] In this view, what was 'stolen' was the entire economy. Insisting on the unqualified right of the owners of property to keep what they have might be used not only to prevent the state from redistributing land, but to block other measures to regulate the market and reduce poverty. If the critics are right that the constitution protects this unqualified right, it could indeed be used to freeze the past.

But they are not right. The critiques – and much of the debate on land expropriation without compensation – mention only part of section 25 of the constitution which protects property from expropriation unless the owner is fairly compensated. They never mention clause 25(8): 'No provision of this section may impede the state from taking legislative and other measures to achieve land, water and related reform, in order to redress the results of past racial discrimination, provided that any departure from the provisions of this section is in accordance with the provisions of section 36(1).'[124] This means that the state can do anything in relation to property as long as it can show it is doing this to redress racial discrimination, and that its actions are 'reasonable and justifiable in an open and democratic society based on human dignity, equality and freedom'.[125] The clause pulls the rug from under the feet of the critiques because it specifically allows that which section 25 is said to obstruct – action to redress racial domination – if it can be shown that it is justifiable in a free society, which, by definition, good-faith attempts to counter racism always are.

This does not necessarily mean the courts would approve any government measure which changes racial ownership patterns. But, as Moseneke has pointed out, we don't know how the courts would interpret the clause because they have never been asked to rule on section 25.[126] The ANC has not once tried to use clause 25(8). It was not the courts which prevented change; the government did not choose to test them. ANC policy documents offer no evidence that it avoided change because it feared it would run afoul of the constitution. This is why Moseneke accuses the Court's critics of blaming it for governing-party decisions. And why Tembeka Ngcukaitobi, an ardent proponent of change to ownership patterns, observes:

> The Constitution is the wrong target. Post-liberation politics have failed the Constitution. Legal constraints to governmental power are necessary. What has slowed down transformation of property relations are the design flaws, inefficiencies of the land administration system, endemic corruption and misapplication of the Constitution, particularly the slavish adherence to market-driven compensation models. For its part, the Constitution is necessarily open-ended and transformative.[127]

The limits on government power Mutua rejects are, Ngcukaitobi points out, necessary to protect citizens' rights. They do not prevent change – as Mutua's own writings show, the post-1994 central government had no interest in the sort of change he believed necessary. His implied claim that central governments are more likely than other levels of government to change society ignores the fact that many of the experiments in empowering people living in poverty around the world have been the work of regional or local governments.[128] The constitution and courts cannot be the cause of preventing something they have never been used to block.

This does not mean that the constitution is an ideal document. It means only that it has not blocked change. It does not even necessarily mean Moseneke is right that the constitution has enabled the courts to develop a framework which points to 'substantive equality', or that Cachalia is right that it expresses popular demands for freedom. It is, as Mamdani points out, a compromise between those aspirations and the interests of private power holders. The ANC would have written a different constitution if it had been able to. But the version which was agreed to, whatever its biases and limitations, does not prevent change to undo the patterns of the past.

Mamdani's suggestion that the constitution reflected the balance of power at the time it was negotiated is also important. None of the liberation movements possessed the military capacity to defeat the apartheid state; they were unlikely to acquire it any time soon. So only negotiation could end apartheid, and a constitution closer to Ramose's decolonisation vision was possible only if the ANC drove a harder bargain than it actually did. But the evidence shows it gained the best bargain going at the time. Critics who argue that the ANC could have used mass mobilisation to shift the NP's position ignore the fact that it did precisely this, particularly in 1992, when negotiations broke down.[129] It pushed the negotiation process as far as it could go – perhaps a little further, because a key feature of the settlement was the NP's late abandonment of its demand for a veto, which prompted Tertius Delport, its first negotiator, to accuse then president FW de Klerk of 'giving the country away'.[130] Had the ANC demanded more, it seems far more likely that the negotiations would have collapsed than that they would have produced a different outcome. Had the ANC continued fighting apartheid, it would still be fighting.

If the constitution reflected social and political reality at the time it was negotiated, then again the 'problem' is the society, not the state. The settlement was, as former deputy minister of finance Mcebisi Jonas points out, the result of a bargain which, for decades after the negotiations, held the society together.[131] It would surely not have done this if it did not reflect the strengths and weaknesses of the parties. Jonas is right to point out that bargains do not last forever and that this one is largely exhausted. But that does not alter the core point: the settlement reflected social reality and did not create it – just as the form of state it established was a product, not a cause, of the path dependence which the critics accurately identify.

The critics discussed here blame the constitution for social realities and political choices it did not create. They also ignore the constitution's potential to provide a vehicle for changing the path dependence they reject. The present is still shot through with the past. But change lies not in another constitution. It lies, rather, in using the possibilities created in 1994 to renegotiate the bargain which produced it. The key to this is to recognise that the problem with the deal which ended apartheid is not too much compromise, but not enough. Those negotiating the settlement bargained compromises which changed the political system, but did not negotiate modifications to the social and economic realities a purely political settlement cannot entirely change.

# 7

# The Power of Negotiation:
# The Prescience of Harold Wolpe

I t may seem new to claim that the patterns of pre-1994 South Africa remain deeply embedded in the new order. But the persistence of the past was anticipated during the negotiation period of the early 1990s, in the writings of a theorist whose concerns seem to be the polar opposite of Douglass North's.

Harold Wolpe never quoted North in his work. Nor did he ever use the term 'path dependence'. This is hardly surprising, for Wolpe was a Marxist who is credited with the first analysis of apartheid as a product of the capitalist system.[1] He was also a committed member of the South African Communist Party (SACP) and the ANC, whose strategic thinking his academic work was meant to assist. But his writing on education and his final journal article – on the Reconstruction and Development Programme (RDP), the development flagship of the 1994 Government of National Unity – warned that a new order would not automatically follow majority rule and hinted that the post-1994 government's thinking could ensure the survival of the old. This work shows how a thinker very different from North discerned that political change would not necessarily bring new social and economic patterns.

Wolpe's work is illuminating for another reason too: it proposes a cure for path dependence which is not usually associated with revolutionary analysis. The most obvious response to realising that the political change of 1994 has left intact many patterns of the apartheid era is to insist on sweeping changes. These should presumably be imposed by an elected governing party which entered the new era committed to a 'national democratic revolution' (NDR), a society which destroyed all remnants of racial minority rule.[2] Wolpe devoted considerable theoretical attention to NDR and we would expect him to urge a militant programme to achieve it – which is how some of his admirers read his critique. But closer reading shows that, for Wolpe, the way to change the patterns of the past lay in negotiating compromises between key economic and social interests.

His analysis offers a diagnosis and a proposed cure, both of which may have been ahead of their time. It took two decades for the diagnosis to gain wide currency. The proposed cure is yet to achieve this, but negotiation is the only workable way out of path dependence and so it too may yet win acceptance. Had either been taken seriously at the time, the trajectory of democracy's first 25 years might have been different. This chapter will examine Wolpe's diagnosis and cure in an attempt to deepen our analysis of path dependence and to begin to chart a possible way out of its limiting effects.

## OLD UNIVERSITIES FOR A NEW ORDER

The early 1990s were, on the surface, a period of great ferment – in ideas as well as in political developments. It was assumed that a new political order would fundamentally change the country, and much debate was devoted to contending views on how a democratic South Africa should fashion its institutions. While some proposed wide-ranging change, others pleaded for the survival of that in which they had a stake.

The future of universities was an arena of contest. Wolpe, who was head of the Education Policy Unit (EPU) at the University of the Western Cape (UWC), wanted fundamental change. According to his friend and fellow radical sociologist Michael Burawoy, Wolpe and his UWC colleagues' work on education was motivated chiefly by a fear that the change in political order would not produce a genuinely new education system. They feared that 'the transformative mission of education would be reduced to a mere footnote'.[3] To prevent this, they advocated an 'overall development plan' for post-apartheid society. In an article, Wolpe argued that without a plan firmly committing the new order to detailed and achievable changes, the elite which dominated the historically white universities would continue to hold sway. Government programmes, however well intentioned, might 'contribute only to a highly limited degree to ... social transformation and, indeed, may ... help reproduce powerfully entrenched structures generated by apartheid'.[4] This concern to prevent the education system's past from surviving into the future prompted the paper by Wolpe and Zenariah Barends[5] which criticised the view that historically white institutions did not have to change.

They argued that both historically white and black universities were products of apartheid. The white institutions had been established to meet the needs of those who relied on racial domination. Elsewhere, Wolpe argued that these universities slavishly accepted 'international standards' which did not fit national realities[6] or meet the needs of most students. Drawing on evidence from South Africa and Britain, Wolpe and Barends suggested that some of the standards imposed by the white universities may have ensured courses that were beyond the reach of many students. So, like the black institutions, they should be 'radically transformed'.

Wolpe and his colleagues were arguing, in effect, that those who wished to leave white universities largely untouched wanted a form of path dependence. Not only would apartheid's hierarchy between universities be maintained, but the white universities would continue operating as they always had, albeit with black students and faculty. What was taught and how it was taught would be determined by the same criteria as those used before 1994, and the new students and teachers would either adapt to the norms set for them or be rejected because they were not measuring up to the required standard. The apartheid university may have died since race was no longer a barrier to admission. But the colonial university, with its assumption that some cultures and experiences were more valuable than others, would remain at the top of the tree. It was this reality, continued over the next two decades, which produced 'Rhodes Must Fall' and 'Fees Must Fall', followed by heated discussions of ways in which universities might 'decolonise' to develop the academic potential of most students.

Wolpe and the EPU proposed a way out of the dead end which could be applied to much more than the education system. They did this in an indirect way, noting that a national debate was raging on what Wolpe and his colleagues called the tension between 'development' and 'equity'. They used 'development' to describe the position of those who believed higher education's purpose was to boost economic growth. For them, this meant privileging universities which economic power holders believed were efficient; condemning historically black universities to inferiority, ensuring that they and white universities still played the roles they played under apartheid, was 'the triumph of development over equity'.[7] The champions of 'development', they argued, favour a particular understanding of efficiency which leaves inequities intact. 'Equity', by contrast, means the desire to end hierarchies created by the past whether or not this serves the economy.

An article by Wolpe, his EPU colleague Saleem Badat and Barends[8] addressed the relationship between 'development' and 'equity'. They argue that both should be important to a new higher education system. But there is a tension between them which requires choices: priority for development could mean less equity, and vice versa. To ignore the need for a balance between them is to adopt 'populist or pragmatist positions which ... may advance neither social equality nor ... development'.[9] In many arguments for equity, 'virtually no explicit attempt is made to propose which educational needs should be given priority'. But the money needed to redress the effects of the past in higher education was not available and so choosing priorities was essential. There were also different types of equity: 'Difficult political choices are entailed.' The article again advocates a national development plan which, the authors say, would provide a framework for choices. But they want priorities to be chosen through a democratic process.

To justify this approach, they quote the Nigerian democratic theorist Claude Ake's criticism of African regimes which insisted that development take precedence over democracy. Even if postponing democracy did promote development, Ake wrote, 'it does not follow that people must be more concerned with improving nutrition than casting votes, or ... with health than with political participation. The primary issue is not whether it is more important to eat well than to vote, but who is entitled to decide which is more important.'[10] This implied, Wolpe and his colleagues argue, that there was no way to determine with certainty which education policy best balances equity and development. The way to arrive at solutions which allowed for both was by ensuring that everyone with an interest in the choice played a role in deciding.[11] Only an inclusive and democratic process could ensure a solution all key interests would accept. Business and the professions must be included; but a say for black students and youth who were rendered 'politically marginal' by the constitutional negotiations is, they argue, particularly important. The outcomes which a democratic process will produce are uncertain, but this uncertainty, and the possibility that this approach would make it more difficult to reach agreement, was 'a small price to pay'[12] since, if it was allowed to succeed, everyone affected would ultimately agree and this would presumably make it easier to implement whatever emerges.

It could be argued that Wolpe and his colleagues' distinction between 'equity' and 'development' contradicts aspects of their critique of Charles van Onselen. It will be recalled that they argued that both historically white and historically black universities were products of apartheid. Given that one is thus not superior to the other, why is privileging historically white institutions a triumph of 'development'? If the white institutions are also products of apartheid, they surely do not represent 'development'. It is confusing to label those who want a dominant role for white universities advocates of 'development' since Wolpe and his co-authors believe this view would make the development of most people impossible. However, our purpose here is not to discuss education policy, but to examine the implications of these ideas for path dependence and its remedies.

We can see the tension between 'development' and 'equity' as that between those with a stake in path dependence and those interested in ending it. Patterns persist because powerful interests want them retained. And so to end path dependence is not only to establish new thinking patterns and values, but also to create new power relationships. Implicitly, Wolpe and his colleagues' approach acknowledges this by recognising that different interests are at stake. Given their view of the world, they know that all these parties are not equally powerful. By advocating a process in which all the interests take part, they acknowledge that engagement between those who hold power and those who do not will enable the latter to acquire the power which comes with having a say in decisions. At the same time, they imply that those who resist change command resources which are essential to improvements. And the only way in which differing or conflicting interests can become parties to an agreed approach is through bargaining, even if the word never appears in their writing on the topic. Thus, moving into the future requires compromises between the past and future – which means bargains between those who hold social, economic and cultural power and those who do not.

Their use of Ake's work on democracy may conjure up images not of a hard bargain between contending interests, but of an earnest dialogue between those who benefit from path dependence and those who do not. But Wolpe and his colleagues must know that there are deep differences between the interests and that the parties will not reach agreement by a meeting of minds. They must also recognise that as important as the participating interests are, they are not representative of all the people of South Africa. So the aim is surely not to give all South Africans a say, but to enable interests with a stake in higher education to bargain. This means that interested parties will use power to press 'the other side' into making concessions. As any trade unionist or employer representative knows, this is not a polite exchange of views between friends; it is a battle for advantage. Parties compromise because they know the others command resources which they need. But they use power to obtain the best possible bargain. So while the paper implies that what is required is an earnest discussion between interest groups, in reality what it proposes can be achieved only by a bargaining process which is an exercise of power by contending parties who recognise that they are forced to acknowledge one another's potency.

In this view, whether the topic is higher education or the economy's structure, the most workable means of ending path dependence's negative consequences is negotiated compromise between the holders of power and those who seek it, those with a stake in the patterns of the past and those with an interest in ending them. A similar assumption informs Wolpe's critique of the RDP White Paper issued by the Government of National Unity.[13]

## CRYING PEACE WHEN THERE IS NONE

Wolpe offered an argument for negotiation as a means of changing inherited realities in the last article he wrote before he died. Published in the journal *Transformation* in 1995, this article offered a critical analysis of the RDP White Paper.[14]

The RDP has achieved hallowed status among many critics of the post-1994 government. The programme began, just before the first universal franchise election, as an attempt by the Congress of South African Trade Unions (Cosatu) to hold an ANC-led government to change favoured by the union movement and some in the SACP. They wanted the new order to redistribute power and resources and feared it might not do this unless the ANC was forced to bind itself to this goal.[15] The RDP was meant to do this. The ANC did adopt it before the 1994 election and then, along with partners in the Government of National Unity, issued a White Paper binding the new government to a version of the RDP. But the programme did not remain the project of the new order for long. In 1996, shaken by a sharp fall in the rand in the wake of the appointment of the country's first ANC (and first black) finance minister, Trevor Manuel, the government embraced the Growth, Employment and Redistribution (GEAR) strategy,[16] which was widely criticised by advocates of change as a 'typically "orthodox" macroeconomic policy'.[17] The strategy advocated cutting spending to protect the currency and opening up trade to international companies in the hope of stimulating growth. In the view of its critics on the left, GEAR was an 'ideologically-generated neoliberal policy', which would undermine the goal of redressing the gross inequalities of the apartheid period'.[18]

This criticism implied that, unlike GEAR, the RDP was a recipe for a fundamental break with the past, a view which became deeply held among GEAR's left critics. But the RDP was not the radical charter later myth held it to be. It was the subject of a lengthy internal negotiation within the ANC alliance: repeated drafts were produced before the published version, the sixth draft, was accepted. These negotiations were necessary because, since the ANC's return from exile, its economic policy had undergone significant revision as its strategists (primarily Manuel and Tito Mboweni, who would become governor of the Reserve Bank and finance minister) sought to soften radicalism to ensure that it did not drive away investment. By the time the final version became ANC policy,[19] the RDP was more a fudged reflection of internal ANC compromises than a call to a new order. Before it became government policy, the RDP was again subject to negotiation, which ensured that the White Paper was even less a blueprint for radical change than the already watered-down ANC version.

Given this – and Wolpe's Marxist perspective – we might expect him to reject the White Paper as a betrayal of radical economic change. His language seems to have convinced some of his readers that this was what he was doing. But a closer look reveals that his problems with the document are more complicated. His core critique was that it assumed that agreement existed between the key interests on how the country should be changed. The White Paper constructed a 'consensual model of society'[20] which assumed broad agreement between all significant political and economic forces on what 'fundamental transformation' meant. Wolpe noted that President Nelson Mandela's preface to the White Paper asserted that the 'interdependence of reconstruction and development and growth' were now widely accepted,[21] which meant broad agreement that tackling inequality was as necessary as addressing growth. Other passages also suggest a consensus on priorities. Where consensus had not yet been achieved, the White Paper assumed it could easily be created.[22] Wolpe insisted that this was impossible.

He argued that all societies have limited resources and so they face 'intractable tensions between development and growth'.[23] Social groups will contest which priorities should take precedence. In South Africa, these differences were pronounced because the inequalities created by apartheid ensured a society whose divisions were particularly sharp. For businesses, export-led growth which focused on the needs of foreign markets was a priority; for much of the ANC constituency, meeting basic needs was far more important. This is only one of many points of contention: 'The tensions cannot be eliminated by fiat of the RDP.'[24] While there might be rhetorical agreement between the conflicting interests, this would quickly fall apart when detail was discussed. Wolpe argued that by assuming that everyone agreed on what was needed, the White Paper made conflict harder to manage by hiding it: radically different, even opposed, ideas are 'presented as falling quite unproblematically within the asserted consensus'.[25]Assuming a false consensus might cause more intense conflict between contending interests.

This critique seemed to argue for a shift to the left, particularly since Wolpe observed that 'what the RDP does not put in issue is … the continuity of the capitalist system in South Africa … The encouragement and development of the private sector is stressed.'[26] He contrasts the RDP's approach with that of the SACP's Draft Strategy and Tactics document, which advocates 'the socialisation of the predominant part of the economy'.[27] But Wolpe stresses that it is not his purpose 'to suggest that the RDP should outline a socialist policy'.[28] Rather, he is adding further evidence that agreement has not already been reached on priorities. The SACP document is, in part, a discussion of the RDP. It 'maps out the broad lines for advance' towards a society 'in which democracy will be extended from the political system into the economy, cultural institutions and gender relations ... the most direct route towards socialism in our country'.[29] Wolpe writes that he mentions this perspective 'to point to the contrasting conceptions of "fundamental transformation" which may themselves become a source of contestation in the future'.[30] The purpose is to show how much those who endorse the RDP can differ. For some, it may be a programme to address poverty without changing current power balances; for others, it is the first step on the route to socialism. If differences on what the RDP means are this great, the White Paper's claimed consensus is an illusion.

Why draw attention to the differences in perspective which the White Paper is at pains to deny? If we place this argument next to Wolpe's positions on education change, the reason becomes clear: to make the case for a bargained transition from the old order. By drawing attention to the lack of consensus over 'transformation', Wolpe is pointing out that despite the atmosphere of goodwill at the time, the White Paper is wishing away the reality that there is still strong and powerful support for the survival of the past. His critique could, therefore, be seen as a very early warning that political change does not necessarily bring other changes in its wake.

But as Wolpe points out, he is not arguing that the past can be swept away by the democratic government – by 1995 he had recognised that socialism was not (at least for a considerable period) a realistic possibility.[31] His purpose is to point to the need to recognise contending interests. And since he assumes that the interests which want the past to continue will not be wished away, the only value in pointing to this contention is to imply the need for negotiation which recognises the power of these interests but assumes that bargaining can extract compromises from them. His criticism of the RDP White Paper's claimed consensus does not mean he believes no compromise between contending views is possible. But no compromise will be sought if it is assumed that the interests already agree. His education writings imply that the reason for choosing compromise is that the interests who want the past to continue command resources which are needed if change is to improve lives. Moreover, his discussion of the RDP White Paper suggests another reason why compromise is the only way out of path dependence: the nature of the state.

Wolpe, following Bob Jessop, argued against 'instrumental' understandings of the state – the belief that control of the government automatically meant control of the society. The state does not automatically do what those who control it want, because 'the state structures are themselves the site of political struggles and class conflict'.[32] If a dominated group gained control of the state, it might be able to use the state to change the structure of society. But this was not inevitable. It depended on concrete conditions, one of which is presumably whether private interests are powerful enough to frustrate what the state wants to do. Wolpe applied these insights to the state which was meant to implement the RDP. The White Paper claimed confidently that 'every office of government, from the smallest village council to the largest national department, will have to be restructured to take forward the RDP'.[33] The assumption here is that it was possible for the democratically elected government to shape all instruments of the administration to the needs of an ambitious programme for change. Government strategists were convinced they could do this: the next decade and a half saw repeated attempts to re-engineer the public service to meet the needs of the new order. But the strategists were repeatedly proved wrong. Their attempts constantly encountered obstacles as dynamics within the public service and those between it and society showed that there were great obstacles to change, and attempts to achieve more than government capacity could bear inevitably took it backwards.

To illustrate, during 2012 the ANC, concerned that it might be losing support, recognised that the problem lay in the state's relative inability to meet the needs of many voters. And so the finance minister's budget speech stressed that government planned to rely less on social grants which enable the poor to make their own choices and more on initiating development itself.[34] Other official documents insisted that the government could serve citizens better by increasing the efficiency of government departments, not by building new partnerships with citizens. This assumed that the government machinery needed no help from within society. The plan failed[35] because the government was unable to place its stamp on society. Even more telling was that same speech's promise that the government would embark on an aggressive campaign to root out corruption and increase efficiency. The following year's budget speech admitted ruefully: 'This is a difficult task with too many points of resistance!'[36] The reformers discovered that many of those whose interests were not served by change were powerful enough to frustrate it. Wolpe anticipated this by distrusting the claim that technicians could make the state reshape the world regardless of the power of interests in society.

For Wolpe, there were also competing priorities within government:

> The most cogent reasons for refusing the instrumentalist conception of the state lies in the structural conditions of the state itself … The contradictions and conflicts between … state departments are pervasive. The most public example in South Africa has been the claim of the Defence Department for the expenditure of two billion rands on new corvettes against the demands from the health, housing and education ministries for this sum to be spent on basic needs programmes.[37]

The state was not 'a simple, homogeneous, consensual … instrument which, in a straightforward and unproblematic manner, will carry out'[38] a government programme – in this case the RDP and its many specific initiatives.

Wolpe's colleague and friend Henry Bernstein has noted that 'instrumentalising the state' became 'a motif of the left in South Africa'.[39] Many intellectuals who harboured hopes that the state could change society had moved into government and engaged in policy work. But their hopes that this would give them power to change society had been largely dashed because the state could do little if the balance of power within society was unfavourable to change. Bernstein noted Hein Marais's argument[40] that the post-1994 government had not addressed inequality because the left within the ANC lost the battle to set the agenda. Wolpe, he believed, knew the state could do very little to change the world unless it won the battle in society.

An instrumental view of the state could not build a new order because it assumed that power in society could be wished away if the state became more efficient. For the same reason, the state could not abolish path dependence by introducing programmes. But that did not mean the state could do nothing at all. Wolpe's insights do not mean path dependence cannot be changed. Rather, Wolpe warned that attempts to create new realities need to move beyond the view that the state can be made to do anything as long as the right technical formula is found.

## FORWARD THROUGH COMPROMISE?

Wolpe's work is important for our purposes firstly because, as early as the 1990s, it began to warn of the possibility of path dependence, albeit not in the same words.

This illustrates a point made earlier: that it is possible to recognise path dependence without endorsing North's framework. Wolpe's perspective was very different from North's, and yet Wolpe too anticipated that if the political order changed, but the patterns of the economy and society did not, many realities which the fight against apartheid sought to end would remain. Using path dependence to understand South African society can rely on a variety of perspectives. The proposed remedies might be different, but the diagnosis remains the same. To argue that South Africa's development has been path dependent is not to embrace a particular theory of society.

Perhaps more important is that Wolpe arrived at his insights using a framework which, far more explicitly than North's, places power at the centre. He and his EPU colleagues did not say why they argued that the tension between equity and development should be resolved by a bargain between interest groups, rather than by a seminar or an awareness campaign. But, as suggested earlier, the answer is obvious. Everyone with a stake in higher education needs to be at the table because they all enjoy the power to derail change if they feel it does not serve their needs. This does not mean they are all willing and able to mobilise protest or resistance. Rather, it means that they may act in ways which make it very difficult for the system to achieve its goals (business may not invest or hire graduates; students may not realise their potential even if they do not protest). This is even clearer in Wolpe's critique of the RDP White Paper: the differences which its 'consensual model' conceals are those between holders of power. The survival of the past into the new order can be addressed only by building strategies which recognise power relationships.

This enables us to develop a point made in the discussion of the theory of path dependence – that it should be seen as a product of power. The old order does not survive into the new simply because people are creatures of habit, but because powerful interests have a stake in its continuation and enough power to persuade others to continue acting in the way they act and valuing what they value. This does not mean power is wielded by force alone. If interests which benefit from a particular arrangement are able to convince others that it should continue, they exercise power even if they never seem to force anyone to do anything.

The power which preserves path dependence is similar to that proposed by the Marxist theorist Antonio Gramsci, who argued that dominant classes retain their power by presenting their values as the only 'common sense' view of the world.[41] Similarly, John Gaventa, following Peter Bachrach and Morton Baratz, argues that power can stem from a 'mobilization of bias': 'a set of predominant values, beliefs, rituals, and … "rules of the game" that operate … to the benefit of certain persons and groups at the expense of others'.[42] Power holders may persuade others that they should endorse power holders' values and rules. They may do this through myths and symbols or by communicating information[43] rather than by force. New leaderships may endorse the rules of the old because these rules fit their view of the world, which happened to be the reality in post-1994 South Africa. Those who are convinced may express hostility to the old elite, but continue to value what it values and do what it does.

But recognising that path dependence is a product of power does not necessarily mean that the only way of ending or modifying it is to forcefully overthrow those who benefit from it. Wolpe's work on these questions is valuable also because it implicitly proposes negotiation as the only way of ending or reducing path dependence. To those impatient for a new society, this may well seem an unjustifiable concession to the past and those who benefit from it. If powerful interests are ensuring the preservation of the past, the obvious solution is to use force – the law in this case – to compel those with a stake in the past to accept the future. To rely on negotiation is surely to compromise with the past and ensure that it survives. To insist that path dependence be cast off entirely is to claim that a new order, without any vestiges of the past, can be created.

This view has inspired many attempts to overthrow existing orders and replace them with something entirely new. None of these attempts succeeded.[44] Even if it is agreed that these efforts improved living standards, they did not achieve their stated goal: a society free of force or conflict. The attempts always imposed a new form of force which created new conflicts. The reason, it has been argued, is that they were guided by the belief that conflicts of interest between people are undesirable and that the ideal society is one in which everyone agrees (on the big issues, at least).[45] But the only way to achieve a society in which everyone agrees is to use extreme force to suppress difference. A world without conflicting interests or values would not be Utopia. It would be a world in which self-expression would be so stifled that human life would lose much of its meaning. New orders can change some realities which governed the old, but not all of them.

The voices who want a South Africa which has shaken off all vestiges of the past are not necessarily hoping for the end of all difference (although some do hope for a future in which all the divisions of the past are dissolved in a common nationhood). But there are clear similarities to other Utopias, because to assume that path dependence can simply be removed by the right laws is also to assume that a substantial part of South African reality, which has long been one of division and difference, can be wished away by an act of political will. Wolpe's critique of the RDP White Paper warned against assuming that simply because the formal rules said the past had ended, it really had. If law and policy were to seek to do now what some hoped the constitution (or the RDP) would do then, Wolpe would, were he still alive, be forced to issue the same warning. Declaring that black and white people are equal did not end racism; declaring men and women equal did not end male domination. Governments often complain that powerful interest groups find ways around measures which regulate what they do. Governments can prevent interest groups from doing this only if they recognise the power of these interests. And whatever laws are passed and policies adopted, important elements of the present and the past will remain.

Given understandable frustration at path dependence in South Africa, it is important to stress that this does not mean that the only changes possible are those acceptable to current power holders. It means, rather, that change must be 'rooted in the present' and 'sensitive to context'.[46] The reality of power – and the interests of those who wield it – cannot be dissolved, and important elements will survive into any workable new path. Negotiation partners are forced to recognise that those with whom they negotiate are not going to disappear and that a compromise with their interests is necessary. But as bargaining in the workplace shows, this does not rule out bold demands for change and strategies which aim to achieve it. Efforts to negotiate compromise recognise the need to ensure that the power holders with a stake in path dependence are part of shaping what will replace it, because a strategy which ignores this necessity will create a future which is either not workable or continues the past while claiming to create something entirely new.

Changes in the balance of power are not achieved simply by decreeing that they should be. It follows that if legal or policy change is imposed where those with a stake in a new path lack anything approaching the power of those who want the old to survive, the likeliest outcome is that the past will survive, dressed up as something new. A concrete example was offered much earlier, in Chapter 1: the Labour Relations Act of 1995. This Act was hailed as a sharp departure from apartheid-era labour legislation, but in reality it continued the pattern established in 1924. The effect was not to create something new, but to preserve the old in new packaging. While the Act did solidify worker bargaining rights, it did not alter the balance of power between unions and employers. The same fate is likely to await attempts to end path dependence by imposing a new future on power holders on the assumption that they will comply because they are told to do so.

A more plausible route to changing the power balance is that suggested by the experience of the trade union movement in its formative period: negotiating compromises which reflect a power relationship but also shift it because, where power relations are unequal, compromises reduce the freedom of action of the power holders and so shift power.[47] This view, often denounced as the preference of 'reformists' who want only to tinker with unjust power relationships, has been endorsed by thinkers who advocate revolutionary change. It can be derived not only from Wolpe's writings but from the work of some Marxists. For example, Boris Kagarlitzky argues that a fundamental break with what exists can be achieved through reforms which point the way to a different future because they create 'elements of the new system within the framework of the old society'.[48] John Saul argues that South African realities can be changed only by 'structural reforms' which do not abolish the existing order but challenge its logic by creating new ways of doing things.[49]

The approach of Wolpe and his colleagues was not a surrender to power. A negotiation process which recognises power relationships and seeks to shift them is a far likelier route to change than adopting policies and laws which wish them away. This approach recognises the balance of power while also seeking to change it. It also opens the way to a different perspective on the constitutional negotiations and their failure to end path dependence, referred to at the end of the previous chapter. Wolpe's proposals for a negotiated compromise between educational 'development' and 'equity' were ignored. Two decades later, 'Rhodes Must Fall' and 'Fees Must Fall' highlighted the consequence: a path dependence which meant that the universities were still doing what James Moulder, Wolpe and his colleagues accused them of: trying to reshape black students to fit the academy rather than shaping it to serve students' needs. Also ignored was Wolpe's espousal of an approach to change which recognised the differences of power and interest the RDP White Paper refused to see. This contributed to the quarter-century of path dependence discussed here. The past was perpetuated not because negotiators compromised too much. Rather, while they compromised to rearrange political power, they did not negotiate its social and economic equivalents. The past survives not because negotiators gave away too much in the constitution, but because they did not, as Wolpe and others urged, supplement the political bargaining with similar negotiations on the economy and the society's key institutions.

Given this, the key to moving away from path dependence is a strategy which attends to the neglected business of the early 1990s and negotiates the reforms needed to ensure that political change is complemented by its economic and social equivalents.

# 8

# Towards a Future:
# A Route Out of Path Dependence

Do South African realities a quarter-century after the achievement of formal democracy offer a route out of path dependence?

Before attempting an answer, it is important to emphasise again that change which would benefit South Africans would not end all aspects of path dependence. In 2017, the governing party responded to the prospect of losing its national majority not by finding ways to stay in power whatever the outcome, but by electing the president it believed could prevent this defeat. After the election, the former president is reported to have asked the military to stage a coup on his behalf but was rebuffed.[1] This indicated not only a respect for parliamentary democracy but also perpetuated another form of path dependence for which most South Africans may be grateful: the subordination of the military to civilian rulers. Under apartheid, despite the militarisation of the state by PW Botha, the military did not take over the government. The ANC's guerrilla army, Umkhonto we Sizwe, was always subject to the authority of its elected civilian leadership. Thus, to abolish all vestiges of path dependence might also be to scrap free elections and civilian government. Respect for court rulings, which played a crucial role in thwarting a particular example of 'state capture', is a product of a path dependence which has served citizens well. A core feature of post-1994 South Africa – vigorous freedom of speech for some, and constraints on speech and action for others – is also a feature of path dependence. A fairer social order would not abolish this freedom; it would ensure that free speech is extended to all. Therefore, the question is not whether the society can rid itself of all vestiges of the past, but whether it can begin to move away from those which ensure continued exclusion and inequality, while retaining those elements which protect citizens' rights.

A credible strategy to move away from path dependence would also need to recognise that not everything has remained the same since 1994. This is yet another argument against smashing all vestiges of the past. The first quarter-century of democracy brought social and economic changes which would need to be preserved and extended in a path which differs fundamentally from that which exists now. This applies not just to the changes which have benefited only those able to take advantage of them, such as access to higher education and entry into the professions and business. It also applies to changes which have affected lives at the grassroots, including access to social grants and life-giving medication for those who need it.

## THE DIALECTIC OF CHANGE

These factors, along with those discussed in the previous chapter – the factors which make a negotiated route out of path dependence the only option likely to ensure a different but sustainable future – suggest that movement away from path dependence is likely to be sustainable and to enhance lives only if it rests on a view of change which does not insist that the only way to alter the patterns described here is to impose, without negotiation, a set of laws which will compel those who benefit from the patterns of the past to accept a new direction.

This alternative approach is further justified by an understanding of precisely how path dependence operates. Because it does not preserve rules and values by force, path dependence will not be abolished simply by compelling obedience. If the way decision-makers think about the economy and society still reflects the patterns of the past, these old patterns will continue as they graft themselves onto new rules. The path dependence described here has survived the early introduction of laws compelling white-owned businesses to open up opportunities for their black counterparts and to negotiate ways of ensuring that people deprived by apartheid enjoy access to skilled jobs: Black Economic Empowerment and the Employment Equity Act. Instead of creating new patterns, the result was to absorb most new black entrants into the old rules and values. As noted in chapters 3 and 6, Karl von Holdt points out that black business was incorporated on unfavourable terms which reduced new entrants to dependants. But why was this path taken? It was argued earlier that the path chosen was a product of the core goal of the post-1994 project: the attempt to ensure that what whites enjoyed under apartheid was available to all. So the goal of policy and strategy was not to open up new ways of creating wealth.

The aim was to shoehorn the excluded into the world of the included. (In reality, that meant as many of the excluded as possible since there is not nearly enough room for all). That choice stemmed from a view of the world which will not change automatically if laws are imposed which purport to abolish the vestiges of the past by breaking the power of those who rely on them.

The approach to change recommended by these realities is, ironically, drawn from the Marxist tradition – an irony because Marxism is often associated with a revolutionary seizure of power. A core Marxist view is that change is dialectical. This does not mean the old is simply swept away and replaced by the new. Rather, the new transcends the old: it retains those features of the past which are of value while building something new.[2] Marxist theory does not see the capitalist order, which it expects and hopes will be replaced, as simply exploitative. It also sees it as a source of progress because it develops productive forces which advance humanity. Given this, change from one order to another was not meant to smash every remnant of the past. Since Marxism believes a viable society needs a firm material base, this type of change would not free people – on the contrary, it would ensure that they remained enslaved. This model of change would destroy all the potential capacity of the old order. It would build the new order on the rubble of the old, and no one is likely to enjoy living in a society built on ruins.[3] Similarly, in the early 1990s, Bill Freund argued that a revolution imposed on an inhospitable environment could produce only 'local devastation ... It would at best be a harsh, militantly policed "barracks socialism".'[4]

A total break with the past order cannot provide a better future even if this rupture is possible, which it may well not be since no one has yet succeeded anywhere in building a new order which contained no traces of that which it replaced. The theory of change which flows from this recognition does not judge progress by whether it entirely destroys the old. A rational measure of change is whether it begins to move society away from path dependence, not whether it catapults it into an entirely new reality. This strengthens the argument in the previous chapter that change may be an advance even if it seems to leave the same power holders in charge. John Hoffman has argued that a ban on smoking in public places is a step towards a new society because it forces participants in the market to take into account human health and is thus a contribution towards 'a gradual process of making the exchange process more and more concrete so that real people replace the abstract individuals of the market'.[5] If we apply this approach to path dependence, a recognition by power holders in government and business that people earning a living in township and shack-settlement backyards are economic assets who need nurturing, rather than embarrassments who need to be changed into something else, would constitute progress away from path dependence, even while many of the rules and values analysed here remain.

This view also insists, with Brian Levy's interpretation of Douglass North, that incremental changes to a path-dependent society can produce fundamental change – if the reforms are consciously designed to erode path dependence. A critique of affirmative action measures and the Labour Relations Act may well be that the new reality they sought to create could never be fundamentally new, because they did not stem from an analysis which recognised that the past was embedded in the present and that this needed to change. But if changes are born of a recognition of path dependence, and are consciously designed to weaken it, there is no reason why the result should entrench the past and the power relationships which sustain it. In contemporary South Africa, a coherent attempt to challenge path dependence has not yet been tried. The arguments assembled here insist that if it was, and the goal was explicitly to ensure change towards a more productive path, incremental changes which move the society away from current patterns are a surer route to sustainable change than an attempt to erase all aspects of the present and past.

What approach, then, is likely to place the society on a new path which will begin to reduce economic exclusion and move away from racial hierarchy, while preserving those elements of current reality which are needed to ensure a functioning democracy and steady improvements in the livelihoods and lives of the majority of South Africans?

## THE CENTRALITY OF NEGOTIATION

The previous chapter argued that the route towards a more promising future lies in negotiation between interests which retain a stake in past patterns and those which seek a new approach.

At the outset, it is important to stress that as central as negotiation is, it is not the only element in a credible process of change. Power is the central reason why path dependence persists, but a particular sort of power is at work. John Gaventa discusses a mode of power in which people are persuaded by those who wield it to accept ways of thinking and doing which are not in their interests: they agree to their own enslavement.[6] This is not the power which underpins South African path dependence. The new elite is willing to fight to protect the market economy in its current form not because it is deluded, but because the market offers it benefits – from a weekly wage for some, through to senior roles in corporations for others. The belief that domination will end only when everyone has what the dominators had may commit elites to unattainable goals, but it required no manipulation from the old elite to persuade the new one to respond in this way. One of its consequences – the belief that people earning a living in shack settlements and backyards are an embarrassment – may hold back economic progress. But it is not the response of slaves embracing values which keep them in bondage. It is the perspective of elites committed to a project which works for them but for no one else, not because the elites are looking for reasons to dominate, but because it makes sense of their experience and the reality they perceive.

This cannot be changed by negotiation alone. If the society was neatly divided into those whose power depended on ensuring that this vision remained dominant and those whose prospects depended on ending it, negotiation might be the only remedy, for it is the most appropriate process to channel conflicts between power holders and those over whom they wield power. But the society is not divided this neatly. Some of the loudest calls for change emanate from interests who want the current reality to persist, albeit with new names and faces in dominant roles. Those who have the clearest interest in ending economic exclusion are, precisely because they are excluded, unorganised and unheard. And so a significant element in a strategy to begin weakening path dependence would be a campaign to change attitudes and win support for the view that the current trajectory stunts growth and that this is why the country lags behind peer economies.[7] Such a campaign would not substitute for negotiation but would complement it.

Path dependence may reflect power relations, but that does not necessarily mean it efficiently serves the elites who perpetuate it. The growth-stunting effects of path dependence may harm the interests of poor and working people far more than the interests of the elites. But the economic effects of path dependence have become debilitating, with negative consequences for the elites too. This is why the limits of the current growth path are widely recognised. But its roots in path dependence are not. Elites respond by blaming not their own attachment to past patterns, but the actions and attitudes of others, assuming that progress is possible only when everyone adopts their view of the world. The standard business response to poor growth is to place the blame on the government[8] or, on occasion, trade unions.[9] Government leadership used to blame business but, given its concern to attract private investment, now mostly blames the previous administration.[10] Trade unions blame business and the government.[11] So none of the key economic actors takes responsibility for their own role, and none recognises that the root of the problem is a path dependence which shapes the way in which the key actors, as well as others, see their roles. None, therefore, recognises the need to change their approach to tackle the problems of which they complain. Nor do they recognise the need to negotiate structural changes which address path dependence.

An example of a recognition that much is amiss which does not acknowledge the roots of the problem is Mcebisi Jonas's book on the country's options, *After Dawn: Hope After State Capture*. The book contains a foreword by Cyril Ramaphosa, which suggests that it reflects a strain in mainstream thinking. As noted previously, in Chapter 6, Jonas observed that the negotiated settlement resulted from a bargain which held the society together for some time. This bargain, he believes, 'is no longer fit for South Africa's prosperity purposes'.[12] The recognition that the problem is rooted in a bargain which gave all the key actors something is an important departure because it holds all key interests responsible. For Jonas, the bargain has four elements. It 'safeguarded the interests of the existing (largely white) economic elite essentially by ensuring that South Africa did not nationalise'; the black elite was 'placated ... primarily through state employment and rents in the form of preferential ownership and procurement schemes'; labour was 'brought on board' by 'putting in place a regime of protective labour laws'; and those who were 'outside the bargain looking in were placated with the rolling out of a comprehensive welfare system for the poorest'.[13] Jonas argues that the bargain is 'unravelling'. Growth remains low, inequality high and ownership highly concentrated.[14] So the bargain does not offer business the returns it seeks, and it has not fundamentally changed racial ownership patterns or addressed inequality and exclusion.

Jonas's analysis describes an important reality: although all of the parties were frustrated by aspects of the bargain, all found in it elements which advanced their interests. This explains why they have continued to cling to the bargain despite the frustrations. To the disappointment of conspiracy theorists, the terms of the compromise were not agreed at secret meetings – rather, they flowed from assumptions each organised interest group made about the others. The government never seriously considered imposing severe constraints on business; the affluent made no serious attempt to mobilise opposition to Black Economic Empowerment (choosing rather to use it strategically) or against an anti-poverty programme. Organised labour was willing to work within its own unstated bargain with the ANC, in which the political organisation set economic policy but ensured that unions remained protected by labour law. Union leadership complained about economic policy but did not do much about it as long as the labour protections remained. So the bargain did not spring from a secret pact, or the constitutional settlement, which does not require that social grants be extended to millions or that the ANC's labour ally cede to the government control over economic policy. Rather, the bargain was a product of how social actors saw their strategic options. They needed no secret deals to settle for their portion of the bargain.

It is possible to quibble with details of Jonas's description. All the parties were dissatisfied with the bargain to some degree. The affluent presumably wanted more than the knowledge that the government would not seize their property. Initially, they wanted stability – a look at company annual reports in the 1980s shows that social conflict was making profit-making activity very difficult. This they received. But they have remained uneasy, for rooted deep in the psyche of the South African middle class and affluent is the fear that the society is always a hair's breadth from violent upheaval, despite the absence of evidence for this dread. The continuation of social protest, although it rarely affects the lives of economic power holders, may encourage the fear that this part of the bargain is under threat. They also wanted latitude to continue growing their wealth. While their property rights were never threatened, growth began to dwindle from 2008. As Von Holdt's discussion of 'class formation' shows, some in the black elite wanted more than share options and seats on boards (although these were important contributors to reducing elite conflict). They wanted a role in the economy which they have not achieved, hence both corruption and middle-class anger. Labour surely wanted rising incomes and opportunities, not simply the right to bargain for them, which is why unions have complained about the bargain even if they have done nothing to opt out of it. And although the excluded do value social grants, most wanted economic inclusion. Jonas's analysis may underestimate the degree to which none of the parties to the bargain received enough of what they wanted, which is why it faces stress, despite the fact that all the parties derive benefit from it.

But Jonas is right that the post-1994 order has been held together by the reality that all the key organised actors and much of the citizenry received enough from the compromises which are made every day to ensure that they found the bargain worth preserving (even if some had no say in it). He is also correct to argue that this bargain is fraying at the edges and is in need of revision, a reality which may be deepened by the effects of Covid-19. This is so not only because student protesters, much of the black middle class, and township residents who have been protesting in the streets for much of the past four decades insist, explicitly or implicitly, that the bargain is not working for them. The bargain is, as Jonas points out, now very obviously frustrating just about everyone. The affluent are as safe from nationalisation as ever, but frustration with weak growth weighs heavily on confidence.[15] The black political elite is riven by factionalism prompted partly by competition for limited opportunities, while much of the black middle class is angry. Trade union leadership may be quiescent because it has become part of the elite it was meant to curb;

yet members remain militant,[16] not least because their pay packets are meant to offer a lifeline to family who cannot find formal work and, in some cases, a means to acquire the consumer goods which bring status. And while the excluded are less immediately affected by changes in the economy as long as grants are maintained (they cannot lose jobs since they have none), continuing local protests are at least partly fuelled by the consequences of exclusion.

Given these realities, the logical consequence of Jonas's analysis would surely be that the bargain must be replaced by a new one. A bargain was needed because a new order could not be imposed on any of the interests, who depend on each other to some degree. Unless something has changed to make it no longer necessary to secure the support of all the key interests, this must still be so. Jonas does not say a bargain is no longer needed; on the contrary, he refers to the need for a 'social compact', an agreement between the key economic actors. This would presumably not be needed if it was not still essential to secure enough consent to ensure that those with the capacity to derail a new path are willing at least to tolerate it.

This makes it all the more remarkable that, despite ending his book with a chapter entitled 'Getting the Politics Right', Jonas does not discuss how a new bargain would be reached and what it might entail. His conclusions reveal that despite the 'social contract' references, he isn't pinning his hopes on a new bargain at all. Instead, he advocates a 'new consensus'[17] to be achieved by 'constructive disruption'[18] which will produce new 'national obsessions'.[19] Stripped of the management language, a new set of ideas – those outlined in the book, which is a wish list of desired changes – will be imposed on the rest of society so successfully that everyone will not only endorse the new approach but become obsessed by it. The 'constructive disruptors' are, of course, those like himself who will unsettle the thinking of everyone else and place them on a new path. Jonas never says how this will be achieved – which is not surprising, since it cannot be achieved. The bulk of his proposals are consistent with pro-market thinking and so will be resisted by unions (who may be weak but are still the representatives of many people) and a significant slice of public opinion. He has little to say about the racial dynamics which anger the black middle class and so is unlikely to find much support from the most vocal and influential black interest group. Some of his proposals do reflect his activist background and advocate more emphasis on poverty and exclusion. These will not be endorsed by conservative interests. And so there will be no 'new consensus' no matter how constructive the disruption may be. This does not mean that none of the changes he (or anyone else) recommends will be accepted. But given the society's divisions, there is no set of proposals which can attract consensus. Some of these ideas might be accepted in negotiations in which parties concede some ground to get some of what they want, but only in altered form, since negotiation always entails compromise.

Jonas's view of economic change is precisely the 'consensual model' which Wolpe criticised. The Reconstruction and Development Programme (RDP) White Paper assumed that a consensus had already been achieved, while Jonas believes one is possible in the future. Both make the mistake criticised by Wolpe: they assume that in a deeply divided society with high levels of inequality, it is possible to secure consensus in support of particular ideas simply because, in the view of those who advocate them, they are logical or moral. If that were so, the negotiations of the 1990s would not have been needed. The National Party and its allies' racial perspective could have been conquered by a careful required reading of the writings of Steve Biko and Chief Albert Luthuli, while the economic radicalism which threatened a settlement could have been dissolved by a diet of World Bank and International Monetary Fund research papers. In reality, the problem was not a lack of knowledge, but interests and values which were starkly different and likely to remain so whatever books and papers the parties read unless they were able to negotiate compromises.

Jonas's book indicates the opportunities and constraints which face a negotiated alternative to path dependence. It is no accident that his book is endorsed by Ramaphosa, because it expresses what is probably the dominant position among the political elites. Current realities are agreed to fall short of what the society needs. But the antidote is found not in hard bargaining but in persuading others that a particular approach is required. When adopted by the government, it takes a particular form – that criticised by Wolpe a year after democracy's arrival. Buffeted between the need to secure investment and the pressures for change in an unequal society, the government falls back on the 'consensus model'. It assumes that despite deep social divisions and the very different perspectives they produce, a common patriotism and goodwill can prompt agreement on goals. This is a deep-rooted view in South Africa: it tends to surface particularly at moments of sporting success, which are said to show that South Africans can achieve anything if they realise how much unites them.[20] Inevitably, the call to 'submerge differences' is, like Jonas's book, an expectation that, in the pursuit of national unity, people will accept ideas which run counter to their understanding of their interests.[21] The concrete result, when the government is directing the process, is that the key interests agree on vague principles and then either interpret them in a way consistent with their interests – which diverge from what the commitment is meant to achieve – or simply ignore them.

This 'consensual model' has produced two related strategies which were pursued by the government of Thabo Mbeki and have been revived by the

Ramaphosa administration. For the achievement of goals which require the support of social interests, it relies on the summit, an event at which the interests are expected to agree to a common programme or course of action. Summits, according to Ramaphosa, aim to 'align the efforts of every sector and every stakeholder' towards a common social goal.[22] As Jonas's book suggests, a core aim of this approach is the achievement of a 'social compact' in which the interests agree to a joint course of action. In his June 2019 State of the Nation Address, Ramaphosa said the compact his government sought would require it to make a commitment to the country's human potential. In return, he asked business 'to consider the country's national strategic objectives and social considerations' and urged labour to 'advance the interests of workers while, at the same time, promoting the sustainability of businesses and the creation of jobs'. Finally, 'civil society needs to continue to play its role in holding government to account but must also join us in practical actions to attain our common goals'.[23] He neglected to say how the government planned to persuade the other parties to do what it believes is needed (or, indeed, what some of the vague and very broad phrases actually require the parties to do).

This strategy will not negotiate a way out of path dependence. The divisions which give some interests a stake in the past, and others a need to seek new paths, run deep and are firmly embedded in experience. The much-lamented lack of trust between business and government[24] (and between labour and business) reflects the fact that they were on opposite sides of the apartheid divide. It is a product of differing experiences and identities which have been a central reality for decades, if not centuries. Differences this deep cannot be resolved by an event which lasts two or three days even if it is preceded by preparatory discussions between the key interests aimed at reaching a consensus.

This is why the summits have failed to trigger substantial changes, and are routinely denounced as 'talk shops' in the media (and why officials feel compelled to insist that they are nothing of the sort).[25] They either commit the parties to generalities so vague that they can happily endorse them without compromising any of their interests – as Ramaphosa's address quoted above does – or parties fail to implement the commitments if they do require them to change. The differences persist, but the parties do not wish to seem lacking in patriotism. Therefore they sign on to commitments which those on whose behalf they make them are unwilling to embrace. This does not mean the differences are unbridgeable – but they can be reconciled only by negotiation over a much longer period during which the parties are likely to test their respective strength before reaching compromises that reflect the balance of power between them. Unlike the 'consensus model', the departure point for such negotiation does not wish difference away. And so it opens the way to bargaining and compromise.

A social compact – an agreement between interest groups – could be the product of a bargaining process which acknowledges difference. But despite much talk of a compact in South Africa during democracy's first quarter-century, none is in sight, because the search for one assumes a far greater capacity for agreement than is possible given the realities discussed here. This too was anticipated in the early days of democracy. Several years into the new order, Jeremy Baskin, a student of and participant in the labour movement, argued that 'corporatism' – structured, binding agreements between government, labour and business (in effect a social compact) – may not be possible in democratic South Africa because none of the parties could ensure that their constituencies would comply with agreements of this sort. He suggested that a more realistic goal was 'concertation': 'an institutional role for interest organisations (mainly economic) in the formulation and implementation/regulation of state policy'. He added: 'In practice, this involves not one event or institution, but a web of collaborative interchanges between state, labour and capital.'[26] In one respect, this lowers the bar – all that is required is that the interests enjoy a say and engage with each other. In another, it raises it by suggesting, in place of a single agreement, a 'web of interchanges', a range of engagements. There is no reason why these should not produce agreements on some issues. A grand compromise is unlikely given the differences, but bargains on specifics have been struck in particular industries and could be achieved again. Over time, small bargains could pave the way for bigger ones, or a succession of 'small' bargains would begin to change the country's development path.

Instead of envisioning a single document binding the interests to move the country from its current dependent path, it is more appropriate to think of a process of engagement, happening at a variety of levels (particular industries or professions or regions), in which parties seek compromises from others and offer their own in return. They could produce agreements which reflect the balance of power in each case. The result would be not a 'social compact', but a series of specific agreements which would significantly change the economy and society and begin to lead it away from path dependence. How might this process begin?

## A WAY FORWARD?

Only hard bargaining between key interests can move the country from path dependence. But this is not possible unless the parties agree that change – and compromise – are needed. This is why it is possible and necessary to challenge the thinking of key interests to prod them to begin to bargain. It follows that any attempt to begin movement away from path dependence must begin with a strategy designed to ensure that bargaining begins because the key interests recognise the need for it.

To recognise that South Africa's post-1994 development has been path dependent is also to challenge the claim that its problems are a consequence of government actions alone. The government elected in 1994 could hardly have created patterns which began well before then; to blame it alone is to ignore history. The preference of private economic interests for the patterns of the past cannot be a consequence of government action. But this does not mean that the government has no role in maintaining path dependence and no power to begin moving the country towards a new course. Path dependence means that the post-1994 political elite has either failed to chart a new path or has not tried. Removing the vestiges of apartheid and the colonialism which preceded it is the core stated goal of the new order's political leadership. Since many of these realities remain, the leadership has not achieved what it promised. Its assumption that the goal of the new order was to extend the benefits of minority privilege to everyone makes the political elite a willing participant in the persistence of the past.

At no point since majority rule was achieved has the governing party developed a strategy clearly designed to end path dependence. While mythology assumes that the RDP was the planned antidote, it was not a coherent plan for a new order. Since then, the government has released policies and programmes designed to stimulate growth and development, but none has broken significantly with past patterns. Even the most innovative-sounding – the attempt to fashion South Africa as a developmental state[27] – was arguably a modified attempt to apply one of the assumptions which underpinned the apartheid era: that the state could be a key motor of a development path which would enable a group excluded from economic power to dominate an economy in which private capital remained central.[28] While the post-1994 government did not create path dependence, it made no serious attempt to dismantle it.

This does not necessarily mean that the government failed because, as left critics argue, it did not impose change. The previous chapter has tried to show why simply imposing change would have kept the past alive in a new guise. A viable strategy for change would have begun by recognising the importance of inherited power, not wishing it away. To recognise that power is not to assume that it must operate unchallenged. It is, rather, to build a strategy for change on an acknowledgement of reality. This would have meant a negotiation strategy which sought to change patterns that lock in long-standing power relationships by compromising with those interests whose resources remain essential to a workable development path. The failure to generate that strategy explains why the core feature of the first quarter-century of democracy has been the attempt to operate a new political order in unchanged economic and social patterns.

The obvious way for the government to address this failure is to do now what it should have done then: initiate bargaining which can move the society away from path dependence. It is hard to see how this could occur without government initiative. For over four decades, business's contribution to change has been not to initiate it but to adapt to it. Business is, therefore, likely to engage in negotiation if pressed to do so, but will not of its own accord seek to remove barriers which sustain economic exclusion. Labour is so weakened by the impact of path dependence that it is in no position to initiate this process even if it wanted to, and it is not clear that it does. It has been turned by developments since 1994 from a movement which initiated change to one whose leaders simply react to it. So a negotiation process will not begin unless the government takes responsibility for prodding the other parties to participate.

To do that, the government would need to move away from the 'consensus model' and the reliance on summits and social compacts it produces. The university fees and land disputes have shown that compromise in post-1994 South Africa is triggered by the perception of crisis, and that this occurs when interests who want change make demands which seem to threaten the status quo, triggering a compromise. If, therefore, the government wants to initiate a negotiation process, it would need to concentrate the minds of interests wedded to path dependence by announcing a programme for fundamental change and inviting those affected by it to respond. Only this is likely to inject the urgency necessary to stimulate bargaining. It presents an important challenge to the government: to produce proposals which recognise existing power balances but also break with path dependence. Even if the process does not rise to that challenge, bargaining may still produce workable alternatives to path dependence once it begins. None of this can happen, however, unless the government begins the process by saying what it wants.

Making proposals for change and inviting others to respond is itself an invitation to negotiation, just as the fees and land disputes have been. As long as key interests are adjusting their assessments of what they are willing to accept in the light of what other interests want, a negotiation has begun. This process cannot be designed to end at a particular time. It will, if it operates effectively, produce a series of agreement and shifts in policy when the parties are able to agree on them, and will continue until the parties are happy enough with the negotiated arrangements not to seek alternatives.

The role of citizens in this process is to press the government to initiate the nego-tiations. Change occurs when there is pressure for it – especially in South Africa. It also occurs when the key interests develop a sense of crisis, which does not mean that they become even more alarmed than media headlines already are, but that they recognise that a new departure is needed. This has occurred before in South Africa. In the late 1980s and the early 1990s, the sense of crisis was palpable; all the key interests recognised that change was necessary and a loud debate (in effect, an informal negotiation) began on which changes were needed. Then, the pressure for change was clear. It is likely to become clear again only when the public debate begins to recognise that the root of South Africa's malaise is not that too much has changed but that not enough has, and that all the power holders, private and public, keep alive patterns which need to change. It would be revived only if the principal voices in the debate press the key interests to recognise that the country will not be able to achieve anything like its potential as long as ways of doing and thinking exclude most people from the mainstream economy. The essential step in begin-ning the process is public pressure on the government to spell out its proposals for change, and to invite other interests to respond with their own ideas.

To some, this will seem impossible. But so did a negotiated end to apartheid. Given sufficient public pressure, a negotiation process that produces an economy and society in which all members of society have a stake, and in which policy and practice are no longer grounded in the assumptions of the past, is no less possible than a political order in which all citizens enjoy the same formal rights.

# NOTES

EPIGRAPH

William Faulkner *Requiem for a Nun* New York, Vintage Books, 1975, p. 80

INTRODUCTION

1   Steven Friedman *Understanding Reform* Johannesburg, South African Institute of Race Relations, 1986
2   Ronelle Burger, Cindy Lee Steenekamp, Asmus Zoch and Servaas van der Berg *The Middle Class in Contemporary South Africa: Comparing Rival Approaches* Working Paper No. 11/2014, Department of Economics, University of Stellenbosch, 25 May 2017
3   Haroon Bhorat and Carlene van der Westhuizen *Poverty, Inequality and the Nature of Economic Growth in South Africa* Development Policy Research Unit Working Paper No. 12/151, University of Cape Town, November 2012
4   South African Social Security Agency (SASSA) *A Statistical Summary of Social Grants in South Africa* Fact Sheet No. 21, December 2018
5   Avert *HIV and AIDS in South Africa* January 2019 https://www.avert.org/professionals/hiv-around-world/sub-saharan-africa/south-africa
6   World Bank Group *An Incomplete Transition: Overcoming the Legacy of Exclusion in South Africa* Systematic Country Diagnostic, World Bank, Washington DC, 2018
7   Rocco Zizzamia, Simone Schotte, Murray Leibbrandt and Vimal Ranchhod *Vulnerability and the Middle Class in South Africa* Southern Africa Labour and Development Research Unit, University of Cape Town, 2016
8   Aubrey Matshiqi 'Why Manuel is right and wrong about Manyi's "racism"' *Business Day* 8 March 2011 http://www.businessday.co.za/articles/Content.aspx?id=136509
9   Trevor Manuel 'Proof of how much we have done – and must still do' *Business Day* 21 October 2012
10  Khehla Shubane and Mark Shaw *Tomorrow's Foundations? Forums as the Second Level of a Negotiated Transition in South Africa* Research Report No. 33, Centre for Policy Studies, Johannesburg, 1993
11  Douglass C North *Institutions, Institutional Change and Economic Performance* Cambridge, Cambridge University Press, 1990

12    Scott E Page 'Path dependence' *Quarterly Journal of Political Science* Vol. 1, No. 1, 2006, pp. 87–115

13    Bonang Mohale, chair Bidvest, interviewed on Newzroom Afrika, 30 December 2019

14    Abhijit Banerjee, Sebastian Galiani, Jim Levinsohn, Zoë McLaren and Ingrid Woolard *Why Has Unemployment Risen in the New South Africa?* National Bureau of Economic Research Working Paper No. 13167, NBER, Cambridge MA, June 2007

## CHAPTER 1

1    Mpumelelo Mkhabela 'Reckless Zuma leaves a country in tatters' *News24* 15 December 2017 https://www.news24.com/Columnists/Mpumelelo_Mkhabela/reckless-zuma-leaves-a-country-in-tatters-20171215

2    Zingisa Mvumvu 'Voters like Cyril Ramaphosa more than they like the ANC: Survey' *TimesLive* 24 February 2019 https://www.timeslive.co.za/politics/2019-02-24-voters-like-cyril-ramaphosa-more-than-they-like-the-anc-survey/

3    Maarten Mittner 'Scary move points to recession' *Finweek* 11 April 2019 https://www.fin24.com/Finweek/Investment/scary-move-points-to-recession-20190411

4    Sarah Smit 'Unemployment rate at 29% – Stats SA' *Mail and Guardian* 30 July 2019 https://mg.co.za/article/2019-07-30-unemployment-rate-at-29-statssa

5    Staff writer 'State-owned Denel unable to pay full salaries to staff' *Business Report* 25 June 2019 https://www.iol.co.za/business-report/economy/state-owned-denel-unable-to-pay-full-salaries-to-staff-27540180

6    Antony Sguazzin and Colleen Goko 'Eskom gets bailout funding. Now it needs a rescue plan' *Bloomberg News* 26 July 2019 https://www.fin24.com/Economy/Eskom/eskom-gets-bailout-funding-now-it-needs-a-rescue-plan-20190726

7    Mikhail Moosa 'Corruption rife throughout our civil service' *Mail and Guardian* 18 April 2019 https://mg.co.za/article/2019-04-18-00-corruption-rife-throughout-our-civil-service

8    Max du Preez 'Unproductive, incompetent state at heart of SA's problems' *News24* 21 August 2018 https://www.news24.com/Columnists/MaxduPreez/unproductive-incompetent-state-at-heart-of-sas-problems-20180821

9    Nompumelelo Runji 'Ramaphosa tightening his grip on control of government' *Sowetan* 14 February 2019 https://www.sowetanlive.co.za/opinion/columnists/2019-02-14-ramaphosa-tightening-his-grip-on-control-of-government/

10    Carol Paton 'Ramaphosa has to set the agenda' *Business Day* 13 August 2019

11    Daniel Friedman 'Ramaphosa is no different to Zuma and his actions are "illegal, period!" – Ndlozi' *The Citizen* 2 July 2019 https://citizen.co.za/news/south-africa/social-media/2157441/ramaphosa-is-no-different-to-zuma-and-his-actions-are-illegal-period-ndlozi/

12    Simnikiwe Hlatshaneni 'Eskom, workers' strike plunge SA into darkness' *The Citizen* 15 June 2018 https://citizen.co.za/news/south-africa/1954517/eskom-workers-strike-plunge-sa-into-darkness/

13    For a list, see Oscar van Heerden 'More haste, less speed, Mr President: Slow but steady wins the race' *Daily Maverick* 14 August 2019 https://www.dailymaverick.co.za/opinionista/2019-08-14-more-haste-less-speed-mr-president-slow-but-steady-wins-the-race/?fbclid=IwAR206NcEGq3eRG9govEFWvQGUPYgCYILkahfSHbShPSKH3_PQDGN7b9xVBM

14  Dudley Horner 'African labour representation up to 1975' in Johann Maree (ed.) *The Independent Trade Unions 1974–1984: Ten Years of the South African Labour Bulletin* Johannesburg, Ravan Press, 1987, pp. 124–137, p. 125

15  Ian Goldin *The Poverty of Coloured Labour Preference: Economics and Ideology in the Western Cape* Southern Africa Labour and Development Research Unit Working Paper No. 59, SALDRU, Cape Town, January 1984 http://opensaldru.uct.ac.za/bitstream/handle/11090/563/1984_goldin_swp59.pdf?sequence=1

16  Statistics South Africa 'Who is most likely to be affected by long-term unemployment?' 30 October 2018 http://www.statssa.gov.za/?p=11688#:~:text=The%20most%20affected%20persons%20were,than%20it%20affects%20the%20adults

17  Centraal Bureau voor de Statistiek (CBS) 'Unemployment in 1930s unprecedentedly high' 17 March 2009 https://www.cbs.nl/en-gb/news/2009/12/unemployment-in-1930s-unprecedentedly-high

18  Statistics South Africa/The World Bank *Overcoming Poverty and Inequality in South Africa: An Assessment of Drivers, Constraints and Opportunities* Washington DC, The World Bank, 2018, p. 7

19  Statistics South Africa/World Bank *Overcoming Poverty* p. 12

20  Statistics South Africa/World Bank *Overcoming Poverty* p. 45

21  Manuel 'Proof of how much we have done'

22  Haroon Bhorat, Carlene van der Westhuizen and Derek Yu *The Silent Success: Delivery of Public Assets Since Democracy* Development Policy Research Unit Working Paper No. 201403, University of Cape Town, July 2014

23  Johannesburg Stock Exchange (JSE) *JSE Presents Findings on Black Ownership on the JSE* 2 September 2010 http://ir.jse.co.za/news-releases/news-release-details/jse-presents-findings-black-ownership-jse

24  Development Network Africa *Professional Services in South Africa: Accounting, Engineering and Law* 25 January 2009 http://www.dnaeconomics.com/assets/Usegareth/SA_Professional_Services.pdf

25  Haroon Bhorat, Carlene van der Westhuizen and Toughedah Jacobs *Income and Non-Income Inequality in Post-Apartheid South Africa: What Are the Drivers and Possible Policy Interventions?* Development Policy Research Unit Working Paper No. 09/138, University of Cape Town, August 2009, p. 4

26  Statistics South Africa 'Economy slips into recession' 3 March 2020 http://www.statssa.gov.za/?p=13049

27  Statistics South Africa/The World Bank *Overcoming Poverty* p. 10

28  Dani Rodrik *The New Global Economy and Developing Countries: Making Openness Work* Washington DC, Overseas Development Council, 1999

29  *Fin24* 'Black ownership dropped in JSE-listed companies – report' 3 August 2018 https://www.fin24.com/Economy/black-ownership-dropped-in-jse-listed-companies-report-20180803

30  *BusinessTech* 'ANC's employment rhetoric – a timeline' 15 January 2014 https://businesstech.co.za/news/government/51660/ancs-employment-rhetoric-a-timeline/

31  *Fin24* 'Black ownership'

32  Neva Makgetla 'Big business's hold on economic power spawns pervasive inequality' *Business Day* 23 October 2018 https://www.businesslive.co.za/bd/opinion/columnists/2018-10-23-neva-makgetla-big-businesss-hold-on-economic-power-spawns-pervasive-inequality/

33  Thando Vilikazi 'Barriers to entry and inclusive growth: A case study of the liquid fuel wholesale industry' Centre for Competition, Regulation and Economic Development (CCRED), University of Johannesburg, May 2017 http://www.energy.gov.za/files/petroleum-sector-transformation-workshop/Barriers-to-entry-and-inclusive-growth-liquid-fuel-wholesale-industry-CCRED.pdf

34  Makgetla 'Big business's hold'

35  Edward Webster 'The promise and the possibility: South Africa's contested industrial relations path' *Transformation* 81/82, 2013, pp. 208–235, p. 211

36  Webster 'The promise and the possibility' pp. 216–219

37  *Fin24* 'SARB: Unsecured lending on the rise' 28 June 2013 http://www.fin24.com/Debt/News/Sarb-Unsecured-lending-on-the-rise-20130628

38  South Africa.info 'South Africa improves access to services' 30 October 2012 http://www.southafrica.info/about/social/census-301012b.htm#.UxzX685_Fec

39  Ryno Schutte and Janine van der Post '"I felt sorry for the victims but I had a job to do" – Former hijackers reveal all, here's how you can protect yourself in SA' *Wheels24* 29 August 2018 https://www.wheels24.co.za/News/Guides_and_Lists/i-felt-sorry-for-the-victims-but-i-had-a-job-to-do-former-hijackers-reveal-all-heres-how-you-can-protect-yourself-in-sa-20180829

40  Ed Stoddard and Jan Harvey 'S Africa miners' strike to drive up platinum over time' Reuters 18 February 2014 https://www.reuters.com/article/safrica-strikes-prices/safrica-miners-strike-to-drive-up-platinum-over-time-idUSL6N0LN2VG20140218

41  Sakhela Buhlungu quoted in Steven Friedman and Sharon Groenmeyer 'A nightmare on the brain of the living? The endurance and limits of the collective bargaining regime' *Transformation* 91, 2016, pp. 63–83, p. 67

42  David Lipton 'Bridging South Africa's economic divide' Speech at University of the Witwatersrand, Johannesburg, International Monetary Fund, 19 July 2016 https://www.imf.org/en/News/Articles/2016/07/18/20/15/SP071916-Bridging-South-Africas-Economic-Divide

43  David Yudelman *The Emergence of Modern South Africa: State, Capital and the Incorporation of Organized Labor on the South African Gold Fields, 1902–1939* Cape Town, David Philip, 1984

44  Jan Cronje 'Africa is "new frontier of economic growth", Ramaphosa tells G7 leaders' *Fin24* 26 August 2019 https://www.fin24.com/Economy/South-Africa/africa-is-new-frontier-of-economic-growth-ramaphosa-tells-g7-leaders-20190826

45  National Treasury 'Economic overview' *2018 Budget Review* chapter 2, 2018 http://www.treasury.gov.za/documents/national%20budget/2018/review/Chapter%202.pdf

46  Siphelele Dludla 'Retail sales remain muted with consumers under pressure' *Business Report* 19 September 2019 https://www.iol.co.za/business-report/economy/retail-sales-remain-muted-with-consumers-under-pressure-33244162

47  Department of Planning, Monitoring and Evaluation, Presidency (DPME) *Twenty Year Review South Africa 1994–2014* 2014, p. 105

48  Statistics South Africa/The World Bank *Overcoming Poverty* p. 20

49  Statistics South Africa/The World Bank *Overcoming Poverty* p. 10

50  Department of Planning, Monitoring and Evaluation, Presidency (DPME) *Twenty Year Review South Africa 1994–2014: Background Paper: Income, Poverty and Inequality* 2014, p. 15

51  Thanthi Mthanti 'Systemic racism behind South Africa's failure to transform its economy' *The Conversation* 31 January 2017 https://theconversation.com/systemic-racism-behind-south-africas-failure-to-transform-its-economy-71499

52  Carin Smith 'Ramaphosa: Growing black anger about "lackadaisical" whites with power' *Fin24* 13 December 2018 https://www.fin24.com/Economy/ramaphosa-growing-black-anger-about-lackadaisical-whites-with-power-20181213

53  Geraldine Martin and Kevin Durrheim 'Racial recruitment in post-apartheid South Africa: Dilemmas of private recruitment agencies' *Psychology in Society* Vol. 33, 2006, pp. 1–15

54  Karl von Holdt 'South Africa: The transition to violent democracy' *Review of African Political Economy* Vol. 40, No. 138, 2013, pp. 589–604

55  Hennie van Vuuren *Apartheid, Guns and Money: A Tale of Profit* Auckland Park, Jacana Media, 2017

56  Valencia Talane 'Bosasa handouts and Zuma's coughing fits: One year of testimony at Zondo Commission' *Independent Online* 20 August 2019 https://www.iol.co.za/news/opinion/bosasa-handouts-and-zumas-coughing-fits-one-year-of-testimony-at-zondo-commission-30952078

57  Peter Alexander, Thapelo Lekgowa, Botsang Mmope, Luke Sinwell and Bongani Xezwi *Marikana: A View from the Mountain and a Case to Answer* Auckland Park, Jacana Media, 2012

58  IG Farlam, PD Hemraj and BR Tokota *Marikana Commission of Inquiry: Report on Matters of Public, National and International Concern Arising Out of the Tragic Incidents at the Lonmin Mine in Marikana, in the North West Province* 31 March 2105 https://www.sahrc.org.za/home/21/files/marikana-report-1.pdf

59  Karl von Holdt *The Political Economy of Corruption: Elite-Formation, Factions and Violence* Society, Politics and Work Institute Working Paper No. 10, University of the Witwatersrand, February 2019, p. 11

60  Staff writer 'Jonas tells the inside story of Nhlanhla Nene's firing' *Business Day* 24 August 2018 https://www.businesslive.co.za/bd/national/2018-08-24-jonas-tells-the-inside-story-of-nhlanhla-nenes-firing/

61  Ahmed Areff 'Timeline: How South Africa got three finance ministers in four days' *News24* 14 December 2015 https://www.news24.com/SouthAfrica/News/timeline-how-south-africa-got-three-finance-ministers-in-four-days-20151214

62  Steven Friedman 'Whose freedom? South Africa's press, middle-class bias and the threat of control' *Ecquid Novi* Vol. 32, No. 2, 2011, pp. 106–121

63  SAFM Radio *Morning Live* April 2008

64  Julian May *Poverty and Inequality in South Africa: Report Prepared for the Office of the Executive Deputy President and the Inter-Ministerial Committee for Poverty and Inequality* Summary Report 13 May 1998

65  Lucille Davie 'Why Alexandra survived apartheid' 6 October 2003 Joburg My City Our Future: Official Website of the City of Johannesburg http://www.joburg.org.za/index.php?option=com_content&task=view&id=888&Itemid=0

66  Christopher Clark 'Immigrants targeted in Alexandra housing battle' *GroundUp* 21 February 2019 https://www.groundup.org.za/article/immigrants-targeted-alexandra-housing-battle/

67  Steven Friedman 'Seeing ourselves as others see us: Racism, technique and the Mbeki administration' in Daryl Glaser (ed.) *Mbeki and After: Reflections on the Legacy of Thabo Mbeki* Johannesburg, Wits University Press, 2010, pp. 163–186

68   Steven Friedman 'Getting better than "world class": The challenge of governing postapartheid South Africa' *Social Research* Vol. 72, No. 3, 2005, pp. 757–784

69   Brand South Africa 'SA targets 5-million new jobs by 2020' 24 November 2010 https://www.brandsouthafrica.com/investments-immigration/business/economy/policies/growth-241110; Democratic Alliance 'BOKAMOSO/DA can put a job every home' 22 January 2019 https://www.da.org.za/2019/01/bokamoso-da-can-put-a-job-every-home

70   This section develops an argument spelled out in Steven Friedman 'Archipelagos of dominance: Party fiefdoms and South African democracy' *Zeitschrift für Vergleichende Politikwissenschaft (Journal of Comparative Politics)* Vol. 9, No. 3, 2015, pp. 139–159

71   Hermann Giliomee and Charles Simkins (eds) *The Awkward Embrace: One-Party Domination and Democracy* Amsterdam, Harwood, 1999; Kimberly Lanegran, 'South Africa's 1999 election: Consolidating a dominant party system' *Africa Today* Vol. 48, No. 2, 2001, pp. 81–102; Thiven Reddy 'The Congress Party model: South Africa's African National Congress (ANC) and India's Indian National Congress (INC) as dominant parties' *African and Asian Studies* Vol. 4, No. 3, 2005, pp. 271–300; Karen Ferree *Framing the Race in South Africa: The Political Origins of Racial Census Elections* Cambridge, Cambridge University Press, 2011

72   Roger Southall 'The "dominant party debate" in South Africa' *Africa Spectrum* Vol. 39, No. 1, 2005, pp. 61–82

73   Southall 'Dominant party debate' p. 64

74   Karl von Holdt, Malose Langa, Sepetla Molapo, Nomfundo Mogapi, Kindi Ngubeni, Jacob Dlamini and Adele Kirsten *The Smoke that Calls: Insurgent Citizenship, Collective Violence and the Search for a Place in the New South Africa* Johannesburg, Centre for the Study of Violence and Reconciliation, Society, Work and Development Institute, July 2011; Von Holdt 'Violent democracy'

75   Setumo Stone 'ANC loses ward near Marikana in by-election' *Business Day* 8 November 2012; *News24* 'ANC loses Nkandla by-election' 6 December 2012 http://www.news24.com/SouthAfrica/Politics/ANC-loses-Nkandla-by-election-20121206-4

76   African News Agency (ANA) reporter 'IFP retains Nkandla ward despite fervent Zuma campaigning' *Independent Online* 1 June 2018 https://www.iol.co.za/news/politics/ifp-retains-nkandla-ward-despite-fervent-zuma-campaigning-15265352

77   Ferree *Framing the Race* p. 2

78   Matshiqi 'Why Manuel is right and wrong'

79   Leila Patel, Yolanda Sadie, Victoria Graham, Aislinn Delaney and Kim Baldry *Voting Behaviour and the Influence of Social Protection: A Study of Voting Behaviour in Three Poor Areas of South Africa* Johannesburg, Centre for Social Development in Africa and Department of Politics, University of Johannesburg, June 2014

80   Tom Lodge and Ursula Scheidegger *Political Parties and Democratic Governance in South Africa* Electoral Institute for Sustainable Democracy in Africa Research Report No. 25, Johannesburg, EISA, 2006

81   *Northern Natal Courier* 'Final election results in: IFP gains ground in KZN at the expense of the ANC and NFP' 12 May 2019 https://northernnatalcourier.co.za/96773/final-election-results-ifp-gains-ground-kzn-expense-anc-nfp/

82   The exercise was conducted by identifying a selection of typical wards held by the ANC and DA (and, in one case, the IFP) derived from http://www.joburg.org.za/index.php?option=com_content&view=article&id=7401:joburgs-

councillors&catid=84:how-it-works&Itemid=13. Results in each were obtained from the website of the Independent Electoral Commission (IEC) http://www.elections. org.za/content/LGEPublicReports/197/Detailed%20Results/GP/JHB/79800103.pdf

83 Steven Friedman and Louise Stack 'The magic moment: The 1994 election' in Steven Friedman and Doreen Atkinson (eds) *The Small Miracle: South Africa's Negotiated Settlement* Johannesburg, Ravan Press, 1994, pp. 301–330, p. 310

84 Truth and Reconciliation Commission (TRC) *Final Report* Vol. 3, chapter 3, subsection 62, 438, TRC, 1998

85 Victoria Eastwood 'Bigger than the army: South Africa's private security forces' CNN 8 February 2013 http://edition.cnn.com/2013/02/08/business/south-africa-private-security

86 Karina Landman *Gated Communities in South Africa: Comparison of Four Case Studies in Gauteng* Pretoria, Council for Scientific and Industrial Research, 2004

87 David MacDonald *World City Syndrome: Neoliberalism and Inequality in Cape Town* New York, Routledge, 2008

88 Matshiqi 'Why Manuel is right and wrong'

89 John Carlin 'Judge shows why constitution is about morals not ceremony' *Business Day* 28 March 2014

90 John Kane-Berman 'ANC corruption is systemic, unlike Nats' incidental version' *Business Day* 24 March 2014

91 Matshiqi 'Why Manuel is right and wrong'

92 Sam C Nolutshungu *Changing South Africa: Political Considerations* Manchester, Manchester University Press, 1982, p. 69

93 Richard Turner 'Black consciousness and white liberals' *Reality* July 1972, p. 20. See also Steven Friedman 'Less a theory of society, more a state of mind? The ambiguous legacy of South African liberalism' in Peter Vale, Lawrence Hamilton and Estelle H Prinsloo (eds) *Intellectual Traditions in South Africa: Ideas, Individuals and Institutions* Pietermaritzburg, University of KwaZulu-Natal Press, 2014

94 Richard Humphries, Thabo Rapoo and Steven Friedman 'The shape of the country: Negotiating regional government' in Steven Friedman and Doreen Atkinson (eds), *The Small Miracle: South Africa's Negotiated Settlement* Johannesburg, Ravan Press, 1994, pp. 148–181

95 Deborah Brautigam 'Contingent consent: Export taxation and state building in Mauritius' Paper presented at the annual meeting of the American Political Science Association, Philadelphia PA, 31 August 2006

96 Anye Nyamnjoh 'The phenomenology of Rhodes Must Fall: Student activism and the experience of alienation at the University of Cape Town' *Strategic Review for Southern Africa* Vol. 39, No. 1, May 2017, pp. 256–277

97 Von Holdt et al. *The Smoke that Calls* p. 20

98 See, for example, Jerry Lavery *Protest and Political Participation in South Africa: Time Trends and Characteristics of Protesters* Afrobarometer Briefing Paper No. 102, May 2012

99 Von Holdt et al. *The Smoke that Calls* p. 9

100 Von Holdt et al. *The Smoke that Calls* p. 13

101 Von Holdt et al. *The Smoke that Calls* p. 21

102 Von Holdt et al. *The Smoke that Calls* p. 3

103 Salim Vally 'The iron fist and the velvet glove' *Mail and Guardian* 20 December 2003

104  Gareth Newham and Hamadziripi Tamukamoyo 'The Tatane case raises hard questions for South Africa's National Prosecuting Authority' *ISS Today* 11 April 2013
105  Richard Pithouse 'The case of the Kennedy 12: No easy path through the embers' *Counterpunch* 1 August 2011 http://www.counterpunch.org/2011/08/01/no-easy-path-through-the-embers/
106  Von Holdt et al. *The Smoke that Calls* p. 21

CHAPTER 2

1   North *Institutional Change and Economic Performance* p. 92
2   Douglass C North 'Economic performance through time' *American Economic Review* Vol. 84, No. 3, 1994, pp. 359–368, p. 364
3   North 'Performance through time' p. 360
4   Douglass C North 'Institutions' *Journal of Economic Perspectives* Vol. 5, No. 1, 1991, pp. 97–112, p. 97
5   North 'Institutions' p. 97
6   North 'Institutions' p. 98
7   North 'Performance through time' pp. 360–361
8   W Brian Arthur 'Increasing returns, and lock-in by historical events' *Economic Journal* Vol. 99, No. 394, 1989, pp. 116–131, p. 116
9   Paul A David 'Clio and the economics of QWERTY' *American Economic Review* Vol. 75, No. 2, 1985, pp. 332–337, p. 332; emphasis in original
10  David 'Economics of QWERTY' p. 332
11  David 'Economics of QWERTY' p. 333
12  David 'Economics of QWERTY' p. 334
13  David 'Economics of QWERTY' p. 335
14  North *Institutional Change and Economic Performance* p. 104
15  North *Institutional Change and Economic Performance* p. 100
16  North *Institutional Change and Economic Performance* p. 94
17  North *Institutional Change and Economic Performance* p. 95
18  North *Institutional Change and Economic Performance* p. 95
19  North *Institutional Change and Economic Performance* p. 96
20  North *Institutional Change and Economic Performance* p. 96
21  North *Institutional Change and Economic Performance* p. 96
22  North *Institutional Change and Economic Performance* p. 100
23  North *Institutional Change and Economic Performance* p. 96
24  North *Institutional Change and Economic Performance* p. 99
25  North *Institutional Change and Economic Performance* p. 97
26  North 'Performance through time' p. 362
27  Dani Rodrik *Second Best Institutions* Centre for Economic Policy Research Discussion Paper No. DP6764, CEPR, London, June 2008
28  Julio Faundez 'Douglass North's theory of institutions: Lessons for law and development' *Hague Journal on the Rule of Law* Vol. 8, No. 2, 2016, pp. 373–419, p. 374
29  North *Institutional Change and Economic Performance* p. 101
30  North *Institutional Change and Economic Performance* p. 102
31  North *Institutional Change and Economic Performance* p. 103

32    North *Institutional Change and Economic Performance* p. 101
33    North *Institutional Change and Economic Performance* p. 100
34    Scott E Page 'Path dependence' *Quarterly Journal of Political Science* Vol. 1, No. 1, 2006, pp. 87–115, p. 89
35    Steven Friedman *Power in Action: Democracy, Citizenship and Social Justice* Johannesburg, Wits University Press, 2018
36    Robert Putnam *Making Democracy Work: Civic Traditions in Modern Italy* Princeton NJ, Princeton University Press, 1994
37    Faundez 'Douglass North's theory' p. 375
38    Alex Field 'North, Douglass' in DA Clark (ed.) *Elgar Companion to Development Studies* Cheltenham, Edward Elgar Publishing, 2006, pp. 423–426, p. 425
39    Webster 'The promise and the possibility'
40    Faundez 'Douglass North's theory' pp. 374–375
41    Joseph Stiglitz 'It's time to retire metrics like GDP. They don't measure everything that matters' *The Guardian* 24 November 2019 https://www.theguardian.com/commentisfree/2019/nov/24/metrics-gdp-economic-performance-social-progress
42    United Nations Development Programme (UNDP) Human Development Reports *Human Development Data (1990–2017)* 2017 http://hdr.undp.org/en/data
43    Douglass C North *Economic Performance Through Time: The Limits to Knowledge* Economic History Working Paper No. 9612004, University Library of Munich, Germany, 1996, p. 7
44    United States – Human Development Index – HDI https://countryeconomy.com/hdi/usa
45    Frances Fox Piven and Richard Cloward *Poor People's Movements: Why They Succeed, How They Fail* New York, Vintage Books, 1979
46    North *Institutional Change and Economic Performance* p. 99
47    North 'Performance through time' p. 361
48    Faundez 'Douglass North's theory' p. 385
49    Douglass C North *Understanding the Process of Economic Change* Princeton NJ, Princeton University Press, 2005, p. 44
50    North *Understanding the Process* p. 136
51    North *Institutional Change and Economic Performance* pp. 99–100
52    Seymour Martin Lipset 'Some social requisites of democracy: Economic development and political legitimacy' *American Political Science Review* Vol. 53, No. 1, 1959, pp. 69–105. For a critique, see Friedman *Power in Action*
53    Douglass C North 'A framework for analyzing the state in economic history' *Explorations in Economic History* Vol. 16, No. 3, 1979, pp. 249–259, p. 251
54    Faundez 'Douglass North's theory' p. 383
55    Terra Lawson-Remer 'Property insecurity' *Brooklyn Journal of International Law* Vol. 38, No. 1, 2013, pp. 145–191, pp. 148, 151
56    Adam Przeworski 'The last instance: Are institutions the primary cause of economic development?' *European Journal of Sociology* Vol. 45, No. 2, 2004, pp. 165–188, p. 173
57    North *Understanding the Process* p. 63
58    Faundez 'Douglass North's theory' p. 386
59    North *Institutional Change and Economic Performance* p. 138
60    Emile Durkheim *Sociology and Philosophy* DF Pocock (trans.) New York, Free Press, 1974
61    North *Understanding the Process* p. 58
62    North *Institutional Change and Economic Performance* pp. 98–99

63    Brian Levy *Working with the Grain: Integrating Governance and Growth in Development Strategies* New York, Oxford University Press, 2014

64    Levy *Working with the Grain* p. 31

65    Levy *Working with the Grain* p. 32

66    North 'Performance through time' pp. 360–361

67    North *Institutional Change and Economic Performance* p. 101

68    North 'Institutions' p. 111

69    George Devenish 'SA's electoral system needs to accommodate individual candidates' *Business Day* 7 May 2019 https://www.businesslive.co.za/bd/opinion/2019-05-07-sas-electoral-system-needs-to-accommodate-individual-candidates/

70    Jonathan Calof and Wilma Viviers 'Internationalization behavior of small- and medium-sized South African enterprises' *Journal of Small Business Management* Vol. 33, No. 4, 1995, pp. 71–79

71    Yudelman *Emergence of Modern South Africa*

72    Author's unpublished interview-based research, 1993

73    Georges Nzongola-Ntalaja *The Congo from Leopold to Kabila: A People's History* London, Zed Press, 2002

74    John Hoffman *John Gray and the Problem of Utopia* Cardiff, University of Wales Press, 2009; Steven Friedman 'Democracy as an open-ended utopia: Reviving a sense of uncoerced political possibility' *Theoria* Vol. 59, No. 130, 2012, pp. 1–21

75    This argument repeats, with some modification, that made in Steven Friedman 'The Janus face of the past: Preserving and resisting South African path dependence' in Xolela Mangcu (ed.) *The Colour of Our Future: Does Race Matter in Post-Apartheid South Africa?* Johannesburg, Wits University Press, 2015, pp. 45–63

76    Saul Dubow *Apartheid 1948–1994* Oxford, Oxford University Press, 2014, pp. 32ff

77    Dan O'Meara *Volkskapitalisme: Class, Capital and Ideology in the Development of Afrikaner Nationalism 1934–1948* Cambridge, Cambridge University Press, 1983

78    Jonathan Hyslop 'Political corruption: Before and after apartheid' *Journal of Southern African Studies* Vol. 31, No. 4, 2005, pp. 773–789, p. 781

79    See, for example, Andre du Toit and Hermann Giliomee, *Afrikaner Political Thought* Vol. 1, Cape Town, David Philip, 1983

80    O'Meara *Volkskapitalisme*

81    Nolutshungu *Changing South Africa*

82    Turner 'Black consciousness and white liberals' p. 20

83    Robert A Hill (editor in chief) *The Marcus Garvey and Universal Negro Improvement Association Papers, Vol. X: Africa for the Africans 1923–1945* Berkeley and Los Angeles, University of California Press, 2006, pp. 487–488

84    See judgment by Judge Dennis Davis in *Mazibuko v Sisulu and Others* High Court of South Africa, Western Cape Division, Case No. 21990/2012, 22 November 2012

85    IOL News 'Malema hate-speech ruling "problematic"' *Independent Online* 15 September 2011 http://www.iol.co.za/news/crime-courts/malema-hate-speech-ruling-problematic-1.1138174#.U0bf3qL2CF4

86    Jackson Mthembu 'ANC statement on remarks of ANCYL and Cosas on the Public Protector' *Politicsweb* 24 March 2014 http://www.politicsweb.co.za/politicsweb/view/politicsweb/en/page71654?oid=576688&sn=Detail&pid=71616

87    Steven Friedman 'Who we are: Voter participation, rationality and the 1999 election' *Politikon* Vol. 26, No. 2, 1999, pp. 213–223

88    For evidence on the dynamics of the protests, see Von Holdt et al. *The Smoke that Calls*

89    Webster 'The promise and the possibility' pp. 216–219

90    Webster 'The promise and the possibility' pp. 225ff

91    Karl von Holdt 'From the politics of resistance to the politics of reconstruction? The union and "ungovernability" in the workplace' in Glenn Adler and Edward Webster (eds) *Trade Unions and Democratization in South Africa, 1985–1997* Johannesburg, Wits University Press, 2000, pp. 106–108

92    Mohamed Motala 'Why strikes are so violent' *Cape Times* 14 July 2014

## CHAPTER 3

1    Thandika Mkandawire 'Neopatrimonialism and the political economy of economic performance in Africa: Critical reflections' *World Politics* Vol. 67, No. 3, 2015, pp. 563–612

2    Victor Levine, *Political Corruption: The Ghana Case* Stanford CA, Stanford University Press, 1975, cited in Tom Lodge 'Political corruption in South Africa' *African Affairs* Vol. 97, No. 387, 1998, pp. 157–187, p. 158

3    Hermann Giliomee and Bernard Mbenga, *New History of South Africa* Cape Town, Tafelberg, 2007, p. 41

4    Johan Fourie, Ada Jansen and Krige Siebrits 'Public finances under private company rule: The Dutch Cape Colony (1652–1795)' *New Contree* Vol. 68, No. 4, 2012, pp. 51–71, p. 65

5    Martin Legassick and Robert Ross 'From slave economy to settler capitalism: The Cape Colony and its extensions' in Caroline Hamilton, Bernard Mbenga and Robert Ross (eds) *The Cambridge History of South Africa: Volume 1: From Early Times to 1885* New York, Cambridge University Press, 2010, pp. 253–318

6    Abel Gwaindepi 'State building in the colonial era: Public revenue, expenditure and borrowing patterns in the Cape Colony, 1820–1910' PhD dissertation, Faculty of Economics and Management Sciences, University of Stellenbosch, March 2018, pp. 168, 171

7    JL McCracken *The Cape Parliament 1854–1910* London, Oxford University Press, 1967, p. 115

8    Hyslop 'Before and after' p. 780

9    Hennie van Vuuren *Apartheid Grand Corruption: Assessing the Scale of Crimes of Profit from 1976 to 1994* A report prepared by civil society in terms of a resolution of the Second National Anti-Corruption Summit for presentation at the National Anti-Corruption Forum, Pretoria, Institute for Security Studies, May 2006, p. 20

10    Howard C Hillegas *The Boers in War: The Story of the British-Boer War of 1899–1900* New York, Appleton and Co., 1900, cited in Van Vuuren *Apartheid Grand Corruption* p. 22

11    Hyslop 'Before and after' p. 780

12    Mushtaq H Khan and Jomo Kwame Sundaram 'Introduction' in Khan and Sundaram (eds) *Rents, Rent Seeking and Economic Development: Theory and Evidence in Asia* Cambridge, Cambridge University Press, 2005, p. 5, cited in Hyslop 'Before and after' p. 775

13    Hadassah Egbedi 'By ignoring corruption's colonial roots, Cameron's summit was destined to fail' *The Guardian* 13 May 2016 https://www.theguardian.com/world/2016/may/13/ignoring-corruptions-colonial-roots-camerons-summit-was-destined-to-fail

14 JN Cloete 'The bureaucracy' in Anthony de Crespigny and Robert Schrire (eds) *The Government and Politics of South Africa* Cape Town, Juta, 1978, p. 74, cited in Lodge 'Political corruption' p. 164

15 Lodge 'Political corruption' p. 164

16 Lodge 'Political corruption' p. 167

17 Mia Brandel Syrier *Reeftown Elite* Abingdon, Routledge and Kegan Paul, 1971, p. 33, cited in Lodge 'Political corruption' p. 170

18 Lodge 'Political corruption' p. 170

19 Lodge 'Political corruption' p. 171

20 Van Vuuren *Apartheid Grand Corruption* p. 21

21 Van Vuuren *Apartheid Grand Corruption* p. 39

22 Dan O'Meara *Forty Lost Years: The Apartheid State and the Politics of the National Party, 1948–1994* Johannesburg, Ravan Press, 1996, cited in Van Vuuren *Apartheid Grand Corruption* p. 24

23 Van Vuuren *Apartheid Grand Corruption* p. 25

24 Van Vuuren *Apartheid Grand Corruption* p. 30

25 Hyslop 'Before and after' p. 781

26 Hyslop 'Before and after' p. 782

27 Hyslop 'Before and after' p. 782

28 Hyslop 'Before and after' p. 783; see also Lodge 'Political corruption' p. 166

29 Hyslop 'Before and after' p. 783

30 Van Vuuren *Apartheid Grand Corruption* p. 41

31 Van Vuuren *Apartheid, Guns and Money*

32 Hyslop 'Before and after' p. 784

33 Van Vuuren *Apartheid, Guns and Money* p. 8

34 Open Secrets *Evidence for the People's Tribunal on Economic Crime (03–07 February 2018)* 2018, p. 56

35 Open Secrets *Evidence* p. 52

36 Open Secrets *Evidence* p. 54

37 Hyslop 'Before and after' p. 787

38 Van Vuuren *Apartheid Grand Corruption* p. 5

39 Van Vuuren *Apartheid Grand Corruption* p. 23

40 Yudelman *Emergence of Modern South Africa*

41 Sampie Terreblanche *A History of Inequality in South Africa: 1652–2002* Pietermaritzburg, University of KwaZulu-Natal Press, 2002, p. 310

42 Interview with Professor Andre Thomashausen, University of South Africa, 2005, cited in Van Vuuren *Apartheid Grand Corruption* p. 57

43 Mark Gevisser *A Legacy of Liberation: Thabo Mbeki and the Future of the South African Dream* New York, Palgrave Macmillan, 2009, p. 217

44 Gevisser *Legacy* p. 217

45 Remarks by Frene Ginwala, Speaker of Parliament, to the Global Forum II, Opening Session, 28 May 2001, The Hague www.gca-cma.org.

46 Lodge 'Political corruption' p. 162

47 Lodge 'Political corruption' p. 172

48 Hyslop 'Before and after' p. 785

49 Lodge 'Political corruption' p. 184

50 Lodge 'Political corruption' p. 161

51 Hyslop 'Before and after' p. 783

52  Von Holdt et al. *The Smoke that Calls* p. 20

53  Numsa 'Numsa on the United Front and the possibilities of establishing a movement for socialism' Press Release, 4 March 2014 https://www.numsa.org.za/article/numsa-united-front-possibilities-establishing-movement-socialism/

54  Panel discussion, Rhodes University, May 2015

55  N Oelofse 'ANC adviser a pricey anomaly for Bitou' *Business Day* 18 August 2011 http://www.bdlive.co.za/articles/2011/08/18/anc-adviser-a-pricey-anomaly-for-bitou

56  African National Congress *Through the Eye of A Needle? Choosing the Best Cadres to Lead Transformation* Johannesburg, ANC, 2001, p. 31

57  ANC *Eye of a Needle* p. 32

58  Febe Potgieter-Gqubule 'Through the Eye of a Needle revisited: A perspective for discussion' *Umrabulo* No. 32, First Quarter, 2010

59  Potgieter-Gqubule 'Revisited' section 12

60  For example, KwaZulu-Natal High Court *Dube and Others v Zikalala and Others* (7904/2016P) [2017] ZAKZPHC 36; [2017] 4 All SA 365 (KZP) (12 September 2017); Eastern Cape High Court *Mgabadeli and Others v African National Congress and Others* (EL1303/2017, ECD3703/2017) [2017] ZAECGHC 131 (12 December 2017)

61  Lizeka Tandwa 'It was a "festival of chairs" – Ramaphosa on violent ANC elective conference' *News24* 1 October 2017 https://www.news24.com/SouthAfrica/News/it-was-a-festival-of-chairs-ramaphosa-on-violent-anc-elective-conference-20171001

62  Qaanitah Hunter 'How David Mabuza outplayed the NDZ camp: Nifty footwork sees "Mpumalanga cat" come out on top' *TimesLive* 23 December 2017 https://www.timeslive.co.za/sunday-times/news/2017-12-22-how-david-mabuza-outplayed-the-ndz-camp/

63  Von Holdt *Political Economy* p. 3

64  Von Holdt *Political Economy* p. 3

65  Haroon Bhorat et al. *Betrayal of the Promise: How South Africa Is Being Stolen,* State Capacity Research Project, Public Affairs Research Institute et al., May 2017

66  Von Holdt *Political Economy* p. 13

67  Bhorat et al. *Betrayal*

68  Von Holdt *Political Economy* p. 14

69  Von Holdt *Political Economy* p. 8

70  Von Holdt *Political Economy* p. 6

71  Von Holdt *Political Economy* p. 7

72  Von Holdt *Political Economy* p. 10

73  Von Holdt *Political Economy* p. 4

74  Roger Southall 'The ANC and black capitalism in South Africa' *Review of African Political Economy* Vol. 31, No. 100, 2004, pp. 313–328

75  Pallo Jordan 'Ruth First lecture' University of the Witwatersrand, 28 August 2000 wits.journalism.co.za/wp-content/uploads/2019/03/Ruth-First-Lecture-by-Pallo-Jordan-2000.pdf

76  Von Holdt *Political Economy* p. 16

77  Von Holdt 'Violent democracy' p. 596

78  Von Holdt 'Violent democracy' p. 594

79  Von Holdt 'Violent democracy' p. 595

80  Von Holdt 'Violent democracy' p. 596

81  Von Holdt 'Violent democracy' p. 594

82  Von Holdt 'Violent democracy' p. 597

83   African News Agency (ANA) reporter 'Magaqa murder: ANC whistle-blowers live in fear' *Independent Online* 10 November 2017 https://www.iol.co.za/news/south-africa/kwazulu-natal/magaqa-murder-anc-whistle-blowers-live-in-fear-11948622

84   Von Holdt et al. *The Smoke that Calls* p. 20

85   Von Holdt *Political Economy* p. 8

86   Von Holdt et al. *The Smoke that Calls* p. 17

87   Von Holdt et al. *The Smoke that Calls* p. 78

88   Malose Langa and Karl von Holdt 'Insurgent citizenship, class formation and the dual nature of community protest: A case study of Kungcatsha' in Marcelle C Dawson and Luke Sinwell (eds) *Contesting Transformation: Popular Resistance in Twenty-First Century South Africa* London, Pluto Press, 2012, pp. 80–100, p. 91

89   Von Holdt 'Violent democracy' p. 598

90   Von Holdt et al. *The Smoke that Calls* p. 17

91   Victoria Graham, Yolanda Sadie and Leila Patel 'Social grants, food parcels and voting behaviour: A case study of three South African communities' *Transformation* 91, 2016, pp. 106–135

92   I am grateful to Oupa Lehulere for this insight

CHAPTER 4

1    Mahmood Mamdani *Citizen and Subject: Contemporary Africa and the Politics of Late Colonialism* Kampala, Fountain, 1995

2    Mamdani *Citizen and Subject* pp. 3–33

3    Jonny Steinberg 'We should've heeded Mahmoud Mamdani's warning' *Business Day* 2 October 2015

4    Mamdani *Citizen and Subject* p. 26

5    Mkandawire 'Neopatrimonialism and the political economy'

6    Mamdani *Citizen and Subject* p. 26

7    Mamdani *Citizen and Subject* p. 27

8    Mamdani *Citizen and Subject* p. 25

9    Mamdani *Citizen and Subject* p. 34

10   Mamdani *Citizen and Subject* p. 28

11   Mamdani *Citizen and Subject* p. 31

12   Mamdani *Citizen and Subject* p. 27

13   Mamdani *Citizen and Subject* p. 29

14   Mamdani *Citizen and Subject* p. 32

15   Von Holdt et al. *The Smoke that Calls*

16   Lungisile Ntsebeza 'Democratic decentralisation and traditional authority: Dilemmas of land administration in rural South Africa' *European Journal of Development Research* Vol. 16, No. 1, 2004, pp. 71–89, p. 72

17   Thuto Tipe 'The boundaries of tradition: An examination of the Traditional Leadership and Governance Framework Act' *Harvard Human Rights Journal* 4 November 2014 http://harvardhrj.com/2014/11/the-boundaries-of-tradition-an-examination-of-the-traditional-leadership-and-governance-framework-act/

18   Tipe 'Boundaries of tradition'

19   Mazibuko Jara 'Beyond social compacting: A power matrix in flux in post-Mandela South Africa' in Mapungubwe Institute for Social Reflection (MISTRA) *20 Years*

*of South African Democracy: So Where to Now?* Johannesburg, MISTRA, 2014, pp. 82–88, p. 86

20  Centre for Law and Society *Questioning the Legal Status of Traditional Councils in South Africa* Rural Women's Action Research Programme, University of Cape Town, August 2013 http://www.cls.uct.ac.za/usr/lrg/downloads/CLS_TCStatus_Factsheet_Aug2013.pdf

21  Mamdani *Citizen and Subject* p. 17

22  Ntsebeza 'Democratic decentralisation' p. 73

23  Ben Cousins 'More than socially embedded: The distinctive character of "communal tenure" regimes in South Africa and its implications for land policy' *Journal of Agrarian Change* Vol. 7, No. 3, 2007, pp. 281–315, p. 290

24  Aninka Claassens '"Communal land", property rights and traditional leadership' Wits Institute for Social and Economic Research, 2014 http://wiser.wits.ac.za/system/files/documents/Claassens2014.pdf

25  Ben Cousins 'Key provisions of the Communal Land Rights Act are declared unconstitutional. Where to now?' *Another Countryside* (blog) Institute for Poverty, Land and Agrarian Studies (PLAAS), University of the Western Cape, 10 November 2009 http://www.plaas.org.za/blog/key-provisions-communal-land-rights-act-are-declared-unconstitutional-where-no

26  Claassens 'Communal land'

27  Cousins 'More than socially embedded' p. 291

28  Ntsebeza 'Democratic decentralisation' p. 81

29  Cousins 'Key provisions'

30  Steven Friedman 'Moves to empower chiefs bad for democracy' *Business Day* 19 November 2014

31  Nomboniso Gasa 'State repeats mistakes in third attempt at courts bill' *Business Day* 22 June 2015

32  Brendan Boyle 'Foxes left to guard the hens that lay community nest eggs' *Business Day* 10 August 2016

33  Andisiwe Makinana 'Zuma questions "lopsided" land reform law, calls for radical action' *City Press* 3 March 2016

34  Claassens 'Communal land'

35  Sarah Evans 'ConCourt hands land back to North West community' *Mail and Guardian* 20 August 2015

36  Parliament of the Republic of South Africa 'National Assembly agrees to Traditional Courts Bill' 12 March 2019 https://www.parliament.gov.za/press-releases/national-assembly-agrees-traditional-courts-bill

37  Babalo Ndenze 'Ramaphosa praises House of Traditional Leaders as essential part of society' *Eyewitness News* 18 February 2019 https://www.msn.com/en-za/news/national/ramaphosa-praises-house-of-traditional-leaders-as-essential-part-of-society/ar-BBTOTfb

38  Steinberg 'We should've heeded Mamdani'

39  Steinberg 'We should've heeded Mamdani'

40  Govan Mbeki *South Africa: The Peasants' Revolt* Harmondsworth, Penguin, 1964

41  Nelson Mandela *Long Walk to Freedom* London, Little, Brown, 1994, p. 31

42  Andrew Manson and Bernard Mbenga 'Bophuthatswana and the North West province: From Pan-Tswanaism to mineral-based ethnic assertiveness' *South African Historical Journal* Vol. 6, No. 1, 2012, pp. 96–116

43 David Hemson 'So long to a fiery spirit' *Mail and Guardian* 27 November 2009 https://mg.co.za/article/2009-11-27-so-long-to-a-fiery-spirit

44 See discussion in Steven Friedman *Race, Class and Power: Harold Wolpe and the Radical Critique of Apartheid* Johannesburg, Ravan Press, 2015

45 Josette Cole *Crossroads: The Politics of Reform and Repression, 1976–1986* Johannesburg, Ravan Press, 1987

46 Author's unpublished research 1986; see also Steven Friedman *Reform Revisited* Johannesburg, South African Institute of Race Relations, 1987

47 Friedman *Understanding Reform*

48 Mamdani *Citizen and Subject* p. 295

49 Cole *Crossroads*

50 Webster 'The promise and the possibility'

51 See, for example, Jo Beall, Owen Crankshaw and Sue Parnell 'Victims, villains and fixers: The urban environment and Johannesburg's poor' *Journal of Southern African Studies* Vol. 26, No. 4, 2000, pp. 803–855

52 Unpublished research on Butterworth, Eastern Cape, directed by Teresa Connor, University of Fort Hare

53 Khehla Shubane 'Black local authorities: A contraption of control' in Mark Swilling, Richard Humphries and Khehla Shubane (eds) *Apartheid City in Transition* Cape Town, Oxford University Press, 1991, pp. 64–77

54 Connor, Butterworth research

55 Steven Robins *From Revolution to Rights in South Africa: Social Movements, NGOs and Popular Politics After Apartheid* London, James Currey, and Pietermaritzburg, University of KwaZulu-Natal Press, 2008, p. 11

56 Staff reporter 'Buthelezi approved Powell's war plans' *Mail and Guardian* 18 June 1999 https://mg.co.za/article/1999-06-18-buthelezi-approved-powells-war-plans

57 Hilary Lynd 'Secret details of the land deal that brought the IFP into the 1994 poll' *Mail and Guardian* 7 August 2019 https://mg.co.za/article/2019-08-07-secret-details-of-the-land-deal-that-brought-the-ifp-into-the-94-poll

58 Aninka Claassens 'Rural vote notions' *Business Day* Letters 12 August 2016

59 Bob Jessop *State Theory: Putting the Capitalist State in Its Place* University Park, Pennsylvania State University Press, 1990

60 Jessop *State Theory* pp. 8–9

61 Steven Friedman and Shauna Mottiar 'A rewarding engagement? The Treatment Action Campaign and the politics of HIV/AIDS' *Politics and Society* Vol. 33, No. 4, 2005, pp. 511–565

62 This chapter is an adapted version of a paper presented by the author at 'On the Subject of Citizenship', a colloquium to mark the 20th anniversary of the publication of *Citizen and Subject*, convened on 18–20 August 2016 by the Centre for Humanities Research at the University of the Western Cape

CHAPTER 5

1 Sakhela Buhlungu *Comrades, Entrepreneurs and Career Unionists: Organisational Modernisation and New Cleavages Among COSATU Union Officials* Occasional Paper No. 17, Friedrich Ebert Stiftung, 2002 http://citeseerx.ist.psu.edu/viewdoc/summary?doi=10.1.1.196.3667; Alex Beresford 'Organised labour and the politics of

class formation in post-apartheid South Africa' *Review of African Political Economy* Vol. 39, No. 134, 2012, pp. 569–589

2   Theto Mahlakoana 'SA experienced highest rise in labour strikes in 2017' *TimesLive* 10 July 2018 https://www.timeslive.co.za/news/south-africa/2018-07-10-sa-experienced-highest-rise-in-labour-strikes-in-2017/

3   Peter Alexander 'Rebellion of the poor: South Africa's service delivery protests – a preliminary analysis' *Review of African Political Economy* Vol. 37, No. 123, 2010, pp. 25–40 DOI: 10.1080/03056241003637870

4   Cosatu Central Executive Committee *Conceptualising a Second Radical Transition* 29 May 2017 https://www.politicsweb.co.za/opinion/conceptualising-a-second-radical-transition--cosat

5   Benson Ngqentsu 'Cosatu must focus on its unions so it can positively change workers' lives' *City Press* 20 September 2018 https://city-press.news24.com/Voices/cosatu-must-focus-on-its-unions-so-it-can-positively-change-workers-lives-20180919

6   Xavier Greenwood 'South Africa is the most unequal country in the world and its poverty is the "enduring legacy of apartheid", says World Bank' *The Independent* 4 April 2018 https://www.independent.co.uk/news/world/africa/south-africa-unequal-country-poverty-legacy-apartheid-world-bank-a8288986.html

7   Anthea Jeffery 'The state of race relations in SA 2019 – IRR' *Politicsweb* 13 June 2019 https://www.politicsweb.co.za/documents/the-state-of-race-relations-in-sa-2019--irr

8   Nomahlubi Jordaan 'Racism complaints by blacks are on the rise, with Gauteng the worst' *TimesLive* 10 December 2018 https://www.timeslive.co.za/news/south-africa/2018-12-10-racism-complaints-by-blacks-are-on-the-rise-with-gauteng-the-worst/

9   Jacob Zuma 'President Jacob Zuma: 2017 State of the Nation Address' 9 February 2017 https://www.gov.za/speeches/president-jacob-zuma-2017-state-nation-address-9-feb-2017-0000

10  David Everatt 'South Africa's black middle class is battling to find a political home' *The Conversation* 1 May 2019 https://theconversation.com/south-africas-black-middle-class-is-battling-to-find-a-political-home-116180

11  Turner 'Black consciousness and white liberals'

12  Lize Booysen 'Barriers to employment equity implementation and retention of blacks in management in South Africa' *South African Journal of Labour Relations* Vol. 31, No. 1, 2007, pp. 47–68

13  Kenneth Jones and Tema Okun *Dismantling Racism: A Workbook for Social Change Groups* Portland OR, Western States Center, 2001 https://www.thc.texas.gov/public/upload/preserve/museums/files/White_Supremacy_Culture.pdf

14  T Abdou Maliqalim Simone *In Whose Image? Political Islam and Urban Practices in Sudan* Chicago and London, University of Chicago Press, 1994

15  Danielle Adeluwoye 'I thought I'd made it when I got to Cambridge University. How wrong I was' *The Guardian* 23 September 2019 https://www.theguardian.com/commentisfree/2019/sep/23/cambridge-university-upward-mobility-working-class-background

16  Steven Friedman 'Land debate in South Africa is about dignity and equality – not the constitution' *The Conversation Africa* 5 March 2018 https://theconversation.com/land-debate-in-south-africa-is-about-dignity-and-equality-not-the-constitution-92862

17  Francis B Nyamnjoh *#RhodesMustFall: Nibbling at Resilient Colonialism in South Africa* Oxford, African Books Collective, 2016

18  Prega Govender 'Blade's puzzle: How to identify "missing middle" students' *Mail and Guardian* 9 December 2016

19  Mo Masedi 'The doors of learning and culture shall be opened or else … ' *Limpopo Online* 28 October 2015 http://limpopoonline.co.za/index.php/opinion-topmenu-15/124-love-struggle/2516-the-doors-of-learning-and-culture-shall-be-opened-or-else

20  Salim Vally, Enver Motala, Mondli Hlatshwayo and Rasigan Maharajh 'Quality, free university education is necessary – and possible' *Mail and Guardian* 28 January 2016

21  Stephen Devereux 'Nearly a third of SA university students go hungry' *The Citizen* 27 August 2018 https://citizen.co.za/news/south-africa/2000969/nearly-a-third-of-sa-university-students-go-hungry/

22  GroundUp 'Insourcing at universities – uneven progress' *Daily Maverick* 15 March 2017 https://www.dailymaverick.co.za/article/2017-03-15-groundup-insourcing-at-universities-uneven-progress/

23  Nyamnjoh *#RhodesMustFall*

24  Charles van Onselen 'Tertiary education in a democratic South Africa' nd Unpublished mimeo cited in Harold Wolpe and Zenariah Barends *A Perspective on Quality and Inequality in South African University Education* Bellville, Education Policy Unit, University of the Western Cape, February 1993

25  James Moulder 'The predominantly white universities: Some ideas for a debate' in Jonathan Jansen (ed.) *Knowledge and Power in South Africa* Johannesburg, Skotaville, 1991, pp. 117–118, cited in Wolpe and Barends *A Perspective*

26  Wolpe and Barends *A Perspective*

27  Sandiso Bazana and Opelo P Mogotsi 'Social identities and racial integration in historically white universities: A literature review of the experiences of black students' *Transformation in Higher Education* Vol. 2, a25, 2017 https://doi.org/10.4102/the.v2i0.25

28  Savo Heleta, 'Decolonisation of higher education: Dismantling epistemic violence and Eurocentrism in South Africa' *Transformation in Higher Education* Vol. 1, No. 1, a9, 2016 http://dx.doi.org/10.4102/the.vlil.9

29  African National Congress *54th National Conference Report and Resolutions* Johannesburg, ANC, 2018, p. 31

30  Tehilla Niselow 'Loud cheers as Ramaphosa says #ANC54 unanimous on land reform' *Fin24* 21 December 2017 https://www.fin24.com/Economy/loud-cheers-as-ramaphosa-says-anc54-unanimous-on-land-reform-20171221

31  Parliament of the Republic of South Africa *Report of the High-Level Panel on the Assessment of Key Legislation and the Acceleration of Fundamental Change* November 2017, p. 202 https://www.parliament.gov.za/storage/app/media/Pages/2017/october/High_Level_Panel/HLP_Report/HLP_report.pdf

32  Mari Harris of Ipsos Markinor cited in Ferial Haffajee 'As its ratings fall precipitously, the EFF goes post-truth on the opinion polls' *Daily Maverick* 12 December 2018 https://www.dailymaverick.co.za/article/2018-12-12-as-its-ratings-fall-precipitously-the-eff-goes-post-truth-in-the-opinion-polls/

33  Mogobe Bernard Ramose and Derek Hook ' "To whom does the land belong?" Mogobe Bernard Ramose talks to Derek Hook' *Psychology in Society* No. 50, 2016, pp. 86–98 DOI: 10.17159/2309-8708/2016/n50a5

34    Friedman 'Land debate'

35    Baruch Hirson 'Bukharin, Bunting and the "Native Republic" slogan' *Searchlight South Africa* Vol. 1, No. 3, 1989, pp. 51–65

36    For opposition to expropriation, see South African Institute of Race Relations 'Help the IRR stop expropriation and promote real land reform: Endorse our solution' nd https://irr.org.za/campaigns/defend-your-property-rights; FW de Klerk Foundation 'Article: Expropriation without compensation' nd https://www.fwdeklerk.org/index. php/en/latest/news/756-article-expropriation-without-compensation. For support, see Economic Freedom Fighters *The EFF's Answers to Your Questions on Land EWC Politicsweb* nd https://www.politicsweb.co.za/documents/the-effs-answers-to-your-questions-on-land-ewc

37    Jackie Cameron 'Land grabs only possible with 75% majority vote in Parliament – legal expert' *Biznews* 14 August 2019 https://www.biznews.com/thought-leaders/2019/08/14/land-grabs-majority-vote-parliament

38    Constitution of the Republic of South Africa, section 25 (8)

39    Steven Friedman 'Changes to the constitution may boost, not weaken, South African property rights' *The Conversation Africa* 3 August 2018 https://theconversation. com/changes-to-the-constitution-may-boost-not-weaken-south-african-property-rights-100979

40    Khwezi Mabasa and Lebogang Mulaisi 'Why South Africans need National Health Insurance' *Daily Maverick* 17 October 2019 https://www.dailymaverick.co.za/opinionista/2019-10-17-why-south-africans-need-national-health-insurance/#gsc. tab=0

41    Paula Gilbert 'SA smartphone penetration now at over 80%, says ICASA' *ITWeb* 3 April 2019 https://www.itweb.co.za/content/GxwQDM1AYy8MlPVo

42    James C Scott *Weapons of the Weak: Everyday Forms of Peasant Resistance* New Haven CT, Yale University Press, 1985

43    Jane Mansbridge *Beyond Adversary Democracy* Chicago and London, University of Chicago Press, 1983

44    Hirson 'The "Native Republic" slogan' p. 56

45    Mikhail Moosa 'SA is becoming a nation of three countries – along class, not racial lines' *Business Day* 7 June 2018

46    Vally et al. 'Quality, free university education'

47    Bhorat and Van der Westhuizen *Poverty, Inequality and the Nature of Economic Growth*

48    Samuel Berlinski, Sebastian Galiani and Paul Gertler 'The effect of pre-primary education on primary school performance' *Journal of Public Economics* Vol. 93, No. 1–2, February 2009, pp. 219–234

49    Ramos Mabugu and Eddie Rakabe 'The need for proper early childhood development infrastructure is urgent' *Mail and Guardian* 23 October 2015

50    Yusuf Sayed 'The governance of public schooling in South Africa and the middle class: Social solidarity for the public good versus class interest' *Transformation* 91, 2016, pp. 84–105

51    Sayed 'Governance of public schooling'

52    Khulekani Magubane, 'Free higher education is a game of cut and balance – Treasury DG' *Mail and Guardian* 28 March 2018 https://mg.co.za/article/2018-03-28-free-higher-education-is-a-game-of-cut-and-balance-treasury-dg

53 Jon Marcus 'Brazil: Where free universities largely serve the wealthy' *Atlantic* 8 April 2015 http://www.theatlantic.com/education/archive/2015/04/brazil-where-free-universities-largely-serve-the-wealthy/389997/

54 Enver Motala, Salim Vally and Rasigan Maharajh *Education, the State, and Class Inequality: The Case for Free Higher Education in South Africa* South African History Online 2016 https://www.sahistory.org.za/sites/default/files/file%20uploads%20/education_the_state_and_class_inequality.pdf

55 Paul Krugman 'Our invisible rich' *New York Times* 28 September 2014

56 Roshuma Phungo 'University fees: Free higher education is possible in South Africa' *Daily Maverick* 21 October 2015 https://www.dailymaverick.co.za/article/2015-10-21-university-fees-free-higher-education-is-possible-in-south-africa/

57 South African Press Association (Sapa) 'Taxis with valid permits exempt from e-tolls, says department' *Mail and Guardian* 4 December 2013

58 Congress of South African Trade Unions (Cosatu) Cosatu Statement on 'new e-tolls dispensation' 21 May 2015 www.cosatu.org.za/show.php?ID=10433

59 Khulekani Magubane 'Clerics call for e-toll resistance' *Business Day* 3 December 2013

60 Wayne Duvenage 'Open road tolling' Avis nd http://www.avis.co.za/OpenRoad Tolling.asp

61 Sizwe Pamla 'Foreign owned e-toll system nothing but an enrichment scheme for the few' Cosatu Press Statement 18 August 2016 www.cosatu.org.za/show.php?ID=11858

62 South African Press Association (Sapa) 'E-toll opposition group heads to court this week' 23 April 2012 http://mybroadband.co.za/news/general/48340-e-toll-opposition-group-heads-to-court-this-week.html

63 For a fuller account of left organisations and their responses to racial and economic inequality, see Steven Friedman 'Beyond race or class: The politics of identity and inequality' *Transformation* 100, 2019, pp. 78–102

64 South African History Online 'Josiah Tshangana Gumede' 2019 https://www.sahistory.org.za/people/josiah-tshangana-gumede

65 Peter Hudson 'The Freedom Charter and the theory of national democratic revolution' *Transformation* 1, 1986, pp. 6–38

66 No Sizwe (Neville Alexander) *One Azania, One Nation: The National Question in South Africa* London, Zed Books, 1979, p. 198

67 IB Tabata 'Review of Neville Alexander's book *One Azania One Nation*' Unity Movement document 14 March 1980 http://www.apdusaviews.co.za/repository/Microsoft%20Word%20-%20Tabata%20on%20BCM.pdf

68 African National Congress 'The state, property relations and social transformation' *Umrabulo* No. 5, Third Quarter, 1998

69 Steven Friedman, Kenny Hlela and Paul Thulare 'A question of voice: Informality and pro-poor policy in Johannesburg, South Africa' in Nabeel Hamdi (ed.) *Urban Futures: Economic Growth and Poverty Reduction* Rugby, ITDG Publishing, 2005, pp. 51–68

70 Tanya Krause 'Oupad community demands proper houses' *SABC News* 17 April 2016

71 Dudley Horner and Francis Wilson *A Tapestry of People: The Growth of Population in the Province of the Western Cape* Southern Africa Labour and Development Research Unit Working Paper No. 21, SALDRU, Cape Town, 2008

72 Alan Lester 'The margins of order: Strategies of segregation on the Eastern Cape frontier, 1806–circa 1850' *Journal of Southern African Studies* Vol. 23, No. 4, 1997, pp. 635–653

73    CLR James *The Black Jacobins: Toussaint L'Ouverture and the San Domingo Revolution* London, Secker and Warburg, 1938

CHAPTER 6

1     'Ramatlhodi: ANC's fatal concessions' *TimesLive* 1 September 2011 http://www.timeslive. co.za/opinion/commentary/2011/09/01/the-big-read-anc-s-fatal-concessions
2     Jane Duncan 'Best of SACSIS: The problem with South Africa's constitution' http:// www.sacsis.org.za/site/article/631
3     Firoz Cachalia 'Democratic constitutionalism in the time of the postcolony: Beyond triumph and betrayal' *South African Journal on Human Rights* Vol. 34, No. 3, 2018, pp. 375–397
4     Joel Malasela Modiri 'The jurisprudence of Steve Biko: A study in race, law and power in the "afterlife" of colonial apartheid' PhD dissertation, Faculty of Law, University of Pretoria, October 2017, p. 333
5     Karl Klare 'Legal culture and transformative constitutionalism' *South African Journal on Human Rights* Vol. 14, No. 1, 1998, pp. 146–188
6     Klare 'Legal culture' p. 146
7     Marius Pieterse cited in Rosa Solange 'Transformative constitutionalism in a demo-cratic developmental state' *Stellenbosch Law Review* Vol. 22, No. 3, 2011, pp. 542–565, p. 544
8     Kenneth Meshoe 'Praise for SA's progressive constitution' *Cape Times* 20 March 2017
9     Steven Friedman 'Enabling agency: The Constitutional Court and social policy' *Transformation* 91, 2016, pp. 19–39
10    Mogobe B Ramose 'Justice and restitution in African political thought' in PH Coetzee and APJ Roux (eds) *The African Philosophy Reader* London, Routledge, 1998, pp. 541–640, p. 572
11    Ramose 'Justice and restitution' p. 570
12    Mogobe Ramose 'Affirming a right and seeking remedies in South Africa' in Leonhard Praeg and Siphokasi Magadla (eds) *Ubuntu: Curating the Archive* Pietermaritzburg, University of KwaZulu-Natal Press, 2014, pp. 121–136, p. 132
13    Ramose 'Justice and restitution' p. 543
14    Ramose 'Justice and restitution' p. 559
15    Mogobe B Ramose 'In memoriam: Sovereignty and the "new" South Africa' *Griffith Law Review* Vol. 16, No. 2, 2007, pp. 310–329, p. 320
16    Ramose 'In memoriam' p. 327
17    Ramose 'In memoriam' p. 325
18    Ramose 'In memoriam' p. 327
19    Ramose 'In memoriam' p. 327
20    Ramose 'In memoriam' p. 325
21    Ramose 'In memoriam' p. 323
22    Cachalia 'Democratic constitutionalism' p. 385
23    David Welsh 'Review of the Buthelezi Commission' Durban, H & H Publications, 1982 https://www.sahistory.org.za/sites/default/files/archive-files2/rejul82.5.pdf
24    Ramose 'In memoriam' p. 326

25  Tshepo Madlingozi 'Social justice in the time of neo-apartheid: Critiquing the anti-black economy of recognition, incorporation and distribution' *Stellenbosch Law Review* Vol. 28, No. 1, 2017, pp. 123–147, p. 124

26  Madlingozi 'Social justice' p. 140

27  Albie Sachs *Protecting Human Rights in the New South Africa* Oxford, Oxford University Press, 1990, p. 12 cited in Madlingozi 'Social justice' p. 141

28  Madlingozi 'Social justice' pp. 141–142

29  Madlingozi 'Social justice' p. 145

30  Joel Modiri 'The crises in legal education' *Acta Academica* Vol. 46, No. 3, 2014, pp. 1–24, pp. 10–11

31  Modiri 'The crises' p. 11

32  Modiri 'Steve Biko' p. 32

33  Modiri 'Steve Biko' p. 73

34  Modiri 'Steve Biko' p. 76

35  Modiri 'Steve Biko' p. 78

36  Modiri 'Steve Biko' p. 378

37  *Azanian Peoples Organization (AZAPO) and Others v President of the Republic of South Africa and Others* (CCT17/96) [1996] ZACC 16; 1996 (8) BCLR 1015; 1996 (4) SA 672 (25 July 1996)

38  Modiri 'Steve Biko' p. 306

39  *City of Tshwane Metropolitan Municipality v Afriforum and Another* (A811/2013) [2015] ZAGPPHC 1056 (26 May 2015)

40  Modiri 'Steve Biko' p. 320

41  Modiri 'Steve Biko' p. 328

42  Joel M Modiri 'The colour of law, power and knowledge: Introducing critical race theory in (post-)apartheid South Africa' *South African Journal on Human Rights* Vol. 28, No. 3, 2012, pp. 405–436, pp. 406–407

43  *Prince v President of the Law Society of the Cape of Good Hope* (CCT36/00) [2002] ZACC 1; 2002 (2) SA 794; 2002 (3) BCLR 231 (25 January 2002)

44  Modiri 'The colour of law' p. 427

45  Anton Kok 'The Promotion of Equality and Prevention of Unfair Discrimination Act 4 of 2000: Court-driven or legislature-driven societal transformation?' *Stellenbosch Law Review* Vol. 19, No. 1, 2008, pp. 122–142, pp. 131–132

46  *City Council of Pretoria v Walker* (CCT8/97) [1998] ZACC 1; 1998 (2) SA 363; 1998 (3) BCLR 257 (17 February 1998)

47  *Minister of Finance and Other v Van Heerden* (CCT 63/03) [2004] ZACC 3; 2004 (6) SA 121 (CC); 2004 (11) BCLR 1125 (CC); [2004] 12 BLLR 1181 (CC) (29 July 2004)

48  Modiri 'The colour of law' p. 431

49  Modiri 'The colour of law' p. 409

50  Modiri 'The colour of law' p. 424

51  Modiri 'The colour of law' p. 434

52  Makau Mutua 'Hope and despair for a new South Africa: The limits of rights discourse' *Harvard Human Rights Journal* Vol. 10, 1997, pp. 63–114, p. 81

53  Mutua 'Hope and despair' p. 68

54  Mutua 'Hope and despair' p. 78

55  Mutua 'Hope and despair' p. 92

56  Mutua 'Hope and despair' p. 83

57  Mutua 'Hope and despair' p. 81

58   Mutua 'Hope and despair' p. 86
59   Mutua 'Hope and despair' p. 88
60   Mutua 'Hope and despair' p. 93
61   Mutua 'Hope and despair' p. 112
62   Sanele Sibanda 'Not purpose-made! Transformative constitutionalism, post-independence constitutionalism and the struggle to eradicate poverty' *Stellenbosch Law Review* Vol. 22, No. 3, 2011, pp. 482–500, p. 484
63   Sibanda 'Not purpose-made' p. 486
64   Dennis Davis 'Transformation: The constitutional promise and reality' *South African Journal on Human Rights* Vol. 26, No. 1, 2010, pp. 85–101, p. 93
65   Sibanda 'Not purpose-made' p. 493
66   Sibanda 'Not purpose-made' p. 493
67   Sibanda 'Not purpose-made' p. 493
68   Sibanda 'Not purpose-made' p. 498
69   Duncan 'Best of SACSIS'
70   Von Holdt 'Violent democracy' p. 592
71   Von Holdt 'Violent democracy' p. 593
72   Jonathan Michie and Vishnu Padayachee *The Political Economy of South Africa's Transition: Policy Perspectives in the Late 1990s* London, Dryden Press, 1997, p. 11
73   Von Holdt 'Violent democracy' p. 594
74   Von Holdt 'Violent democracy' p. 596
75   Von Holdt 'Violent democracy' p. 600
76   Von Holdt 'Violent democracy' p. 593
77   Von Holdt 'Violent democracy' pp. 592–593
78   Hein Marais *South Africa Pushed to the Limit: The Political Economy of Change* Claremont, UCT Press, 2011, p. 79
79   Von Holdt 'Violent democracy' p. 593
80   Cachalia 'Democratic constitutionalism' p. 377
81   Cachalia 'Democratic constitutionalism' p. 380
82   Cachalia 'Democratic constitutionalism' p. 379
83   Cachalia 'Democratic constitutionalism' p. 382
84   Cachalia 'Democratic constitutionalism' p. 390, emphasis in original
85   Cachalia 'Democratic constitutionalism' p. 391
86   Basil Davidson *The Black Man's Burden: Africa and the Curse of the Nation-State* New York, Times Books/Random House, 1992, pp. 61–62 cited in Cachalia 'Democratic constitutionalism' p. 391
87   Cachalia 'Democratic constitutionalism' p. 387
88   Stuart Woolman 'South Africa's aspirational constitution and our problems of collective action' *South African Journal on Human Rights* Vol. 32, No. 1, 2016, pp. 156–183 cited in Cachalia 'Democratic constitutionalism'
89   Cachalia 'Democratic constitutionalism' p. 387, emphasis in original
90   Cachalia 'Democratic constitutionalism' p. 395
91   Cachalia 'Democratic constitutionalism' p. 384
92   Cachalia 'Democratic constitutionalism' p. 396
93   Cachalia 'Democratic constitutionalism' p. 397
94   Dikgang Moseneke *My Own Liberator: A Memoir* Johannesburg, Picador, 2016
95   Dikgang Moseneke 'The constitution twenty years after its adoption' Address to Nelson Mandela Foundation Centre of Memory, 17 March 2016, p. 15

96  Moseneke 'Twenty years' p. 11
97  Richard Pithouse 'Dikgang Moseneke: Constitution allows for land expropriation' Land and Accountability Research Centre, 5 March 2015 https://www.customcontested. co.za/dikgang-moseneke-constitution-allows-for-land-expropriation/
98  Mahmood Mamdani 'Beyond Nuremberg: The historical significance of the post-apartheid transition in South Africa' *Politics and Society* Vol. 43, No. 1, 2015, pp. 61–88
99  Mamdani 'Beyond Nuremberg' p. 63
100 Mamdani 'Beyond Nuremberg' p. 70
101 Mamdani 'Beyond Nuremberg' p. 71
102 Mamdani 'Beyond Nuremberg' p. 67
103 Mamdani 'Beyond Nuremberg' p. 71
104 Mamdani 'Beyond Nuremberg' pp. 81–82
105 Mamdani 'Beyond Nuremberg' p. 82
106 South African History Online 'NP set to withdraw from GNU' 10 May 1996 https:// www.sahistory.org.za/dated-event/np-set-withdraw-gnu
107 Modiri 'The colour of law' p. 425
108 Modiri 'The colour of law' p. 426
109 Modiri 'The colour of law' p. 433
110 Niren Tolsi 'Grootboom win a house of cards' *Mail and Guardian* 9 March 2012 http://mg.co.za/article/2012-03-09-grootboom-win-a-house-of-cards
111 The discussion which follows relies heavily on Friedman 'Enabling agency'
112 *Government of the Republic of South Africa and Others v Grootboom and Others* (CCT11/00) [2000] ZACC 19; 2001 (1) SA 46; 2000 (11) BCLR 1169 (4 October 2000)
113 *Minister of Health and Others v Treatment Action Campaign and Others* (No 2) (CCT8/02) [2002] ZACC 15; 2002 (5) SA 721; 2002 (10) BCLR 1033 (5 July 2002)
114 *Minister of Health v Treatment Action Campaign*
115 Jackie Dugard 'Courts and the poor in South Africa: A critique of systemic judicial failures to advance transformative justice' *South African Journal on Human Rights* Vol. 24, No. 2, 2008, pp. 214–238; Catherine Albertyn 'Gendered transformation in South African jurisprudence: Poor women and the Constitutional Court' *Stellenbosch Law Review* Vol. 22, No. 3, 2011, pp. 591–613
116 The role of 'minimum core content' in constitutional jurisprudence is discussed in Theunis Roux 'Legitimating transformation: Political resource allocation in the South African Constitutional Court' *Democratization* Vol. 1, No. 4, 2003, pp. 92–111
117 *Mazibuko v City of Johannesburg* (2010) (Centre on Housing Rights and Evictions as amicus curiae) 4 SA 1 (CC)
118 *Mazibuko and Others v City of Johannesburg and Others* (CCT 39/09) [2009] ZACC 28; 2010 (3) BCLR 239 (CC); 2010 (4) SA 1 (CC) (8 October 2009)
119 *Residents of Joe Slovo Community, Western Cape v Thubelisha Homes and Others* (CCT 22/08) [2009] ZACC 16; 2009 (9) BCLR 847 (CC); 2010 (3) SA 454 (CC) (10 June 2009); *Occupiers of 51 Olivia Road, Berea Township and 197 Main Street Johannesburg v City of Johannesburg and Others* (24/07) [2008] ZACC 1; 2008 (3) SA 208 (CC); 2008 (5) BCLR 475 (CC) (19 February 2008)
120 Stuart Wilson 'Litigating housing rights in Johannesburg's inner city: 2004–2008' *South African Journal on Human Rights* Vol. 27, No. 1, 2011, pp. 127–151; Brian Ray 'Proceduralisation's triumph and engagement's promise in socio-economic rights litigation' *South African Journal on Human Rights* Vol. 27, No. 1, 2011, pp. 107–126

121 Ray 'Proceduralisation's triumph'

122 For the origins and implications of the idea of property, see CB Macpherson (ed.) *Property: Mainstream and Critical Positions* Toronto and Buffalo, University of Toronto Press, 1978

123 Tembeka Ngcukaitobi 'What section 25 means for land reform' *Mail and Guardian* 13 December 2019 https://mg.co.za/article/2019-12-13-00-what-section-25-means-for-land-reform

124 Constitution of the Republic of South Africa, section 36, clause 1

125 Greg Nicholson 'Inner city blues: Joburg considers test case for expropriation of run-down buildings' *Daily Maverick* 7 March 2018 https://www.dailymaverick.co.za/article/2018-03-07-inner-city-blues-joburg-considers-test-case-for-expropriation-of-run-down-buildings/

126 Ngcukaitobi 'What section 25 means'

127 Hilary Wainwright *Reclaim the State: Experiments in Popular Democracy* London, Verso, 2003; Md Anisur Rahman 'Science for social revolution: The Kerala experiment' *Economic and Political Weekly* Vol. 14, No. 2, 1979, pp. 59+61–62

128 Steven Friedman (ed.) *The Long Journey: South Africa's Quest for a Negotiated Settlement* Johannesburg, Ravan Press, 1993

129 Patti Waldmeir *Anatomy of a Miracle: The End of Apartheid and the Birth of the New South Africa* New Brunswick NJ, Rutgers University Press, 1998

130 Mcebisi Jonas *After Dawn: Hope After State Capture* Johannesburg, Picador Africa, 2019, p. 1

## CHAPTER 7

1   For Wolpe's work and life, see Friedman *Race, Class and Power*; sections of this book also underpin the analysis offered in this chapter

2   For a full discussion of the theory of national democratic revolution, see Peter Hudson 'The concept of class and the class concept of national liberation in South Africa: Empiricism and essentialism in the theory of the South African revolution' in Mark Swilling (ed.) *Views on the South African State* Pretoria, HSRC, 1990, pp. 209–222

3   Michael Burawoy 'From liberation to reconstruction: Theory and practice in the life of Harold Wolpe' *Review of African Political Economy* Vol. 31, No. 102, 2004, pp. 657–675, p. 669

4   Harold Wolpe 'Education and social transformation: Problems and dilemmas' in Elaine Unterhalter, Harold Wolpe and Thozamile Botha (eds) *Education in a Future South Africa* Trenton NJ, Africa World Press, 1992, p. 16

5   Wolpe and Barends *A perspective*

6   Harold Wolpe 'The debate on university transformation in South Africa: The case of the University of the Western Cape' *Comparative Education* Vol. 31, No. 2, 1995, pp. 398–399

7   Wolpe and Barends *A perspective*

8   Saleem Badat, Zenariah Barends and Harold Wolpe *The Post-Secondary Education System: Towards Policy Formulation for Equality and Development* Working Paper No. 1, Education Policy Unit, University of the Western Cape, May 1993

9   Badat, Barends and Wolpe *The Post-Secondary System*

10    Claude Ake 'Rethinking African democracy' *Journal of Democracy* Vol. 2, No. 1, 1991, pp. 32–44, p. 36 cited in Badat, Barends and Wolpe *The Post-Secondary System*

11    Badat, Barends and Wolpe *The Post-Secondary System*

12    Badat, Barends and Wolpe *The Post-Secondary System*

13    South African Government *White Paper on Reconstruction and Development: A Strategy for Fundamental Transformation* 1994

14    Harold Wolpe 'The uneven transition from apartheid in South Africa' *Transformation* 27, 1995, pp. 88–101

15    Graeme Gotz 'Shoot anything that flies, claim anything that falls: Labour and the changing definition of the Reconstruction and Development Plan' in Glen Adler and Edward Webster (eds) *Trade Unions and Democratization in South Africa 1985–1997* New York, St Martin's Press, 2000, pp. 159–189

16    National Treasury *Growth, Employment and Redistribution: A Macroeconomic Strategy* South African Government, Pretoria, 1996

17    John R Weeks 'Stuck in low GEAR? Macroeconomic policy in South Africa, 1996–98' *Cambridge Journal of Economics* Vol. 23, No. 6, 1999, pp. 795–811, p. 795

18    Weeks 'Low GEAR' p. 796

19    African National Congress *The Reconstruction and Development Programme: A Policy Framework* 1994 https://www.sahistory.org.za/sites/default/files/the_reconstruction_and_development_programm_1994.pdf

20    Wolpe 'Uneven transition' p. 91

21    Wolpe 'Uneven transition' p. 96

22    Wolpe 'Uneven transition' p. 97

23    Wolpe 'Uneven transition' p. 97

24    Wolpe 'Uneven transition' p. 97

25    Wolpe 'Uneven transition' p. 99

26    Wolpe 'Uneven transition' p. 100

27    South African Communist Party *Draft Strategy and Tactics* 1994, p. 13 cited in Wolpe 'Uneven transition' p. 101

28    Wolpe 'Uneven transition' p. 101

29    South African Communist Party *Draft Tactics* p. 7 cited in Wolpe 'Uneven transition' p. 101

30    Wolpe 'Uneven transition' p. 101

31    Friedman *Race, Class and Power*

32    Harold Wolpe 'Towards an analysis of the South African state' *International Journal of the Sociology of Law* Vol. 8, No. 4, 1980, pp. 399–421

33    South African Government *White Paper on Reconstruction and Development* p. 12 cited in Wolpe 'Uneven transition' p. 93

34    Pravin Gordhan '2012 budget speech' 22 February 2012 http://www.treasury.gov.za/documents/national%20budget/2012/speech/speech.pdf

35    Nontsikelelo Mpulo '"Second transition" is non-existent' *Grocott's Mail Online* 2 August 2012 http://www.grocotts.co.za/content/second-transition-premature-says-analyst-02-08-2012

36    Pravin Gordhan '2013 budget speech' 27 February 2013 http://www.treasury.gov.za/documents/national%20budget/2013/speech/speech.pdfp.27

37    Wolpe 'Uneven transition' pp. 94–95

38    Wolpe 'Uneven transition' p. 95

39    Friedman *Race, Class and Power* p. 266

40 Hein Marais *South Africa: Limits to Change – the Political Economy of Transition* New York, Palgrave Macmillan, 1998

41 Antonio Gramsci *Prison Notebooks* Joseph Buttigieg (ed.) New York, Columbia University Press, 1992, pp. 233ff

42 Peter Bachrach and Morton S Baratz *Power and Poverty: Theory and Practice* New York, Oxford University Press, 1970, p. 43 cited in John Gaventa *Power and Powerlessness: Quiescence and Rebellion in an Appalachian Valley* Urbana and Chicago, University of Illinois Press, 1982, p. 14

43 Gaventa *Power and Powerlessness* pp. 15–16

44 Friedman 'Democracy as an open-ended utopia'

45 Hoffman *John Gray*

46 Hoffman *John Gray* p. 137

47 Steven Friedman *Building Tomorrow Today: African Workers in Trade Unions 1970–1984* Johannesburg, Ravan Press, 1985

48 Boris Kagarlitzky *The Dialectic of Change* London, Verso, 1990, p. 8

49 John Saul 'Structural reform: A model for the revolutionary transformation of South Africa?' *Transformation* 20, 1992, pp. 1–16, p. 3

## CHAPTER 8

1 Setumo Stone 'How Ramaphosa "dodged a coup" – security bosses reveal all' *City Press* 22 July 2018

2 Hoffman *John Gray*; Friedman 'Democracy as open-ended utopia'

3 Friedman 'Democracy as open-ended utopia' p. 11

4 Bill Freund 'Review: Four books on the economy' *South African Labour Bulletin* Vol. 16, No. 5, 1992, pp. 78–85, p. 85

5 Hoffman *John Gray* p. 92

6 Gaventa *Power and Powerlessness*

7 World Bank *South Africa Update: Jobs and Inequality* Washington DC, The World Bank, 2018, p. 20

8 Sandile Mchunu 'Nedbank CEO issues strong warning to government as SA runs out of time, money' *Business Report* 7 August 2019 https://www.iol.co.za/business-report/companies/nedbank-ceo-issues-strong-warning-to-government-as-sa-runs-out-of-time-money-30412721

9 Sunita Menon 'Business blames unions for weak economy' *Business Day* 1 May 2019 https://www.businesslive.co.za/bd/economy/2019-05-01-business-blames-unions-for-weak-economy/

10 Natasha Marrian 'ANC blames Jacob Zuma's maladministration for SA's economic mess' *Business Day* 6 September 2018 https://www.businesslive.co.za/bd/national/2018-09-06-jacob-zumas-maladministration-led-to-sas-economic-mess/

11 South African Federation of Trade Unions (SAFTU) 'SAFTU condemns Ramaphosa's pro-big business and "business as usual" SONA' 8 February 2019 https://saftu.org.za/saftu-condemns-ramaphosas-pro-big-business-and-business-as-usual-sona/

12 Jonas *After Dawn* p. 1

13 Jonas *After Dawn* p. 1

14 Jonas *After Dawn* p. 2

15  Lameez Omarjee 'SA edging closer to IMF bailout – Sipho Pityana' *Fin24* 2 November 2019 https://www.fin24.com/Economy/sa-edging-closer-to-imf-bailout-sipho-pityana-20191102

16  Theto Mahlakoana 'SA sets a new record for industrial action' *Business Day* 10 July 2018 https://www.businesslive.co.za/bd/national/labour/2018-07-10-sa-sets-a-new-record-for-industrial-action/

17  Jonas *After Dawn* p. 257

18  Jonas *After Dawn* p. 252

19  Jonas *After Dawn* p. 253

20  TransUnion '#StrongerTogether: Lessons from the 2019 Rugby World Cup' 18 November 2019 https://www.transunion.co.za/blog/strongertogether-lessons-from-the-2019-rugby-world-cup

21  Eustace Davie 'Working together, South Africans can grow a strong economy' *Business Report* 10 November 2019 https://www.iol.co.za/business-report/opinion/working-together-south-africans-can-grow-a-strong-economy-36885220. The author is a director of the Free Market Foundation and the article argued, inevitably, that the country's victory in the Rugby World Cup showed that much could be achieved by uniting behind free-market economics

22  Cyril Ramaphosa 'President Cyril Ramaphosa: State of the Nation Address 2018' 16 February 2018 https://www.gov.za/speeches/president-cyril-ramaphosa-2018-state-nation-address-16-feb-2018-0000

23  Cyril Ramaphosa 'President Cyril Ramaphosa: State of the Nation Address 2019' 20 June 2019 https://www.gov.za/speeches/2SONA2019

24  Lameez Omarjee 'Business trust deficit in SA started long before Zuma – Scopa chair' *Fin24* 14 August 2017 https://www.fin24.com/Economy/business-trust-deficit-in-sa-started-long-before-zuma-scopa-chair-20170814

25  Phanuel Shuma 'Presidential GBV summit not another talk shop: Dlamini' *SABC News Online* 2 November 2018 http://www.sabcnews.com/sabcnews/presidential-gbv-summit-not-another-talk-shop-dlamini/

26  Jeremy Baskin 'Labour in South Africa's transition to democracy: Concertation in a third world setting' in Glen Adler and Edward Webster (eds) *Trade Unions and Democratization* New York, St Martin's Press, 2000, pp. 42–56, p. 48

27  Omano Edigheji (ed.) *Constructing a Developmental State in South Africa: Potentials and Challenges* Cape Town, HSRC Press, 2010

28  O'Meara *Volkskapitalisme*

# REFERENCES

## SECONDARY SOURCES

Ake, Claude 1991 'Rethinking African democracy' *Journal of Democracy* Vol. 2, No. 1, pp. 32–44

Albertyn, Catherine 2011 'Gendered transformation in South African jurisprudence: Poor women and the Constitutional Court' *Stellenbosch Law Review* Vol. 22, No. 3, pp. 591–613

Alexander, Peter 2010 'Rebellion of the poor: South Africa's service delivery protests – a preliminary analysis' *Review of African Political Economy* Vol. 37, No. 123, pp. 25–40 DOI: 10.1080/03056241003637870

Alexander, Peter, Thapelo Lekgowa, Botsang Mmope, Luke Sinwell and Bongani Xezwi 2012 *Marikana: A View from the Mountain and a Case to Answer* Auckland Park, Jacana Media

Arthur, W Brian 1989 'Increasing returns, and lock-in by historical events' *Economic Journal* Vol. 99, No. 394, pp. 116–131

Bachrach, Peter and Morton S Baratz 1970 *Power and Poverty: Theory and Practice* New York, Oxford University Press

Badat, Saleem, Zenariah Barends and Harold Wolpe 1993 *The Post-Secondary Education System: Towards Policy Formulation for Equality and Development* Working Paper No. 1, Education Policy Unit, University of the Western Cape, May

Banerjee, Abhijit, Sebastian Galiani, Jim Levinsohn, Zoë McLaren and Ingrid Woolard 2007 *Why Has Unemployment Risen in the New South Africa?* National Bureau of Economic Research Working Paper No. 13167, NBER, Cambridge MA, June

Baskin, Jeremy 2000 'Labour in South Africa's transition to democracy: Concertation in a third world setting' in Glenn Adler and Edward Webster (eds) *Trade Unions and Democratization in South Africa 1985–1997* New York, St Martin's Press, pp. 42–56

Bazana, Sandiso and Opelo P Mogotsi 2017 'Social identities and racial integration in historically white universities: A literature review of the experiences of black students' *Transformation in Higher Education* Vol. 2, a25 DOI: 10.4102/the.v2i0.25/

Beall, Jo, Owen Crankshaw and Sue Parnell 2000 'Victims, villains and fixers: The urban environment and Johannesburg's poor' *Journal of Southern African Studies* Vol. 26, No. 4, pp. 803–855

Beresford, Alex 2012 'Organised labour and the politics of class formation in post-apartheid South Africa' *Review of African Political Economy* Vol. 39, No. 134, pp. 569–589

Berlinski, Samuel, Sebastian Galiani and Paul Gertler 2009 'The effect of pre-primary education on primary school performance' *Journal of Public Economics* Vol. 93, No. 1–2, pp. 219–234

Bhorat, Haroon and Carlene van der Westhuizen 2012 *Poverty, Inequality and the Nature of Economic Growth in South Africa* Development Policy Research Unit Working Paper No. 12/151, University of Cape Town, November

Bhorat, Haroon, Carlene van der Westhuizen and Toughedah Jacobs 2009 *Income and Non-Income Inequality in Post-Apartheid South Africa: What Are the Drivers and Possible Policy Interventions?* Development Policy Research Unit Working Paper No. 09/138, University of Cape Town, August

Bhorat, Haroon, Carlene van der Westhuizen and Derek Yu 2014 *The Silent Success: Delivery of Public Assets Since Democracy* Development Policy Research Unit Working Paper No. 201403, University of Cape Town, July

Booysen, Lize 2007 'Barriers to employment equity implementation and retention of blacks in management in South Africa' *South African Journal of Labour Relations* Vol. 31, No. 1, pp. 47–68

Brandel Syrier, Mia 1971 *Reeftown Elite* Abingdon, Routledge and Kegan Paul

Brautigam, Deborah 2006 'Contingent consent: Export taxation and state building in Mauritius' Paper presented at the annual meeting of the American Political Science Association, Philadelphia PA, 31 August

Buhlungu, Sakhela 2002 *Comrades, Entrepreneurs and Career Unionists: Organisational Modernisation and New Cleavages Among COSATU Union Officials* Occasional Paper No. 17, Friedrich Ebert Stiftung http://citeseerx.ist.psu.edu/viewdoc/summary?doi=10.1.1.196.3667

Burawoy, Michael 2004 'From liberation to reconstruction: Theory and practice in the life of Harold Wolpe' *Review of African Political Economy* Vol. 31, No. 102, pp. 657–675

Burger, Ronelle, Cindy Lee Steenekamp, Asmus Zoch and Servaas van der Berg 2017 *The Middle Class in Contemporary South Africa: Comparing Rival Approaches* Working Paper No. 11/2014, Department of Economics, Stellenbosch University, 25 May

Cachalia, Firoz 2018 'Democratic constitutionalism in the time of the postcolony: Beyond triumph and betrayal' *South African Journal on Human Rights* Vol. 34, No. 3, pp. 375–397

Calof, Jonathan and Wilma Viviers 1995 'Internationalization behavior of small- and medium-sized South African enterprises' *Journal of Small Business Management* Vol. 33, No. 4, pp. 71–79

Claassens, Aninka 2014 '"Communal land", property rights and traditional leadership' Wits Institute for Social and Economic Research http://wiser.wits.ac.za/system/files/documents/Claassens2014.pdf

Cloete, JN 1978 'The bureaucracy' in Anthony de Crespigny and Robert Schrire (eds) *The Government and Politics of South Africa* Cape Town, Juta

Cole, Josette 1987 *Crossroads: The Politics of Reform and Repression, 1976–1986* Johannesburg, Ravan Press

Cousins, Ben 2007 'More than socially embedded: The distinctive character of "communal tenure" regimes in South Africa and its implications for land policy' *Journal of Agrarian Change* Vol. 7, No. 3, pp. 281–315

Cousins, Ben 2009 'Key provisions of the Communal Land Rights Act are declared unconstitutional. Where to now?' *Another Countryside* (blog) Institute for Poverty, Land and Agrarian Studies (PLAAS), University of the Western Cape, 10 November http://www.plaas.org.za/blog/key-provisions-communal-land-rights-act-are-declared-unconstitutional-where-no

David, Paul A 1985 'Clio and the economics of QWERTY' *American Economic Review* Vol. 75, No. 2, pp. 332–337

Davidson, Basil 1992 *The Black Man's Burden: Africa and the Curse of the Nation-State* New York, Times Books/Random House

Davis, Dennis 2010 'Transformation: The constitutional promise and reality' *South African Journal on Human Rights* Vol. 26, No. 1, pp. 85–101

Dubow, Saul 2014 *Apartheid 1948–1994* Oxford, Oxford University Press

Dugard, Jackie 2008 'Courts and the poor in South Africa: A critique of systemic judicial failures to advance transformative justice' *South African Journal on Human Rights* Vol. 24, No. 2, pp. 214–238

Duncan, Jane 2011 'Best of SACSIS: The problem with South Africa's constitution' http://www.sacsis.org.za/site/article/631

Durkheim, Emile 1974 *Sociology and Philosophy* DF Pocock (trans.) New York, Free Press

Du Toit, Andre and Hermann Giliomee 1983 *Afrikaner Political Thought* Vol. 1 Cape Town, David Philip

Edigheji, Omano (ed.) 2010 *Constructing a Developmental State in South Africa: Potentials and Challenges* Cape Town, HSRC Press

Faundez, Julio 2016 'Douglass North's theory of institutions: Lessons for law and development' *Hague Journal on the Rule of Law* Vol. 8, No. 2, pp. 373–419

Ferree, Karen 2011 *Framing the Race in South Africa: The Political Origins of Racial Census Elections* Cambridge, Cambridge University Press

Field, Alex 2006 'North, Douglass' in DA Clark (ed.) *Elgar Companion to Development Studies* Cheltenham, Edward Elgar Publishing, pp. 423–426

Fourie, Johan, Ada Jansen and Krige Siebrits 2012 'Public finances under private company rule: The Dutch Cape Colony (1652–1795)' *New Contree* Vol. 68, No. 4, pp. 51–71

Fox Piven, Frances and Richard Cloward 1979 *Poor People's Movements: Why They Succeed, How They Fail* New York, Vintage Books

Freund, Bill 1992 'Review: Four books on the economy' *South African Labour Bulletin* Vol. 16, No. 5, pp. 78–85

Friedman, Steven 1985 *Building Tomorrow Today: African Workers in Trade Unions 1970–1984* Johannesburg, Ravan Press

Friedman, Steven 1986 *Understanding Reform* Johannesburg, South African Institute of Race Relations

Friedman, Steven 1987 *Reform Revisited* Johannesburg, South African Institute of Race Relations

Friedman, Steven (ed.) 1993 *The Long Journey: South Africa's Quest for a Negotiated Settlement* Johannesburg, Ravan Press

Friedman, Steven 1999 'Who we are: Voter participation, rationality and the 1999 election' *Politikon* Vol. 26, No. 2, pp. 213–223

Friedman, Steven 2005 'Getting better than "world class": The challenge of governing postapartheid South Africa' *Social Research* Vol. 72, No. 3, pp. 757–784

Friedman, Steven 2010 'Seeing ourselves as others see us: Racism, technique and the Mbeki administration' in Daryl Glaser (ed.) *Mbeki and After: Reflections on the Legacy of Thabo Mbeki* Johannesburg, Wits University Press, pp. 163–186

Friedman, Steven 2011 'Whose freedom? South Africa's press, middle-class bias and the threat of control' *Ecquid Novi* Vol. 32, No. 2, pp. 106–121

Friedman, Steven 2012 'Democracy as an open-ended utopia: Reviving a sense of uncoerced political possibility' *Theoria* Vol. 59, No. 130, pp. 1–21

Friedman, Steven 2014 'Less a theory of society, more a state of mind? The ambiguous legacy of South African liberalism' in Peter Vale, Lawrence Hamilton and Estelle H Prinsloo (eds) *Intellectual Traditions in South Africa: Ideas, Individuals and Institutions* Pietermaritzburg, University of KwaZulu-Natal Press

Friedman, Steven 2015 'Archipelagos of dominance: Party fiefdoms and South African democracy' *Zeitschrift für Vergleichende Politikwissenschaft (Journal of Comparative Politics)* Vol. 9, No. 3, pp. 139–159

Friedman, Steven 2015 'The Janus face of the past: Preserving and resisting South African path dependence' in Xolela Mangcu (ed.) *The Colour of Our Future: Does Race Matter in Post-Apartheid South Africa?* Johannesburg, Wits University Press, pp. 45–63

Friedman, Steven 2015 *Race, Class and Power: Harold Wolpe and the Radical Critique of Apartheid*, Johannesburg, Ravan Press

Friedman, Steven 2016 'Enabling agency: The Constitutional Court and social policy' *Transformation* 91, pp. 19–39

Friedman, Steven 2018 *Power in Action: Democracy, Citizenship and Social Justice* Johannesburg, Wits University Press

Friedman, Steven 2019 'Beyond race or class: The politics of identity and inequality' *Transformation* 100, pp. 78–102

Friedman, Steven and Sharon Groenmeyer 2016 'A nightmare on the brain of the living? The endurance and limits of the collective bargaining regime' *Transformation* 91, pp. 63–83

Friedman, Steven, Kenny Hlela and Paul Thulare 2005 'A question of voice: Informality and pro-poor policy in Johannesburg, South Africa' in Nabeel Hamdi (ed.) *Urban Futures: Economic Growth and Poverty Reduction* Rugby, ITDG Publishing, pp. 51–68

Friedman, Steven and Shauna Mottiar 2005 'A rewarding engagement? The Treatment Action Campaign and the politics of HIV/AIDS' *Politics and Society* Vol. 33, No. 4, pp. 511–565

Friedman, Steven and Louise Stack 1994 'The magic moment: The 1994 election' in Steven Friedman and Doreen Atkinson (eds) *The Small Miracle: South Africa's Negotiated Settlement* Johannesburg, Ravan Press, pp. 301–330

Gaventa, John 1982 *Power and Powerlessness: Quiescence and Rebellion in an Appalachian Valley* Urbana and Chicago, University of Illinois Press

Gevisser, Mark 2009 *A Legacy of Liberation: Thabo Mbeki and the Future of the South African Dream* New York, Palgrave Macmillan

Giliomee, Hermann and Bernard Mbenga 2007 *New History of South Africa* Tafelberg, Cape Town

Giliomee, Hermann and Charles Simkins (eds) 1999 *The Awkward Embrace: One-Party Domination and Democracy* Amsterdam, Harwood

Goldin, Ian 1984 *The Poverty of Coloured Labour Preference: Economics and Ideology in the Western Cape* Southern Africa Labour and Development Research Unit Working Paper No. 59, SALDRU, Cape Town, January http://opensaldru.uct.ac.za/bitstream/handle/11090/563/1984_goldin_swp59.pdf?sequence=1

Gotz, Graeme 2000 'Shoot anything that flies, claim anything that falls: Labour and the changing definition of the Reconstruction and Development Plan' in Glenn Adler and Edward Webster (eds) *Trade Unions and Democratization in South Africa 1985–1997* New York, St Martin's Press, pp. 159–189

Graham, Victoria, Yolanda Sadie and Leila Patel 2016 'Social grants, food parcels and voting behaviour: A case study of three South African communities' *Transformation* 91, pp. 106–135

Gramsci, Antonio 1992 *Prison Notebooks* Joseph Buttigieg (ed.) New York, Columbia University Press

Gwaindepi, Abel 2018 'State building in the colonial era: Public revenue, expenditure and borrowing patterns in the Cape Colony, 1820–1910' PhD dissertation, Faculty of Economics and Management Sciences, University of Stellenbosch, March

Heleta, Savo 2016 'Decolonisation of higher education: Dismantling epistemic violence and Eurocentrism in South Africa' *Transformation in Higher Education* Vol. 1, No. 1, a9 http://dx.doi.org/10.4102/the.vlil.9

Hill, Robert A (editor in chief) 2006 *The Marcus Garvey and Universal Negro Improvement Association Papers, Volume X: Africa for the Africans 1923–1945* Berkeley and Los Angeles, University of California Press

Hillegas, Howard C 1900 *The Boers in War: The Story of the British-Boer War of 1899–1900* New York, Appleton and Co.

Hirson, Baruch 1989 'Bukharin, Bunting and the "Native Republic" slogan' *Searchlight South Africa* Vol. 1, No. 3, pp. 51–65

Hoffman, John 2009 *John Gray and the Problem of Utopia* Cardiff, University of Wales Press

Horner, Dudley 1987 'African labour representation up to 1975' in Johann Maree (ed.) *The Independent Trade Unions 1974–1984: Ten Years of the South African Labour Bulletin* Johannesburg, Ravan Press, pp. 124–137

Horner, Dudley and Francis Wilson 2008 *A Tapestry of People: The Growth of Population in the Province of the Western Cape* Southern Africa Labour and Development Research Unit Working Paper No. 21, SALDRU, Cape Town

Hudson, Peter 1986 'The Freedom Charter and the theory of national democratic revolution' *Transformation* 1, pp. 6–38

Hudson, Peter 1990 'The concept of class and the class concept of national liberation in South Africa – empiricism and essentialism in the theory of the South African revolution' in Mark Swilling (ed.) *Perspectives on the South African State* Pretoria, HSRC, pp. 209–222

Humphries, Richard, Thabo Rapoo and Steven Friedman 1994 'The shape of the country: Negotiating regional government' in Steven Friedman and Doreen Atkinson (eds) *The Small Miracle: South Africa's Negotiated Settlement*, Johannesburg, Ravan Press, pp. 148–181

Hyslop, Jonathan 2005 'Political corruption: Before and after apartheid' *Journal of Southern African Studies* Vol. 31, No. 4, pp. 773–789

James, CLR 1938 *The Black Jacobins: Toussaint L'Ouverture and the San Domingo Revolution* London, Secker and Warburg

Jara, Mazibuko 2014 'Beyond social compacting: A power matrix in flux in post-Mandela South Africa' in Mapungubwe Institute for Social Reflection (MISTRA) *20 Years of South African Democracy: So Where to Now?* Johannesburg, MISTRA, pp. 82–88

Jessop, Bob 1990 *State Theory: Putting the Capitalist State in Its Place* University Park, Pennsylvania State University Press

Jonas, Mcebisi 2019 *After Dawn: Hope After State Capture* Johannesburg, Picador Africa

Jones, Kenneth and Tema Okun 2001 *Dismantling Racism: A Workbook for Social Change Groups* Portland OR, Western States Center https://www.thc.texas.gov/public/upload/preserve/museums/files/White_Supremacy_Culture.pdf

Kagarlitzky, Boris 1990 *The Dialectic of Change* London, Verso

Khan, Mushtaq H and Jomo Kwame Sundaram 2005 'Introduction' in Khan and Sundaram (eds) *Rents, Rent Seeking and Economic Development: Theory and Evidence in Asia* Cambridge, Cambridge University Press

Klare, Karl 1998 'Legal culture and transformative constitutionalism' *South African Journal on Human Rights* Vol. 14, No. 1, pp. 146–188

Kok, Anton 2008 'The Promotion of Equality and Prevention of Unfair Discrimination Act 4 of 2000: Court-driven or legislature-driven societal transformation?' *Stellenbosch Law Review* Vol. 19, No. 1, pp. 122–142

Landman, Karina 2004 *Gated Communities in South Africa: Comparison of Four Case Studies in Gauteng* Pretoria, Council for Scientific and Industrial Research

Lanegran, Kimberly 2001 'South Africa's 1999 election: Consolidating a dominant party system' *Africa Today* Vol. 48, No. 2, pp. 81–102

Langa, Malose and Karl von Holdt 2012 'Insurgent citizenship, class formation and the dual nature of community protest: A case study of Kungcatsha' in Marcelle C Dawson and Luke Sinwell (eds) *Contesting Transformation: Popular Resistance in Twenty-First Century South Africa* London, Pluto Press, pp. 80–100

Lavery, Jerry 2012 *Protest and Political Participation in South Africa: Time Trends and Characteristics of Protesters* Afrobarometer Briefing Paper No. 102, May

Lawson-Remer, Terra 2013 'Property insecurity' *Brooklyn Journal of International Law* Vol. 38, No. 1, pp. 145–191

Legassick, Martin and Robert Ross 2010 'From slave economy to settler capitalism: The Cape Colony and its extensions' in Caroline Hamilton, Bernard Mbenga and Robert Ross (eds) *The Cambridge History of South Africa: Volume 1: From Early Times to 1885* New York, Cambridge University Press, pp. 253–318

Lester, Alan 1997 'The margins of order: Strategies of segregation on the Eastern Cape frontier, 1806–circa 1850' *Journal of Southern African Studies* Vol. 23, No. 4, pp. 635–653

Levine, Victor 1975 *Political Corruption: The Ghana Case* Stanford CA, Stanford University Press

Levy, Brian 2014 *Working with the Grain: Integrating Governance and Growth in Development Strategies* New York, Oxford University Press

Lipset, Seymour Martin 1959 'Some social requisites of democracy: Economic development and political legitimacy' *American Political Science Review* Vol. 53, No. 1, pp. 69–105

Lodge, Tom 1998 'Political corruption in South Africa' *African Affairs* Vol. 97, No. 387, pp. 157–187

Lodge, Tom and Ursula Scheidegger 2006 *Political Parties and Democratic Governance in South Africa* Electoral Institute for Sustainable Democracy in Africa Research Report No. 25, Johannesburg, EISA

MacDonald, David 2008 *World City Syndrome: Neoliberalism and Inequality in Cape Town* New York, Routledge

Macpherson, CB (ed.) 1978 *Property: Mainstream and Critical Positions* Toronto and Buffalo, University of Toronto Press

Madlingozi, Tshepo 2017 'Social justice in the time of neo-apartheid: Critiquing the anti-black economy of recognition, incorporation and distribution' *Stellenbosch Law Review* Vol. 28, No. 1, pp. 123–147

Mamdani, Mahmood 1995 *Citizen and Subject: Contemporary Africa and the Politics of Late Colonialism* Kampala, Fountain

Mamdani, Mahmood 2015 'Beyond Nuremberg: The historical significance of the post-apartheid transition in South Africa' *Politics and Society* Vol. 43, No. 1, pp. 61–88

Mandela, Nelson 1994 *Long Walk to Freedom* London, Little, Brown

Mansbridge, Jane 1983 *Beyond Adversary Democracy* Chicago and London, University of Chicago Press

Manson, Andrew and Bernard Mbenga 2012 'Bophuthatswana and the North West Province: From Pan-Tswanaism to Mineral-Based Ethnic Assertiveness' *South African Historical Journal* Vol. 6, No. 1, pp. 96–116

Marais, Hein 1998 *South Africa: Limits to Change – the Political Economy of Transition* New York, Palgrave Macmillan

Marais, Hein 2011 *South Africa Pushed to the Limit: The Political Economy of Change* Claremont, UCT Press

Martin, Geraldine and Kevin Durrheim 2006 'Racial recruitment in post-apartheid South Africa: Dilemmas of private recruitment agencies' *Psychology in Society* Vol. 33, pp. 1–15

Mbeki, Govan 1964 *South Africa: The Peasants' Revolt* Harmondsworth, Penguin

McCracken, JL 1967 *The Cape Parliament 1854–1910* London, Oxford University Press

Michie, Jonathan and Vishnu Padayachee 1997 *The Political Economy of South Africa's Transition: Policy Perspectives in the Late 1990s* London, Dryden Press

Mkandawire, Thandika 2015 'Neopatrimonialism and the political economy of economic performance in Africa: Critical reflections' *World Politics* Vol. 67, No. 3, pp. 563–612

Modiri, Joel M 2012 'The colour of law, power and knowledge: Introducing critical race theory in (post-)apartheid South Africa' *South African Journal on Human Rights* Vol. 28, No. 3, pp. 405–436

Modiri, Joel 2014 'The crises in legal education' *Acta Academica* Vol. 46, No. 3, pp. 1–24

Modiri, Joel Malasela 2017 'The jurisprudence of Steve Biko: A study in race, law and power in the "afterlife" of colonial apartheid' PhD dissertation, Faculty of Law, University of Pretoria, October

Moseneke, Dikgang 2016 'The constitution twenty years after its adoption' Address to Nelson Mandela Foundation Centre of Memory, 17 March

Moseneke, Dikgang 2016 *My Own Liberator: A Memoir* Johannesburg, Picador

Motala, Enver, Salim Vally and Rasigan Maharajh 2016 *Education, the State, and Class Inequality: The Case for Free Higher Education in South Africa* South African History Online https://www.sahistory.org.za/sites/default/files/file%20uploads%20/education_the_state_and_class_inequality.pdf

Moulder, James 1991 'The predominantly white universities: Some ideas for a debate' in Jonathan Jansen (ed.) *Knowledge and Power in South Africa* Johannesburg: Skotaville, pp. 117–118

Mutua, Makau 1997 'Hope and despair for a new South Africa: The limits of rights discourse' *Harvard Human Rights Journal* Vol. 10, pp. 63–114

Newham, Gareth and Hamadziripi Tamukamoyo 2013 'The Tatane case raises hard questions for South Africa's National Prosecuting Authority' *ISS Today* 11 April

Nolutshungu, Sam C 1982 *Changing South Africa: Political Considerations* Manchester, Manchester University Press

North, Douglass C 1979 'A framework for analyzing the state in economic history' *Explorations in Economic History* Vol. 16, No. 3, pp. 249–259

North, Douglass C 1990 *Institutions, Institutional Change and Economic Performance* Cambridge, Cambridge University Press

North, Douglass C 1991 'Institutions' *Journal of Economic Perspectives* Vol. 5, No. 1, pp. 97–112

North, Douglass C 1994 'Economic performance through time' *American Economic Review* Vol. 84, No. 3, pp. 359–368

North, Douglass C 1996 *Economic Performance Through Time: The Limits to Knowledge* Economic History Working Paper No. 9612004, University Library of Munich, Germany

North, Douglass C 2005 *Understanding the Process of Economic Change* Princeton NJ, Princeton University Press

No Sizwe (Neville Alexander) 1979 *One Azania, One Nation: The National Question in South Africa* London, Zed Books

Ntsebeza, Lungisile 2004 'Democratic decentralisation and traditional authority: Dilemmas of land administration in rural South Africa' *European Journal of Development Research* Vol. 16, No. 1, pp. 71–89

Nyamnjoh, Anye 2017 'The phenomenology of Rhodes Must Fall: Student activism and the experience of alienation at the University of Cape Town' *Strategic Review for Southern Africa* Vol. 39, No. 1, pp. 256–277

Nyamnjoh, Francis B 2016 *#RhodesMustFall: Nibbling at Resilient Colonialism in South Africa* Oxford, African Books Collective

Nzongola-Ntalaja, Georges 2002 *The Congo from Leopold to Kabila: A People's History* London, Zed Press

O'Meara, Dan 1983 *Volkskapitalisme: Class, Capital and Ideology in the Development of Afrikaner Nationalism 1934–1948* Cambridge, Cambridge University Press

O'Meara, Dan 1996 *Forty Lost Years: The Apartheid State and the Politics of the National Party, 1948–1994* Johannesburg, Ravan Press

Page, Scott E 2006 'Path dependence' *Quarterly Journal of Political Science* Vol. 1, No. 1, pp. 87–115

Patel, Leila, Yolanda Sadie, Victoria Graham, Aislinn Delaney and Kim Baldry 2014 *Voting Behaviour and the Influence of Social Protection: A Study of Voting Behaviour in Three Poor Areas of South Africa* Johannesburg, Centre for Social Development in Africa and Department of Politics, University of Johannesburg, June

Potgieter-Gqubule, Febe 2010 'Through the Eye of a Needle revisited: A perspective for discussion' *Umrabulo* No. 32, First Quarter

Przeworski, Adam 2004 'The last instance: Are institutions the primary cause of economic development?' *European Journal of Sociology* Vol. 45, No. 2, pp. 165–188

Putnam, Robert 1994 *Making Democracy Work: Civic Traditions in Modern Italy* Princeton NJ, Princeton University Press

Rahman, Md Anisur 1979 'Science for social revolution: The Kerala experiment' *Economic and Political Weekly* Vol. 14, No. 2, pp. 59+61–62

Ramose, Mogobe B 1998 'Justice and restitution in African political thought' in PH Coetzee and APJ Roux (eds) *The African Philosophy Reader* London, Routledge, pp. 541–640

Ramose, Mogobe B 2007 'In memoriam: Sovereignty and the "new" South Africa' *Griffith Law Review* Vol. 16, No. 2, pp. 310–329

Ramose, Mogobe 2014 'Affirming a right and seeking remedies in South Africa' in Leonhard Praeg and Siphokasi Magadla (eds) *Ubuntu: Curating the Archive* Pietermaritzburg, University of KwaZulu-Natal Press, pp. 121–136

Ramose, Mogobe Bernard and Derek Hook 2016 '"To whom does the land belong?" Mogobe Bernard Ramose talks to Derek Hook' *Psychology in Society* No. 50, pp. 86–98 DOI: 10.17159/2309-8708/2016/n50a5

Ray, Brian 2011 'Proceduralisation's triumph and engagement's promise in socio-economic rights litigation' *South African Journal on Human Rights* Vol. 27, No. 1, pp. 107–126

Reddy, Thiven 2005 'The Congress Party model: South Africa's African National Congress (ANC) and India's Indian National Congress (INC) as dominant parties' *African and Asian Studies* Vol. 4, No. 3, pp. 271–300

Robins, Steven 2008 *From Revolution to Rights in South Africa: Social Movements, NGOs and Popular Politics After Apartheid* London, James Currey, and Pietermaritzburg, University of KwaZulu-Natal Press

Rodrik, Dani 1999 *The New Global Economy and Developing Countries: Making Openness Work* Washington DC, Overseas Development Council

Rodrik, Dani 2008 *Second Best Institutions* Centre for Economic Policy Research Discussion Paper No. DP6764, CEPR, London, June

Roux, Theunis 2003 'Legitimating transformation: Political resource allocation in the South African Constitutional Court' *Democratization* Vol. 1, No. 4, pp. 92–111

Sachs, Albie 1990 *Protecting Human Rights in the New South Africa* Oxford, Oxford University Press

Saul, John 1992 'Structural reform: A model for the revolutionary transformation of South Africa?' *Transformation* 20, pp. 1–16

Sayed, Yusuf 2016 'The governance of public schooling in South Africa and the middle class: Social solidarity for the public good versus class interest' *Transformation* 91, pp. 84–105

Scott, James C 1985 *Weapons of the Weak: Everyday Forms of Peasant Resistance* New Haven CT, Yale University Press

Shubane, Khehla 1991 'Black local authorities: A contraption of control' in Mark Swilling, Richard Humphries and Khehla Shubane (eds) *Apartheid City in Transition* Cape Town, Oxford University Press, pp. 64–77

Shubane, Khehla and Mark Shaw 1993 *Tomorrow's Foundations? Forums as the Second Level of a Negotiated Transition in South Africa* Research Report No. 33, Centre for Policy Studies, Johannesburg

Sibanda, Sanele 2011 'Not purpose-made! Transformative constitutionalism, post-independence constitutionalism and the struggle to eradicate poverty' *Stellenbosch Law Review* Vol. 22, No. 3, pp. 482–500

Simone, T Abdou Maliqalim 1994 *In Whose Image? Political Islam and Urban Practices in Sudan* Chicago and London, University of Chicago Press

Solange, Rosa 2011 'Transformative constitutionalism in a democratic developmental state' *Stellenbosch Law Review* Vol. 22, No. 3, pp. 542–565

Southall, Roger 2004 'The ANC and black capitalism in South Africa' *Review of African Political Economy* Vol. 31, No. 100, pp. 313–328

Southall, Roger 2005 'The "dominant party debate" in South Africa' *Africa Spectrum* Vol. 39, No. 1, pp. 61–82

Statistics South Africa/The World Bank 2018 *Overcoming Poverty and Inequality in South Africa: An Assessment of Drivers, Constraints and Opportunities* Washington DC, The World Bank

Terreblanche, Sampie 2002 *A History of Inequality in South Africa: 1652–2002* Pietermaritzburg, University of KwaZulu-Natal Press

Tipe, Thuto 2014 'The boundaries of tradition: An examination of the Traditional Leadership and Governance Framework Act' *Harvard Human Rights Journal* 4 November http://harvardhrj.com/2014/11/the-boundaries-of-tradition-an-examination-of-the-traditional-leadership-and-governance-framework-act/

Turner, Richard 1972 'Black consciousness and white liberals' *Reality* July, pp. 20–22

Van Vuuren, Hennie 2017 *Apartheid, Guns and Money: A Tale of Profit* Auckland Park, Jacana Media

Vilikazi, Thando 2017 'Barriers to entry and inclusive growth: A case study of the liquid fuel wholesale industry' Centre for Competition, Regulation and Economic Development (CCRED), University of Johannesburg, May http://www.energy.gov.za/files/petroleum-sector-transformation-workshop/Barriers-to-entry-and-inclusive-growth-liquid-fuel-wholesale-industry-CCRED.pdf

Von Holdt, Karl 2000 'From the politics of resistance to the politics of reconstruction? The union and "ungovernability" in the workplace' in Glenn Adler and Edward Webster (eds) *Trade Unions and Democratization in South Africa, 1985–1997* Johannesburg, Wits University Press, pp. 106–108

Von Holdt, Karl 2013 'South Africa: The transition to violent democracy' *Review of African Political Economy* Vol. 40, No. 138, pp. 589–604

Von Holdt, Karl 2019 *The Political Economy of Corruption: Elite-Formation, Factions and Violence* Society, Politics and Work Institute Working Paper No. 10, University of the Witwatersrand, February

Von Holdt, Karl, Malose Langa, Sepetla Molapo, Nomfundo Mogapi, Kindi Ngubeni, Jacob Dlamini and Adele Kirsten 2011 *The Smoke that Calls: Insurgent Citizenship, Collective Violence and the Search for a Place in the New South Africa* Johannesburg, Centre for the Study of Violence and Reconciliation, Society, Work and Development Institute, July

Wainwright, Hilary 2003 *Reclaim the State: Experiments in Popular Democracy* London, Verso

Waldmeir, Patti 1998 *Anatomy of a Miracle: The End of Apartheid and the Birth of the New South Africa* New Brunswick NJ, Rutgers University Press

Webster, Edward 2013 'The promise and the possibility: South Africa's contested industrial relations path' *Transformation* 81/82, pp. 208–235

Weeks, John R 1999 'Stuck in low GEAR? Macroeconomic policy in South Africa, 1996–98' *Cambridge Journal of Economics* Vol. 23, No. 6, pp. 795–811

Welsh, David 1982 'Review of the Buthelezi Commission' Durban, H & H Publications https://www.sahistory.org.za/sites/default/files/archive-files2/rejul82.5.pdf

Wilson, Stuart 2011 'Litigating housing rights in Johannesburg's inner city: 2004–2008' *South African Journal on Human Rights* Vol. 27, No. 1, pp. 127–151

Wolpe, Harold 1980 'Towards an analysis of the South African state' *International Journal of the Sociology of Law* Vol. 8, No. 4, pp. 399–421

Wolpe, Harold 1992 'Education and social transformation: Problems and dilemmas' in Elaine Unterhalter, Harold Wolpe and Thozamile Botha (eds) *Education in a Future South Africa* Trenton NJ, Africa World Press

Wolpe, Harold 1995 'The debate on university transformation in South Africa: The case of the University of the Western Cape' *Comparative Education* Vol. 31, No. 2, pp. 398–399

Wolpe, Harold 1995 'The uneven transition from apartheid in South Africa' *Transformation* 27, pp. 88–101

Wolpe, Harold and Zenariah Barends 1993 *A Perspective on Quality and Inequality in South African University Education* Belville, Education Policy Unit, University of the Western Cape, February

Woolman, Stuart 2016 'South Africa's aspirational constitution and our problems of collective action' *South African Journal on Human Rights* Vol. 32, No. 1, pp. 156–183

World Bank 2018 *South Africa Update: Jobs and Inequality* Washington DC, The World Bank

World Bank Group 2018 *An Incomplete Transition: Overcoming the Legacy of Exclusion in South Africa* Systematic Country Diagnostic, World Bank, Washington DC

Yudelman, David 1984 *The Emergence of Modern South Africa: State, Capital and the Incorporation of Organized Labor on the South African Gold Fields, 1902–1939* Cape Town, David Philip

Zizzamia, Rocco, Simone Schotte, Murray Leibbrandt and Vimal Ranchhod 2016 *Vulnerability and the Middle Class in South Africa* Southern African Labour and Development Research Unit, University of Cape Town

## MEDIA ARTICLES

Adeluwoye, Danielle 2019 'I thought I'd made it when I got to Cambridge University. How wrong I was' *The Guardian* 23 September https://www.theguardian.com/commentisfree/2019/sep/23/cambridge-university-upward-mobility-working-class-background

African News Agency (ANA) reporter 2017 'Magaqa murder: ANC whistle-blowers live in fear' *Independent Online* 10 November https://www.iol.co.za/news/south-africa/kwazulu-natal/magaqa-murder-anc-whistle-blowers-live-in-fear-11948622

African News Agency (ANA) reporter 2018 'IFP retains Nkandla ward despite fervent Zuma campaigning' *Independent Online* 1 June https://www.iol.co.za/news/politics/ifp-retains-nkandla-ward-despite-fervent-zuma-campaigning-15265352

Areff, Ahmed 2015 'Timeline: How South Africa got three finance ministers in four days' *News24* 14 December https://www.news24.com/SouthAfrica/News/timeline-how-south-africa-got-three-finance-ministers-in-four-days-20151214

Boyle, Brendan 2016 'Foxes left to guard the hens that lay community nest eggs' *Business Day* 10 August

*BusinessTech* 2014 'ANC's employment rhetoric – a timeline' 15 January https://businesstech.co.za/news/government/51660/ancs-employment-rhetoric-a-timeline/

Cameron, Jackie 2019 'Land grabs only possible with 75% majority vote in Parliament – legal expert' *Biznews* 14 August https://www.biznews.com/thought-leaders/2019/08/14/land-grabs-majority-vote-parliament

Carlin, John 2014 'Judge shows why constitution is about morals not ceremony' *Business Day* 28 March

Claassens, Aninka 2016 'Rural vote notions' *Business Day* Letters 12 August

Clark, Christopher 2019 'Immigrants targeted in Alexandra housing battle' *GroundUp* 21 February https://www.groundup.org.za/article/immigrants-targeted-alexandra-housing-battle/

Cronje, Jan 2019 'Africa is "new frontier of economic growth", Ramaphosa tells G7 leaders' *Fin24* 26 August https://www.fin24.com/Economy/South-Africa/africa-is-new-frontier-of-economic-growth-ramaphosa-tells-g7-leaders-20190826

Davie, Eustace 2019 'Working together, South Africans can grow a strong economy' *Business Report* 10 November https://www.iol.co.za/business-report/opinion/working-together-south-africans-can-grow-a-strong-economy-36885220

Davie, Lucille 2003 'Why Alexandra survived apartheid' 6 October Joburg My City Our Future: Official Website of the City of Johannesburg http://www.joburg.org.za/index.php?option=com_content&task=view&id=888&Itemid=0

Devenish, George 2019 'SA's electoral system needs to accommodate individual candidates' *Business Day* 7 May https://www.businesslive.co.za/bd/opinion/2019-05-07-sas-electoral-system-needs-to-accommodate-individual-candidates/

Devereux, Stephen 2018 'Nearly a third of SA university students go hungry' *The Citizen* 27 August https://citizen.co.za/news/south-africa/2000969/nearly-a-third-of-sa-university-students-go-hungry/

Dludla, Siphelele 2019 'Retail sales remain muted with consumers under pressure' *Business Report* 19 September https://www.iol.co.za/business-report/economy/retail-sales-remain-muted-with-consumers-under-pressure-33244162

Du Preez, Max 2018 'Unproductive, incompetent state at heart of SA's problems' *News24* 21 August https://www.news24.com/Columnists/MaxduPreez/unproductive-incompetent-state-at-heart-of-sas-problems-20180821

Eastwood, Victoria 2013 'Bigger than the army: South Africa's private security forces' CNN 8 February http://edition.cnn.com/2013/02/08/business/south-africa-private-security

Egbedi, Hadassah 2016 'By ignoring corruption's colonial roots, Cameron's summit was destined to fail' *The Guardian* 13 May https://www.theguardian.com/world/2016/may/13/ignoring-corruptions-colonial-roots-camerons-summit-was-destined-to-fail

Evans, Sarah 2015 'ConCourt hands land back to North West community' *Mail and Guardian* 20 August

Everatt, David 2019 'South Africa's black middle-class is battling to find a political home' *The Conversation* 1 May https://theconversation.com/south-africas-black-middle-class-is-battling-to-find-a-political-home-116180

*Fin24* 2013 'SARB: Unsecured lending on the rise' 28 June http://www.fin24.com/Debt/News/Sarb-Unsecured-lending-on-the-rise-20130628

*Fin24* 2018 'Black ownership dropped in JSE-listed companies – report' 3 August https://www.fin24.com/Economy/black-ownership-dropped-in-jse-listed-companies-report-20180803

Friedman, Daniel 2019 'Ramaphosa is no different to Zuma and his actions are "illegal, period!" – Ndlozi' *The Citizen* 2 July https://citizen.co.za/news/south-africa/social-media/2157441/ramaphosa-is-no-different-to-zuma-and-his-actions-are-illegal-period-ndlozi/

Friedman, Steven 2014 'Moves to empower chiefs bad for democracy' *Business Day* 19 November

Friedman, Steven 2018 'Changes to the constitution may boost, not weaken, South African property rights' *The Conversation Africa* 3 August https://theconversation.com/changes-to-the-constitution-may-boost-not-weaken-south-african-property-rights-100979

Friedman, Steven 2018 'Land debate in South Africa is about dignity and equality – not the constitution' *The Conversation Africa* 5 March https://theconversation.com/land-debate-in-south-africa-is-about-dignity-and-equality-not-the-constitution-92862

Gasa, Nomboniso 2015 'State repeats mistakes in third attempt at courts bill' *Business Day* 22 June

Gilbert, Paula 2019 'SA smartphone penetration now at over 80%, says ICASA' *ITWeb* 3 April https://www.itweb.co.za/content/GxwQDM1AYy8MlPVo

Govender, Prega 2016 'Blade's puzzle: How to identify "missing middle" students' *Mail and Guardian* 9 December

Greenwood, Xavier 2018 'South Africa is the most unequal country in the world and its poverty is the "enduring legacy of apartheid", says World Bank' *The Independent* 4 April https://www.independent.co.uk/news/world/africa/south-africa-unequal-country-poverty-legacy-apartheid-world-bank-a8288986.html

GroundUp 2017 'Insourcing at universities – uneven progress' *Daily Maverick* 15 March https://www.dailymaverick.co.za/article/2017-03-15-groundup-insourcing-at-universities-uneven-progress

Haffajee, Ferial 2018 'As its ratings fall precipitously, the EFF goes post-truth on the opinion polls' *Daily Maverick* 12 December https://www.dailymaverick.co.za/article/2018-12-12-as-its-ratings-fall-precipitously-the-eff-goes-post-truth-in-the-opinion-polls/

Hemson, David 2009 'So long to a fiery spirit' *Mail and Guardian* 27 November https://mg.co.za/article/2009-11-27-so-long-to-a-fiery-spirit

Hlatshaneni, Simnikiwe 2018 'Eskom, workers' strike plunge SA into darkness' *The Citizen* 15 June https://citizen.co.za/news/south-africa/1954517/eskom-workers-strike-plunge-sa-into-darkness/

Hunter, Qaanitah 2017 'How David Mabuza outplayed the NDZ camp: Nifty footwork sees "Mpumalanga cat" come out on top' *TimesLive* 23 December https://www.timeslive.co.za/sunday-times/news/2017-12-22-how-david-mabuza-outplayed-the-ndz-camp/

IOL News 2011 'Malema hate-speech ruling "problematic"' *Independent Online* 15 September http://www.iol.co.za/news/crime-courts/malema-hate-speech-ruling-problematic-1.1138174#.U0bf3qL2CF4

Jeffery, Anthea 2019 'The state of race relations in SA 2019 – IRR' *Politicsweb* 13 June https://www.politicsweb.co.za/documents/the-state-of-race-relations-in-sa-2019--irr

Jordaan, Nomahlubi 2018 'Racism complaints by blacks are on the rise, with Gauteng the worst' *TimesLive* 10 December https://www.timeslive.co.za/news/south-africa/2018-12-10-racism-complaints-by-blacks-are-on-the-rise-with-gauteng-the-worst/

Kane-Berman, John 2014 'ANC corruption is systemic, unlike Nats' incidental version' *Business Day* 24 March

Krause, Tanya 2016 'Oupad community demands proper houses' *SABC News* 17 April

Krugman, Paul 2014 'Our invisible rich' *New York Times* 28 September

Lynd, Hilary 2019 'Secret details of the land deal that brought the IFP into the 1994 poll' *Mail and Guardian* 7 August https://mg.co.za/article/2019-08-07-secret-details-of-the-land-deal-that-brought-the-ifp-into-the-94-poll

Mabasa, Khwezi and Lebogang Mulaisi 2019 'Why South Africans need National Health Insurance' *Daily Maverick* 17 October https://www.dailymaverick.co.za/opinionista/2019-10-17-why-south-africans-need-national-health-insurance/#gsc.tab=0

Mabugu, Ramos and Eddie Rakabe 2015 'The need for proper early childhood development infrastructure is urgent' *Mail and Guardian* 23 October

Magubane, Khulekani 2013 'Clerics call for e-toll resistance' *Business Day* 3 December

Magubane, Khulekani 2018 'Free higher education is a game of cut and balance – Treasury DG' *Mail and Guardian* 28 March https://mg.co.za/article/2018-03-28-free-higher-education-is-a-game-of-cut-and-balance-treasury-dg

Mahlakoana, Theto 2018 'SA experienced highest rise in labour strikes in 2017' *TimesLive* 10 July https://www.timeslive.co.za/news/south-africa/2018-07-10-sa-experienced-highest-rise-in-labour-strikes-in-2017/

Mahlakoana, Theto 2018 'SA sets a new record for industrial action' *Business Day* 10 July https://www.businesslive.co.za/bd/national/labour/2018-07-10-sa-sets-a-new-record-for-industrial-action/

Makgetla, Neva 2018 'Big business's hold on economic power spawns pervasive inequality' *Business Day* 23 October https://www.businesslive.co.za/bd/opinion/columnists/2018-10-23-neva-makgetla-big-businesss-hold-on-economic-power-spawns-pervasive-inequality/

Makinana, Andisiwe 2016 'Zuma questions "lopsided" land reform law, calls for radical action' *City Press* 3 March

Manuel, Trevor 2012 'Proof of how much we have done – and must still do' *Business Day* 21 October

Marcus, Jon 2015 'Brazil: Where free universities largely serve the wealthy' *Atlantic* 8 April http://www.theatlantic.com/education/archive/2015/04/brazil-where-free-universities-largely-serve-the-wealthy/389997/

Marrian, Natasha 2018 'ANC blames Jacob Zuma's maladministration for SA's economic mess' *Business Day* 6 September https://www.businesslive.co.za/bd/national/2018-09-06-jacob-zumas-maladministration-led-to-sas-economic-mess/

Masedi, Mo 2015 'The doors of learning and culture shall be opened or else …' *Limpopo Online* 28 October http://limpopoonline.co.za/index.php/opinion-topmenu-15/124-love-struggle/2516-the-doors-of-learning-and-culture-shall-be-opened-or-else

Matshiqi, Aubrey 2011 'Why Manuel is right and wrong about Manyi's "racism"' *Business Day* 8 March http://www.businessday.co.za/articles/Content.aspx?id=136509

Mchunu, Sandile 2019 'Nedbank CEO issues strong warning to government as SA runs out of time, money' *Business Report* 7 August https://www.iol.co.za/business-report/companies/nedbank-ceo-issues-strong-warning-to-government-as-sa-runs-out-of-time-money-30412721

Menon, Sunita 2019 'Business blames unions for weak economy' *Business Day* 1 May https://www.businesslive.co.za/bd/economy/2019-05-01-business-blames-unions-for-weak-economy/

Meshoe, Kenneth 2017 'Praise for SA's progressive constitution' *Cape Times* 20 March

Mittner, Maarten 2019 'Scary move points to recession' *Finweek* 11 April https://www.fin24.com/Finweek/Investment/scary-move-points-to-recession-20190411

Mkhabela, Mpumelelo 2017 'Reckless Zuma leaves a country in tatters'*News24* 15 December https://www.news24.com/Columnists/Mpumelelo_Mkhabela/reckless-zuma-leaves-a-country-in-tatters-20171215

Moosa, Mikhail 2018 'SA is becoming a nation of three countries – along class, not racial lines' *Business Day* 7 June

Moosa, Mikhail 2019 'Corruption rife throughout our civil service' *Mail and Guardian* 18 April https://mg.co.za/article/2019-04-18-00-corruption-rife-throughout-our-civil-service

Motala, Mohamed 2014 'Why strikes are so violent' *Cape Times* 14 July

Mpulo, Nontsikelelo 2012 '"Second transition" is non-existent' *Grocott's Mail Online* 2 August http://www.grocotts.co.za/content/second-transition-premature-says-analyst-02-08-2012

Mthanti, Thanthi 2017 'Systemic racism behind South Africa's failure to transform its economy' *The Conversation* 31 January https://theconversation.com/systemic-racism-behind-south-africas-failure-to-transform-its-economy-71499

Mvumvu, Zingisa 2019 'Voters like Cyril Ramaphosa more than they like the ANC: survey' *TimesLive* 24 February https://www.timeslive.co.za/politics/2019-02-24-voters-like-cyril-ramaphosa-more-than-they-like-the-anc-survey/

Ndenze, Babalo 2019 'Ramaphosa praises House of Traditional Leaders as essential part of society' *Eyewitness News* 18 February https://www.msn.com/en-za/news/national/ramaphosa-praises-house-of-traditional-leaders-as-essential-part-of-society/ar-BBTOTfb

*News24* 2012 'ANC loses Nkandla by-election' 6 December http://www.news24.com/SouthAfrica/Politics/ANC-loses-Nkandla-by-election-20121206-4

Ngcukaitobi, Tembeka 2019 'What section 25 means for land reform' *Mail and Guardian* 13 December https://mg.co.za/article/2019-12-13-00-what-section-25-means-for-land-reform

Ngqentsu, Benson 2018 'Cosatu must focus on its unions so it can positively change workers' lives' *City Press* 20 September https://city-press.news24.com/Voices/cosatu-must-focus-on-its-unions-so-it-can-positively-change-workers-lives-20180919

Nicholson, Greg 2018 'Inner city blues: Joburg considers test case for expropriation of run-down buildings' *Daily Maverick* 7 March https://www.dailymaverick.co.za/article/2018-03-07-inner-city-blues-joburg-considers-test-case-for-expropriation-of-run-down-buildings/

Niselow, Tehilla 2017 'Loud cheers as Ramaphosa says #ANC54 unanimous on land reform' *Fin24* 21 December https://www.fin24.com/Economy/loud-cheers-as-ramaphosa-says-anc54-unanimous-on-land-reform-20171221

*Northern Natal Courier* 2019 'Final election results in: IFP gains ground in KZN at the expense of the ANC and NFP' 12 May https://northernnatalcourier.co.za/96773/final-election-results-ifp-gains-ground-kzn-expense-anc-nfp/

Oelofse, N 2011 'ANC adviser a pricey anomaly for Bitou' *Business Day* 18 August http://www.bdlive.co.za/articles/2011/08/18/anc-adviser-a-pricey-anomaly-for-bitou

Omarjee, Lameez 2017 'Business trust deficit in SA started long before Zuma – Scopa chair' *Fin24* 14 August https://www.fin24.com/Economy/business-trust-deficit-in-sa-started-long-before-zuma-scopa-chair-20170814

Omarjee, Lameez 2019 'SA edging closer to IMF bailout – Sipho Pityana' *Fin24* 2 November https://www.fin24.com/Economy/sa-edging-closer-to-imf-bailout-sipho-pityana-20191102

Pamla, Sizwe 2016 'Foreign owned e-toll system is nothing but an enrichment scheme for the few' Cosatu Press Statement 18 August www.cosatu.org.za/show.php?ID=11858

Paton, Carol 2019 'Ramaphosa has to set the agenda' *Business Day* 13 August

Phungo, Roshuma 2015 'University fees: Free higher education is possible in South Africa' *Daily Maverick* 21 October https://www.dailymaverick.co.za/article/2015-10-21-university-fees-free-higher-education-is-possible-in-south-africa/

Pithouse, Richard 2011 'The case of the Kennedy 12: No easy path through the embers' *Counterpunch* 1 August http://www.counterpunch.org/2011/08/01/no-easy-path-through-the-embers/

Ramatlhodi, Ngoako 2011 'ANC's fatal concessions' *TimesLive* 1 September http://www.timeslive.co.za/opinion/commentary/2011/09/01/the-big-read-anc-s-fatal-concessions

Runji, Nompumelelo 2019 'Ramaphosa tightening his grip on control of government' *Sowetan* 14 February https://www.sowetanlive.co.za/opinion/columnists/2019-02-14-ramaphosa-tightening-his-grip-on-control-of-government/

Schutte, Ryno and Janine van der Post 2018 ' "I felt sorry for the victims but I had a job to do" – former hijackers reveal all, here's how you can protect yourself in SA' *Wheels24* 29 August https://www.wheels24.co.za/News/Guides_and_Lists/i-felt-sorry-for-the-victims-but-i-had-a-job-to-do-former-hijackers-reveal-all-heres-how-you-can-protect-yourself-in-sa-20180829

Sguazzin, Antony and Colleen Goko 2019 'Eskom gets bailout funding. Now it needs a rescue plan' *Bloomberg News* 26 July https://www.fin24.com/Economy/Eskom/eskom-gets-bailout-funding-now-it-needs-a-rescue-plan-20190726

Shuma, Phanuel 2018 'Presidential GBV summit not another talk shop: Dlamini' *SABC News Online* 2 November http://www.sabcnews.com/sabcnews/presidential-gbv-summit-not-another-talk-shop-dlamini/

Smit, Sarah 2019 'Unemployment rate at 29% – StatsSA' *Mail and Guardian* 30 July https://mg.co.za/article/2019-07-30-unemployment-rate-at-29-statssa

Smith, Carin 2018 'Ramaphosa: Growing black anger about "lackadaisical" whites with power' *Fin24* 13 December https://www.fin24.com/Economy/ramaphosa-growing-black-anger-about-lackadaisical-whites-with-power-20181213

South Africa.info 2012 'South Africa improves access to services' 30 October http://www.southafrica.info/about/social/census-301012b.htm#.UxzX685_Fec

South African History Online 2019 'Josiah Tshangana Gumede' https://www.sahistory.org.za/people/josiah-tshangana-gumede

South African Press Association (Sapa) 2012 'E-toll opposition group heads to court this week' 23 April http://mybroadband.co.za/news/general/48340-e-toll-opposition-group-heads-to-court-this-week.html

South African Press Association (Sapa) 2013 'Taxis with valid permits exempt from e-tolls, says department' *Mail and Guardian* 4 December

Staff reporter 1999 'Buthelezi approved Powell's war plans' *Mail and Guardian* 18 June https://mg.co.za/article/1999-06-18-buthelezi-approved-powells-war-plans

Staff writer 2018 'Jonas tells the inside story of Nhlanhla Nene's firing' *Business Day* 24 August https://www.businesslive.co.za/bd/national/2018-08-24-jonas-tells-the-inside-story-of-nhlanhla-nenes-firing/

Staff writer 2019 'State-owned Denel unable to pay full salaries to staff' *Business Report* 25 June https://www.iol.co.za/business-report/economy/state-owned-denel-unable-to-pay-full-salaries-to-staff-27540180

Steinberg, Jonny 2015 'We should've heeded Mahmoud Mamdani's warning' *Business Day* 2 October

Stiglitz, Joseph 2019 'It's time to retire metrics like GDP. They don't measure everything that matters' *The Guardian* 24 November https://www.theguardian.com/commentisfree/2019/nov/24/metrics-gdp-economic-performance-social-progress

Stoddard, Ed and Jan Harvey 2014 'S Africa miners' strike to drive up platinum over time' Reuters 18 February https://www.reuters.com/article/safrica-strikes-prices/safrica-miners-strike-to-drive-up-platinum-over-time-idUSL6N0LN2VG20140218

Stone, Setumo 2012 'ANC loses ward near Marikana in by-election' *Business Day* 8 November

Stone, Setumo 2018 'How Ramaphosa "dodged a coup" – security bosses reveal all' *City Press* 22 July

Talane, Valencia 2019 'Bosasa handouts and Zuma's coughing fits: One year of testimony at Zondo Commission' *Independent Online* 20 August https://www.iol.co.za/news/opinion/bosasa-handouts-and-zumas-coughing-fits-one-year-of-testimony-at-zondo-commission-30952078

Tandwa, Lizeka 2017 'It was a "festival of chairs" – Ramaphosa on violent ANC elective conference' *News24* 1 October https://www.news24.com/SouthAfrica/News/it-was-a-festival-of-chairs-ramaphosa-on-violent-anc-elective-conference-20171001

Tolsi, Niren 2012 'Grootboom win a house of cards' *Mail and Guardian* 9 March http://mg.co.za/article/2012-03-09-grootboom-win-a-house-of-cards

Vally, Salim 2003 'The iron fist and the velvet glove' *Mail and Guardian* 20 December

Vally, Salim, Enver Motala, Mondli Hlatshwayo and Rasigan Maharajh 2016 'Quality, free university education is necessary – and possible' *Mail and Guardian* 28 January

Van Heerden, Oscar 2019 'More haste, less speed, Mr President: Slow but steady wins the race' *Daily Maverick* 14 August https://www.dailymaverick.co.za/opinionista/2019-08-14-more-haste-less-speed-mr-president-slow-but-steady-wins-the-race/?fbclid=IwAR206NcEGq3eRG9govEFWvQGUPYgCYILkahfSHbShPSKH3_PQDGN7b9xVBM

## REPORTS AND DOCUMENTS

African National Congress 1994 *The Reconstruction and Development Programme: A Policy Framework* https://www.sahistory.org.za/sites/default/files/the_reconstruction_and_development_programm_1994.pdf

African National Congress 1998 'The state, property relations and social transformation' *Umrabulo* No. 5, Third Quarter

African National Congress 2001 *Through the Eye of A Needle? Choosing the Best Cadres to Lead Transformation* Johannesburg, ANC

African National Congress 2018 *54th National Conference Report and Resolutions* Johannesburg, ANC

Avert 2019 *HIV and AIDS in South Africa* January https://www.avert.org/professionals/hiv-around-world/sub-saharan-africa/south-africa

*Azanian Peoples Organization (AZAPO) and Others v President of the Republic of South Africa and Others* (CCT17/96) [1996] ZACC 16; 1996 (8) BCLR 1015; 1996 (4) SA 672 (25 July 1996)

Bhorat, Haroon et al. 2017 *Betrayal of the Promise: How South Africa Is Being Stolen* State Capacity Research Project, Public Affairs Research Institute et al., May

Brand South Africa 2010 'SA targets 5-million new jobs by 2020' 24 November https://www.brandsouthafrica.com/investments-immigration/business/economy/policies/growth-241110

Centraal Bureau voor de Statistiek (CBS) 2009 'Unemployment in 1930s unprecedently high' 17 March https://www.cbs.nl/en-gb/news/2009/12/unemployment-in-1930s-unprecedentedly-high

Centre for Law and Society 2013 *Questioning the Legal Status of Traditional Councils in South Africa* Rural Women's Action Research Programme, University of Cape

Town, August http://www.cls.uct.ac.za/usr/lrg/downloads/CLS_TCStatus_Factsheet_Aug2013.pdf

City Council of Pretoria v Walker (CCT8/97) [1998] ZACC 1; 1998 (2) SA 363; 1998 (3) BCLR 257 (17 February 1998)

City of Tshwane Metropolitan Municipality v Afriforum and Another (A811/2013) [2015] ZAGPPHC 1056 (26 May 2015)

Congress of South African Trade Unions (Cosatu) 2015 Cosatu Statement on 'new e-tolls dispensation' 21 May www.cosatu.org.za/show.php?ID=10433

Cosatu Central Executive Committee 2017 Conceptualising a Second Radical Transition 29 May https://www.politicsweb.co.za/opinion/conceptualising-a-second-radical-transition--cosat

Davis, Judge Dennis 2012 Judgment: Mazibuko v Sisulu and Others High Court of South Africa, Western Cape Division, Case No. 21990/2012 (22 November)

Democratic Alliance 2019 'BOKAMOSO/DA can put a job every home' 22 January https://www.da.org.za/2019/01/bokamoso-da-can-put-a-job-every-home

Department of Planning, Monitoring and Evaluation, Presidency (DPME) 2014 Twenty Year Review South Africa 1994–2014

Department of Planning, Monitoring and Evaluation, Presidency (DPME) 2014 Twenty Year Review South Africa 1994–2014: Background Paper: Income, Poverty and Inequality

Development Network Africa 2009 Professional Services in South Africa: Accounting, Engineering and Law 25 January http://www.dnaeconomics.com/assets/Usegareth/SA_Professional_Services.pdf

Duvenage, Wayne nd 'Open road tolling' Avis http://www.avis.co.za/OpenRoadTolling.asp

Eastern Cape High Court 2017 Mgabadeli and Others v African National Congress and Others (EL1303/2017, ECD3703/2017) [2017] ZAECGHC 131 (12 December)

Economic Freedom Fighters nd The EFF's Answers to Your Questions on Land EWC Politicsweb https://www.politicsweb.co.za/documents/the-effs-answers-to-your-questions-on-land-ewc

Farlam, IG, PD Hemraj and BR Tokota 2015 Marikana Commission of Inquiry: Report on Matters of Public, National and International Concern Arising Out of the Tragic Incidents at the Lonmin Mine in Marikana, in the North West Province 31 March https://www.sahrc.org.za/home/21/files/marikana-report-1.pdf

FW de Klerk Foundation nd 'Article: Expropriation without compensation' https://www.fwdeklerk.org/index.php/en/latest/news/756-article-expropriation-without-compensation

Gordhan, Pravin 2012 '2012 budget speech' 22 February http://www.treasury.gov.za/documents/national%20budget/2012/speech/speech.pdf

Gordhan, Pravin 2013 '2013 budget speech' 27 February http://www.treasury.gov.za/documents/national%20budget/2013/speech/speech.pdfp.27

Government of National Unity 1994 White Paper on Reconstruction and Development

Government of the Republic of South Africa and Others v Grootboom and Others (CCT11/00) [2000] ZACC 19; 2001 (1) SA 46; 2000 (11) BCLR 1169 (4 October 2000)

Johannesburg Stock Exchange (JSE) 2010 JSE Presents Findings on Black Ownership on the JSE 2 September http://ir.jse.co.za/news-releases/news-release-details/jse-presents-findings-black-ownership-jse

Jordan, Pallo 2000 'Ruth First lecture' University of the Witwatersrand, 28 August wits.journalism.co.za/wp-content/uploads/2019/03/Ruth-First-Lecture-by-Pallo-Jordan-2000.pdf

KwaZulu-Natal High Court 2017 *Dube and Others v Zikalala and Others* (7904/2016P) [2017] ZAKZPHC 36; [2017] 4 All SA 365 (KZP) (12 September 2017)

Lipton, David 2016 'Bridging South Africa's economic divide' Speech at University of the Witwatersrand, Johannesburg, International Monetary Fund, 19 July https://www.imf.org/en/News/Articles/2016/07/18/20/15/SP071916-Bridging-South-Africas-Economic-Divide

May, Julian 1998 *Poverty and Inequality in South Africa: Report prepared for the Office of the Executive Deputy President and the Inter-Ministerial Committee for Poverty and Inequality* Summary Report 13 May

*Mazibuko v City of Johannesburg* (2010) (Centre on Housing Rights and Evictions as amicus curiae) 4 SA 1 (CC)

*Mazibuko and Others v City of Johannesburg and Others* (CCT 39/09) [2009] ZACC 28; 2010 (3) BCLR 239 (CC); 2010 (4) SA 1 (CC) (8 October 2009)

*Minister of Finance and Other v Van Heerden* (CCT 63/03) [2004] ZACC 3; 2004 (6) SA 121 (CC); 2004 (11) BCLR 1125 (CC); [2004] 12 BLLR 1181 (CC) (29 July 2004)

*Minister of Health v Treatment Action Campaign* (No 2) 2002 (5) SA 721 (CC)

*Minister of Health and Others v Treatment Action Campaign and Others* (No 2) (CCT8/02) [2002] ZACC 15; 2002 (5) SA 721; 2002 (10) BCLR 1033 (5 July 2002)

Mthembu, Jackson 2014 'ANC statement on remarks of ANCYL and Cosas on the Public Protector' 24 March http://www.politicsweb.co.za/politicsweb/view/politicsweb/en/page71654?oid=576688&sn=Detail&pid=71616

National Treasury 1996 *Growth, Employment and Redistribution: A Macroeconomic Strategy* South African Government, Pretoria

National Treasury 2018 'Economic overview' *2018 Budget Review,* chapter 2 http://www.treasury.gov.za/documents/national%20budget/2018/review/Chapter%202.pdf

Numsa 2014 'Numsa on the United Front and the possibilities of establishing a movement for socialism' Press Release, 4 March https://www.numsa.org.za/article/numsa-united-front-possibilities-establishing-movement-socialism/

*Occupiers of 51 Olivia Road, Berea Township and 197 Main Street Johannesburg v City of Johannesburg and Others* (24/07) [2008] ZACC 1; 2008 (3) SA 208 (CC); 2008 (5) BCLR 475 (CC) (19 February 2008)

Open Secrets 2018 *Evidence for the People's Tribunal on Economic Crime (03–07 February 2018)*

Parliament of the Republic of South Africa 2017 *Report of the High-Level Panel on the Assessment of Key Legislation and the Acceleration of Fundamental Change* November https://www.parliament.gov.za/storage/app/media/Pages/2017/october/High_Level_Panel/HLP_Report/HLP_report.pdf

Parliament of the Republic of South Africa 2019 'National Assembly agrees to Traditional Courts Bill' 12 March https://www.parliament.gov.za/press-releases/national-assembly-agrees-traditional-courts-bill

Pithouse, Richard 2015 'Dikgang Moseneke: Constitution allows for land expropriation' Land and Accountability Research Centre, 5 March https://www.customcontested.co.za/dikgang-moseneke-constitution-allows-for-land-expropriation/

*Prince v President of the Law Society of the Cape of Good Hope* (CCT36/00) [2002] ZACC 1; 2002 (2) SA 794; 2002 (3) BCLR 231 (25 January 2002)

Ramaphosa, Cyril 2018 'President Cyril Ramaphosa: State of the Nation Address 2018' 16 February https://www.gov.za/speeches/president-cyril-ramaphosa-2018-state-nation-address-16-feb-2018-0000

Ramaphosa, Cyril 2019 'President Cyril Ramaphosa: State of the Nation Address 2019' 20 June https://www.gov.za/speeches/2SONA2019

*Residents of Joe Slovo Community, Western Cape v Thubelisha Homes and Others* (CCT 22/08) [2009] ZACC 16; 2009 (9) BCLR 847 (CC); 2010 (3) SA 454 (CC) (10 June 2009)

Restitution of Land Rights Act No. 22 of 1994

South African Communist Party 1994 *Draft Strategy and Tactics*

South African Federation of Trade Unions (SAFTU) 2019 'SAFTU condemns Ramaphosa's pro-big business and "business as usual" SONA' 8 February https://saftu.org.za/saftu-condemns-ramaphosas-pro-big-business-and-business-as-usual-sona/

South African Government 1994 *White Paper on Reconstruction and Development: A Strategy for Fundamental Transformation*

South African History Online 1996 'NP set to withdraw from GNU' 10 May https://www.sahistory.org.za/dated-event/np-set-withdraw-gnu

South African Institute of Race Relations nd 'Help the IRR stop expropriation and promote real land reform: Endorse our solution' https://irr.org.za/campaigns/defend-your-property-rights

South African Social Security Agency (SASSA) 2018 *A Statistical Summary of Social Grants in South Africa* Fact Sheet No. 21, December

Statistics South Africa 2018 'Who is most likely to be affected by long-term unemployment?' 30 October http://www.statssa.gov.za/?p=11688#:~:text=The%20most%20affected%20persons%20were,than%20it%20affects%20the%20adults

Statistics South Africa 2020 'Economy slips into recession' 3 March http://www.statssa.gov.za/?p=13049

Tabata, IB 1980 'Review of Neville Alexander's book *One Azania One Nation*' Unity Movement document, 14 March http://www.apdusaviews.co.za/repository/Microsoft%20Word%20-%20Tabata%20on%20BCM.pdf

TransUnion 2019 '#StrongerTogether: Lessons from the 2019 Rugby World Cup' 18 November https://www.transunion.co.za/blog/strongertogether-lessons-from-the-2019-rugby-world-cup

Truth and Reconciliation Commission (TRC) 1998 *Final Report* Volume 3, chapter 3, subsection 62, 438

United Nations Development Programme (UNDP) 2017 Human Development Reports *Human Development Data (1990–2017)* http://hdr.undp.org/en/data

United States – Human Development Index – HDI https://countryeconomy.com/hdi/usa

Van Onselen, Charles nd 'Tertiary education in a democratic South Africa' Unpublished mimeo

Van Vuuren, Hennie 2006 *Apartheid Grand Corruption: Assessing the Scale of Crimes of Profit from 1976 to 1994* A report prepared by civil society in terms of a resolution of the Second National Anti-Corruption Summit for presentation at the National Anti-Corruption Forum, Pretoria, Institute for Security Studies, May

Zuma, Jacob 2017 'President Jacob Zuma: 2017 State of the Nation Address' 9 February https://www.gov.za/speeches/president-jacob-zuma-2017-state-nation-address-9-feb-2017-0000

Milton Keynes UK ·
Ingram Content Group UK Ltd.
UKHW011443031123
431797UK00014B/185

9 781776 146840